JOURNEYS WITH THE MESSIAH

GUIDE BOOK and FILM SERIES

A journey of discovery through Jesus' teachings with 34 stories, photographs and free videos.

Photographed & Written by **Michael Belk**

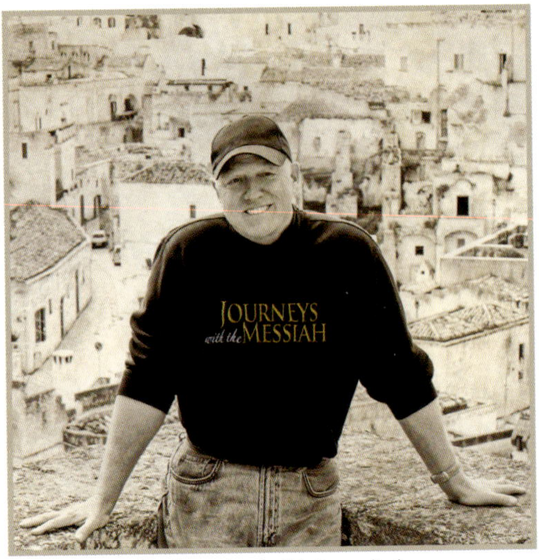

On location in Matera, Italy

A Message from The Author

Seeing a film and reading the book about the film offers a greater experience than either the film or book can provide on its own. Our new **Film Series** and companion **Guide Book** work in tandem to take you on an exciting journey of discovery with Jesus.

In 2008, feeling a nudge from God to create these unique images, I left my career as a fashion photography to begin production on this collection of photographs. Little did I know it would be the beginning of a personal journey with the Messiah — a journey for which God had been grooming me for over 30 years.

The concept: Juxtapose first century Jesus against twentieth century characters and elements to depict the relevance of His timeless messages. Like Jesus' parables, the images are simple, thought-provoking stories designed to draw you closer to Him.

Since Journeys with the Messiah's photographs premiered in 2009, we have witnessed their impact as they travel the world through our website, our books and artwork and as they are shared in newspapers and magazines and on social media and television. We are blessed by testimonies of how they are engaging, encouraging and comforting to so many people.

In 2017, I sensed God nudging me again, this time to create a series of short films to expand the messages each image depicts. Then, through the internet, we would share them with unlimited audiences around the world. And thus, the new Journeys Film Series evolved.

Through the Guide Book, each chapter will direct you to the corresponding film which can be streamed to your television, computer and mobile devices. As your host, I will bring the stories to life with photos, graphics, film clips (including behind-the-scenes) and music. I believe you will find these short films exciting, engaging, thought-provoking, memorable and easy to share.

The Guide Book includes adaptations of the film scripts, allowing you to read and wonder through the messages at your own pace. Each chapter is independent of the others and connected only through the common theme of Jesus and what He said on a variety of subjects. There's no beginning or end. So read them in any order you like.

At the end of each chapter are my *Thoughts to Ponder.* I say "my" because these are questions and ideas I have pondered and researched during the many years of the project. They are not a test, just ideas for consideration! Even when written as a question, you are not obligated to answer. Just take time to think about it!

Produced in the ancient city of Matera, Italy, I hope this one-of-a-kind magnificently beautiful collection of photographs and films will provide a fresh, delightful and inviting perspective of Jesus.

Come along on this Journey with the Messiah!

Michael Belk. *Photographer & Author*

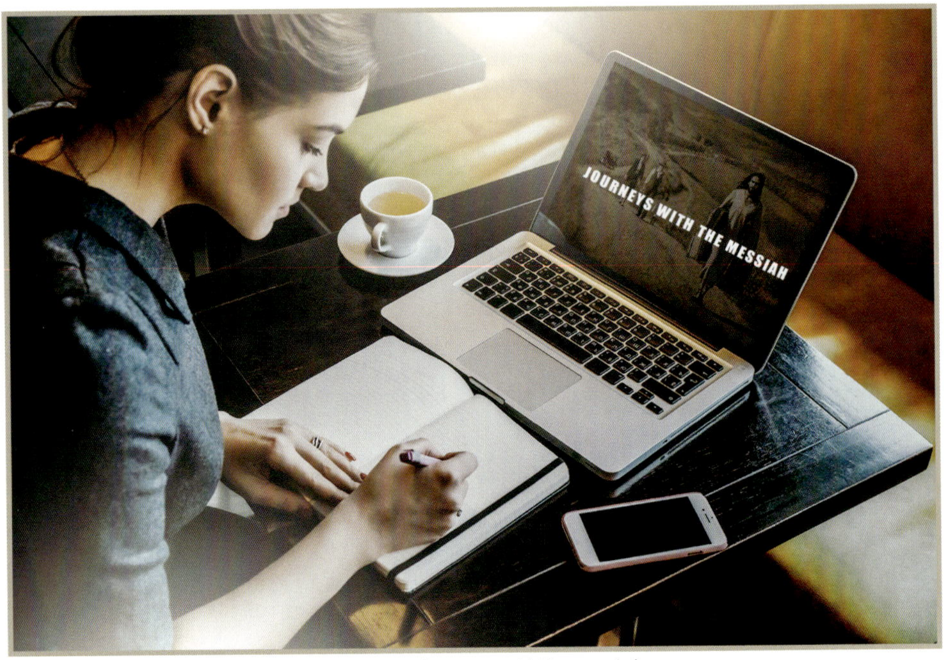

Register at www.journeyswiththemessiah.org

How to use the Guide Book & Film Series

Start Here>

1. Register for free access to the films.
Go to our website — journeyswiththemessiah.org — and register if you do not already have an account. Once your account is set, you will have free access to all of the films.

2. About the Guide Book.
Journeys with the Messiah Guide Book and Film Series is your official guide to these powerful messages. Each chapter contains the original photograph and an adapted version of the film script. Plus it will guide you to the corresponding film on our website.

3. Watch the film.
I suggest that you begin each chapter by watching the corresponding film on your tablet, mobile phone, computer or television. (Films average ten minutes.)

4. Read the chapter.
While the film is fresh in your mind, read the corresponding chapter, taking time to absorb the content.

5. Thoughts to Ponder.
At the end of each chapter is a section of thoughts, ideas and questions called *Thoughts to Ponder*. They invite us to think about things that matter in our spiritual walk with Jesus. They are not a test! They reflect back to us how we are doing relative to what Jesus says and to remind us of things He shared. Use them intentionally. In other words, don't just read them and move on, but select different ones to ponder as you go through each day.

Great for Small Groups.
The Film Series and Guide Book is an ideal resource for small groups. *Thoughts to Ponder* offers an assortment of discussion topics to consider after each film.

Journeys with the Messiah Guide Book & Film Series
Photographed and Written by Michael Belk

First published in the United States in 2020 by
Journeys with the Messiah, Inc
28679 Alessandria Circle
Bonita Springs, FL 34135 USA
www.journeyswiththemessiah.org

ISBN Number 978-0-578-80862-8

Printed in the United States

Multiple scripture sources have been quoted and paraphrased for clarity of content. Versions include the New International Version, English Standard Version and The Message.

Table of Contents & Film Number

R.S.V.P.

A Lesson in Spiritual Etiquette

View film at ▶ journeyswiththemessiah.org

Most of us have received invitations to weddings, dinner parties and other events with a request to respond or R.S.V.P. Have you ever received such an invitation from a friend and then sent regrets with an excuse as to why you couldn't attend, although you could have if you wanted to? In Luke's account of Jesus' life, He tells a story about such an incident.

The French phrase *Répondez s'il vous plaît* is where we get the initials R.S.V.P. Translated, it means *respond if you please.* We add R.S.V.P. to invitations so that we may know who is coming and how much to prepare. In biblical times, someone planning a banquet would send out an initial invitation, usually delivered in person. When preparations were ready, a second invitation would go to the people who had responded favorably to the original invitation.

As it remains in some societies today, a person's social standing was often determined by whose dinners and parties they were invited to. It was considered a serious social faux pas and insult to the host to accept an invitation and then not attend. For a whole group of invitees to reject the second invitation after the first was accepted, may even appear to be a conspiracy to discredit the host.

Rules of social etiquette would have been known among the Pharisees, who were the religious elite of the Jewish people of Jesus' time. It was at the home of a prominent Pharisee when Jesus told His parable about a man who planned a great banquet.

In Jesus' story, the man planning the banquet had sent the first invitation to guests who had R.S.V.P.'d accepting the invitation (Luke 14:15-24). Once preparations were made and it was time for the banquet, the host sent the second invitation, "Come now, everything is ready!" This time, the guests sent regrets offering questionable excuses as to why they would not attend (Luke 14:17).

One of the invited guests responded, "I have just bought a field, and I must go and see it. Please excuse me" (Luke 14:18). It was not likely that he purchased land before he saw it?

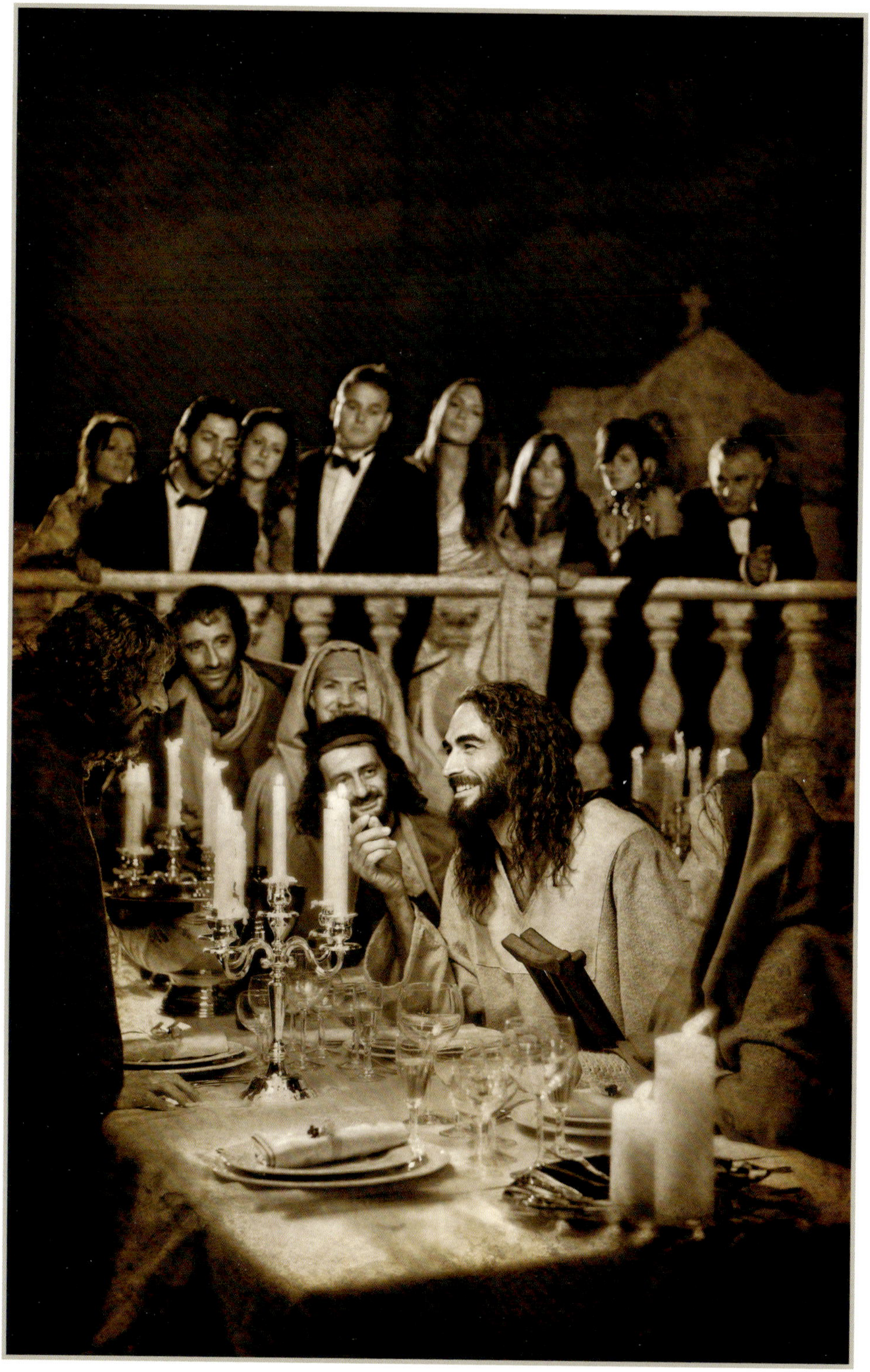

Another said, "I have just bought five yoke of oxen and I'm on my way to try them out. Please excuse me" (Luke 14:19). Today, this would be the equivalent of saying you could not attend because you bought a car before you took it for a test drive! Still, another said, "I just got married, so I can't come" (Luke 14:20). And, why couldn't his wife go with him?

Insulted with these lame excuses, the host got angry and told his servant, "Go out quickly into the streets and alleys of the town and bring in the poor, the crippled, the blind and the lame" (Luke 14:21).

Then the master of the house made a declaration that I believe represents one of the most explicit warnings in the Gospels. He said, "I tell you, not one of those who were invited will taste my great banquet" (Luke 14:24).

I find it interesting that in the verses just before this story, Jesus said, "When you give a luncheon or dinner, do not invite your friends, your brothers or sisters, your relatives, or your rich neighbors; if you do, they may invite you back, and so you will be repaid. But when you give a banquet, invite the poor, the crippled, the lame, the blind, and you will be blessed (Luke 14:13-14).

So in Jesus' parable, the host invited his friends, family and rich neighbors but ends up having the poor, the crippled, the blind and the lame as his guests.

This is such a great story and a powerful message to depict through a photograph. Imagine a scene of Jesus interacting with the poor, blind and lame who have joined Him at the banquet table while the original invitees — the friends, family and rich neighbors — look on from outside the gate. **In real life, it is a photograph in which we must all take part!**

The parable of the great banquet reminds us that Jesus has invited everyone to the greatest party that will ever be given, a life in Eternity with Him! While many people have already responded with an exuberant, "Yes, I cannot wait to attend," the parable reveals that many will foolishly be too busy to accept His invitation — or even consider it — until the gates of the party are closed. Then it will be too late!

Imagine the hurt your father would feel if he planned a great banquet, and after you said you would come, you didn't show up? In Jesus' parable, the master of the house is God, and the banquet is The Kingdom that has been prepared for all who have accepted and have R.S.V.P.'d "Yes" to His invitation.

Think about the excuses the invited guests made. Are they really any different from the ones we make? They are laughable at best, for there is no acceptable reason to reject God's invitation, especially when there is 2,000 years of overwhelming evidence pointing to Jesus as the Messiah, the Son of God.

For those who have accepted His invitation, Jesus has written our names on the royal guest list. As the master told his servant, "Go out to the roads and country lanes and compel them to come in so that my house will be full" (Luke 14:23), this verse is instruction to us to continue to send out our invitations.

Jesus said to send invitations out into the world to all nations, all people, and especially to our neighbors across the street, our co-workers where we work, and our family and friends. Tell them that they too are invited to His great banquet, for this is a party no one will want to miss!

"Blessed is the one who will eat at the feast in The Kingdom of God."

Amen! Let's eat!

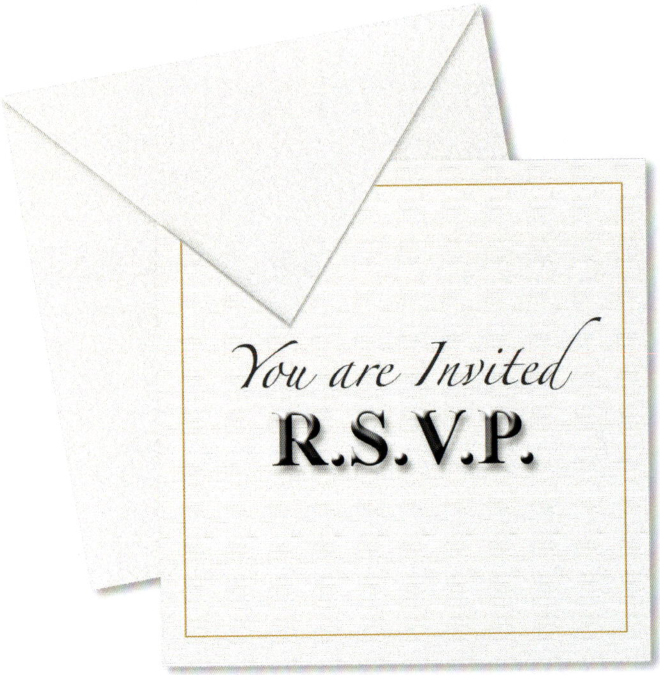

An invitation to a life in Eternity.

Thoughts to Ponder

View film at ▶ journeyswiththemessiah.org

- Have you R.S.V.P.'d favorably to an event and then not attended? Did you offer an excuse?
- Have you had anyone R.S.V.P. favorably to your invitation and then not attend? Did they offer a questionable excuse? Do you recall how you felt? (It could be as simple as an invite to meet for lunch.)
- Jesus said, "When you give a luncheon or dinner, do not invite your friends, your brothers or sisters, your relatives or your rich neighbors; if you do, they may invite you back, and so you will be repaid. But when you give a banquet, invite the poor, the crippled, the lame, the blind, and you will be blessed (Luke 14:13-14). It is comfortable to invite only our friends and people of the same social-economic class to our banquets. Jesus says that we should examine our guest lists and consider reaching out in love to share our homes with "unexpected guests?"
- The image *R.S.V.P.* is simple, exciting, and powerful. Its message tells us that Jesus has invited everyone to the most lavish banquet that will ever be given — a life in Eternity with Him. Will you consider using this image and story to let a neighbor, co-worker, family, and friends know they are invited to His banquet?
- Consider having a banquet (dinner party, lunch, any gathering), making this image the theme and sharing the story that goes with it.

Best is Yet to Come

Your Best Life is Just Over the Horizon

View film at ▶ journeyswiththemessiah.org

When I was a child, I was taught to eat my vegetables before eating my dessert and do my homework before going out to play. My parents wanted me to learn the value of saving the best for last.

The inspiration for *Best is Yet to Come* came from the biblical story of Jesus' first miracle when He turned water into wine at a wedding in Cana.

At a conference my wife and I attended, we heard Bruce Wilkinson (author of Prayer of Jabez) say that God does not speak to us through burning bushes, and seldom uses angels; God speaks to us primarily through people — through the words they write and speak. So as I study — reading the Bible, books and articles, hearing sermons and even music — I'm excited when something new is revealed to me.

The meaning of Jesus' first miracle at the Wedding in Cana was revealed in *The Training of the Twelve*, a book written by A. B. Bruce in 1871. It's an enlightening book about Jesus' discipleship of the first twelve men to carry His message into the world. (You can download a free workbook version written by my friend, John Musselman, at TJI.org.)

The story of Jesus' first miracle is recorded in the Book of John. The miracle occurred while Jesus was attending a wedding in Cana with His mother and several disciples (John 2:1-11). In many cultures, running out of wine at a wedding is considered an unacceptable social blunder. At this wedding, such a situation was about to occur and it would have caused great embarrassment for the bridegroom and others.

Jesus' mother brought the news of this impending doom, saying to her son, "They have no more wine!" Jesus' response seems odd to us. "What is that to you and to Me? My time to be revealed has not yet come" (John 2:3-4).

A. B. Bruce explained that Jesus was cautious about performing any public miracles if the time and place were not according to God's will. Jesus would not reveal His divine power sooner than God intended.

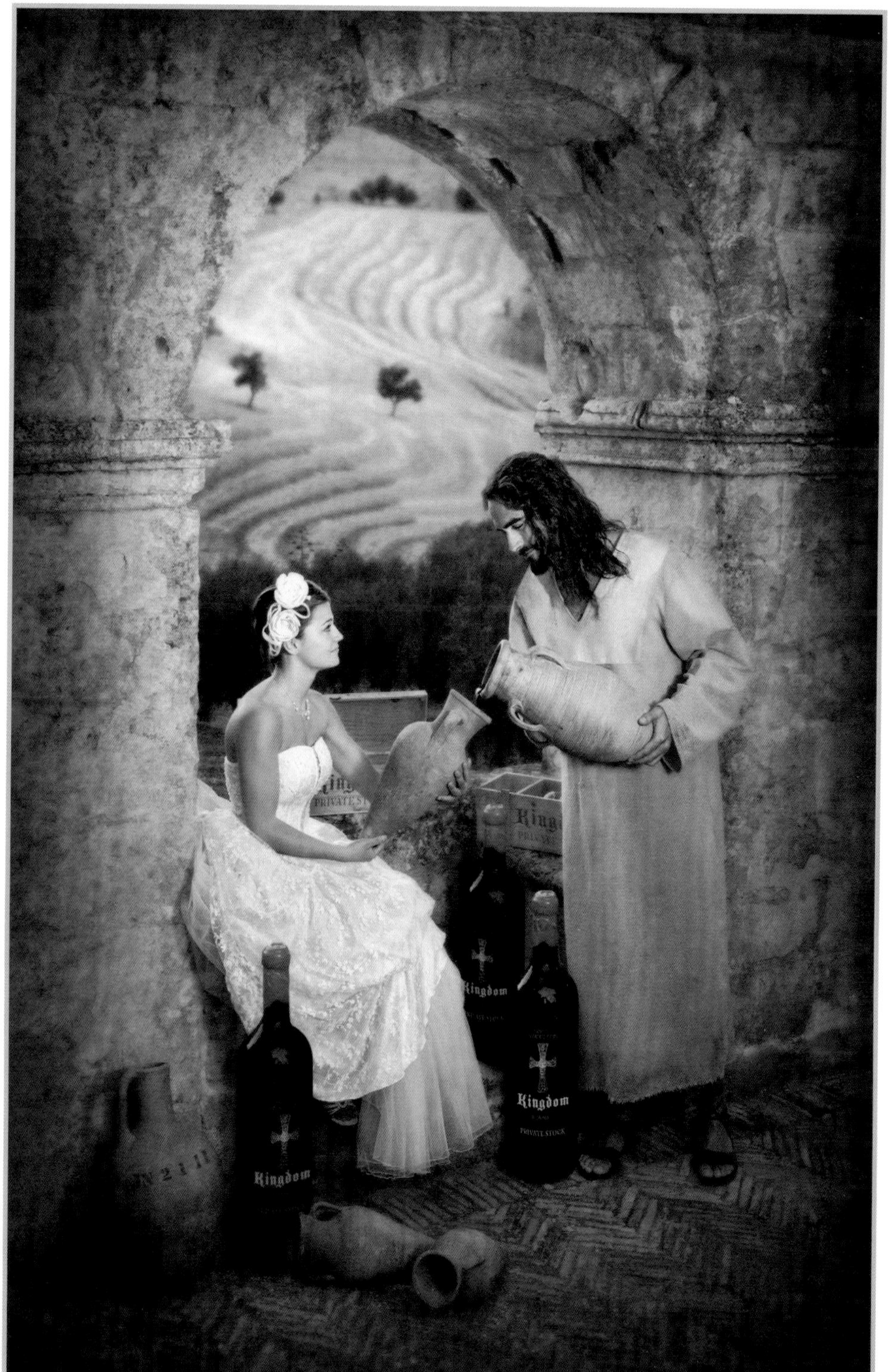
Kingdom
PRIVATE STOCK
Kingdom
Kingdom

You have to love the way Jesus' mother responded to Him as if she was completely ignoring what Jesus said. She turned to the servants and instructed them, "Do whatever he tells you to!" (John 2:5). So Jesus did as his mother wished and went about saving the day.

First, He directed the servants to get six large pots customarily used by the Jews for ceremonial washing and to fill them with water. And then, without any fanfare, the water was turned into wine (John 2:6-7).

It is significant for us to understand that Jesus did not do this in front of the wedding guests. It was done out of sight of everyone except his mother, a few servants and several disciples. Again, He was not ready for the public to see His divine power, especially since it might appear that He was showing off.

With the pots now filled with wine, He told the servants to draw some and give it to the master of the wedding banquet.

The master had no idea from where the wine had come. Yet, after tasting it and realizing just how good it was, he called the bridegroom over and said, "Most people serve the choice wine first, and when the guests have had a lot to drink, the host brings out the cheaper wine. But you, sir, have saved the best for last!" (John 2:10).

The miracles Jesus performed were not only to show His divine power from God but to convey the truths He came to share about his Father's Kingdom. At the wedding in Cana, it was important for Jesus to introduce His disciples to His divinity through the miracle of turning water into wine. This miracle also serves to reiterate God's promise of provision to us. It illustrates that we will not run out of wine, meaning that God will provide for all of our needs.

Yet there is a message that can be overlooked in the comment the master of the banquet made to the bridegroom after tasting the wine: "You sir, have saved the best for last!" (John 2:10). This is the message of hope that Jesus brings: "The wine we drink now is the cheaper wine compared to the wine in The Kingdom to come." The result of Jesus' miracle in Cana, when the best wine was served last, is a promise to us that the lives we are living on earth will not compare to the magnificent lives that await us in Eternity with Him.

In God's Kingdom, our lives never run out of anything. They will be never-ending lives filled with health and wholeness. There will be no pain or tears and we will have no needs of any kind because everything will be provided. It's impossible for our carnal minds to grasp the greatness that has been "saved for last" in God's Kingdom to come. Yet there's even more to the story!

While writing this chapter and its companion film, my attention continued to be drawn to the statement made by the master to the bridegroom after tasting Jesus' miracle wine. He said, "Most people serve the choice wine first, and when the guests have had a lot to drink, the host brings out the cheaper wine" (John 2:10).

Suddenly, I realized why my attention had been drawn to this passage! You see, the master of the banquet honestly believed that the best wine had already been served. This is evidenced by his statement, "Most people serve the choice wine first" (John 2:10). He had no idea that there would be even better wine served later.

This is the same reason why we settle for this world instead of staying focused on the Kingdom to come. We think "the best has already been served!" So, we get intoxicated on the "here and now." Our lack of understanding results in false feelings that we should throw caution to the wind and live it all now — often at any cost. When life is going well, we're lured into believing it cannot get any better. We have it all! What can Jesus offer?

Yet, until God's promise of Heaven and eternal life through Jesus is revealed, people will remain blinded by the world and hold on tightly to the first wine served — to what they already have. Many people think, "This is all there's going to be, so I'd better store up and hoard a disproportionate share for myself." They are reluctant to share it with others. When we believe we have the best, it keeps us from seeing the best is still to come!

Jesus warns us to not be deceived by what this world promises. The world's glitter may dazzle us now, yet when we turn our eyes to Heaven and the road ahead, we'll realize, "We're not home yet!" The best is still yet to come, for He has saved the best for last!

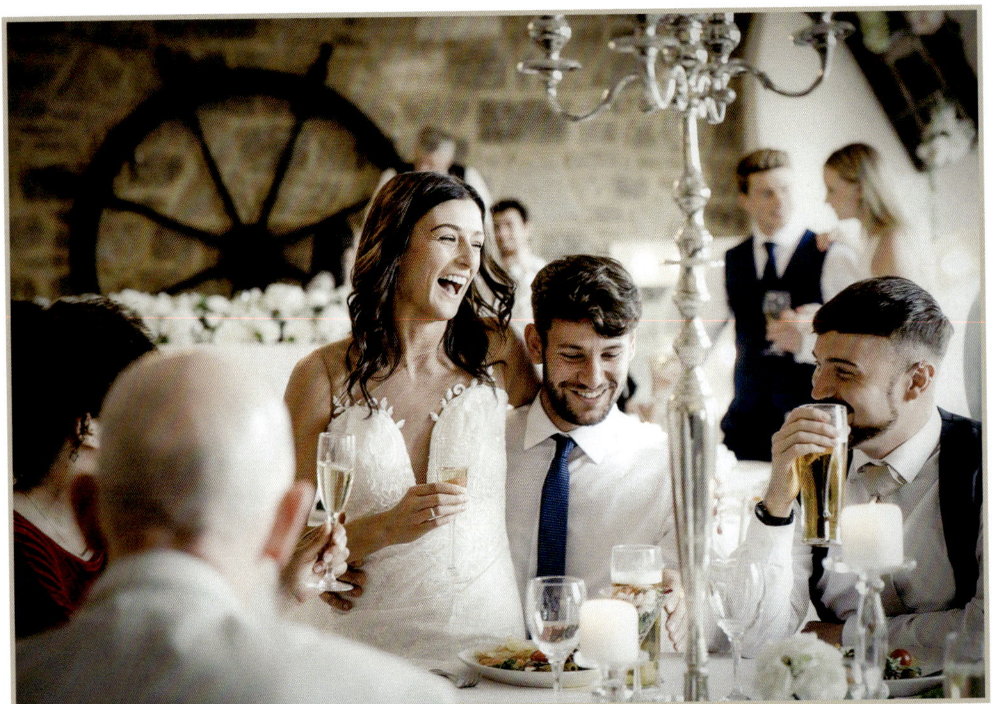

The best has yet to be served!

Thoughts to Ponder

View film at ▶ journeyswiththemessiah.org

- Jesus was reluctant to respond to His mother's announcement, "They have no more wine," and He did not perform his "water-to-wine" miracle in front of the crowds. Consider the correlation here with Matthew 6:5-6: "And when you pray...go into your room, close the door and pray to your Father, who is unseen. Then your Father, who sees what is done in secret, will reward you." Why would God want our prayers hidden?

- When Jesus sent the new miracle wine to the master, the master had no idea from where it had come. As you scurry about picking up groceries, filling your car with gas, shopping here and there, or even running to the doctor or dentist, do you lose sight of "where the wine comes from?" Do we take God's provision for granted and fail to give thanks in all things, moment by moment? Consider purchasing a click counter and picking a day to "click" and give thanks for everything God provides to you. Check the total at the end of the day.

- The Wedding in Cana reminds us of the new wine God offers to everyone through salvation. If we have confessed Jesus as our Lord and Savior, then the best has been saved for last! Consider that we are living "the days of cheap wine." The miraculous wine awaits us in Eternity with Him. And, make sure that "The Host" knows you will be attending!

- The master of the wedding ceremony was convinced that the best wine had already been served. Yet, Jesus' miracle wine indicates the best remains in the bottle and it will not be uncorked until we arrive in His Kingdom. While we wait, avoid getting intoxicated on the here and now.

- When the helicopter dropped us off on the Napali Coast in Hawaii, leaving us one thousand feet above the Pacific Ocean, I recalled saying to my film crew, "It just doesn't get better than this!" Later, Jesus revealed to me that with Him, it does get better! When we think we have the best now, it keeps us from longing for the best that is still to come! Hang on! We're not home yet!

3

Lighten the Load

Help for Whatever is Weighing You Down

View film at ▶ journeyswiththemessiah.org

Who among us is without burdens? Perhaps it's a delayed flight or a late mortgage payment, a term paper due on Friday or a family member who is seriously ill. All of us have burdens that cause us to be anxious and discouraged as we travel along our way. Sometimes, it feels as if we have more baggage than we can bear.

The term *baggage* is a part of today's culture. We hear statements like, "He has

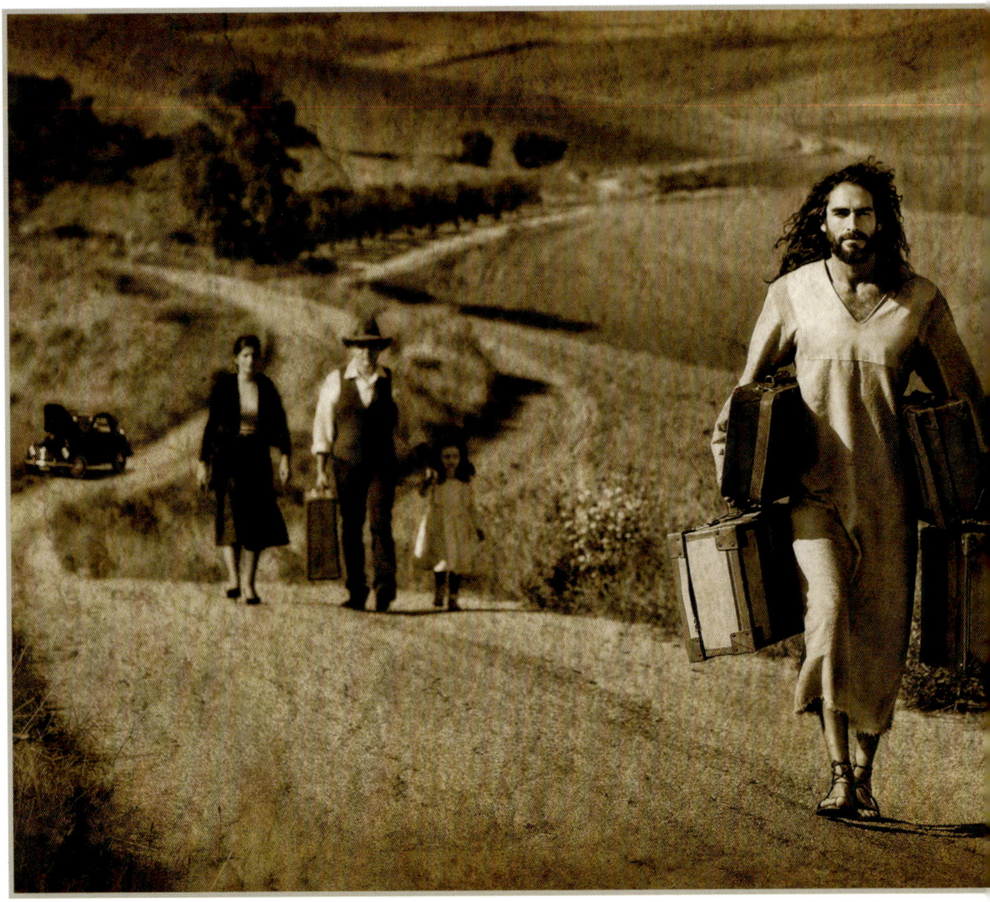

a lot of baggage" or "she comes with a lot of baggage." The Urban Dictionary defines baggage as *an issue regarding a person's past that can affect their current disposition.* Past baggage can definitely affect your future!

As defined here, baggage comes in many shapes and sizes, both physical and emotional. Like the baggage fees charged by today's commercial airlines, there is a price we pay for the baggage we carry in our lives — the more baggage, the higher the cost.

If you have lived for any significant amount of time, you have collected some baggage or issues that can affect your future. The longer you have lived, the more baggage you have accumulated and often through no specific fault of your own. Let's face it, everyone has difficulties to overcome. It is just an inevitable part of life.

Baggage is not spoken of as a positive thing. In many cases, it doesn't amount to much, it's just part of life; just part of being human. Some people can process the events of their lives and move on. For others, their difficulties can linger and turn into emotional baggage they carry around forever. People are seldom aware of how much baggage they actually have or how it affects them.

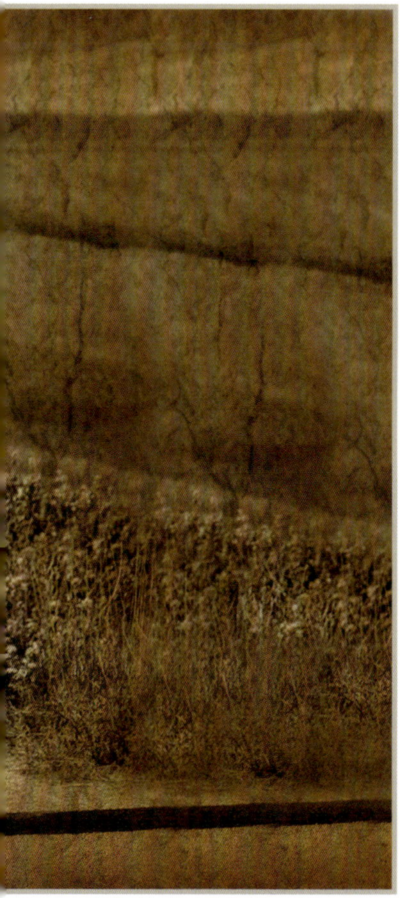

Too much baggage weighs us down, and certain types of baggage weigh us down more than others. Not only does our baggage cause emotional and physical struggle, it often affects the people around us. Some people allow their baggage to get so heavy they become hostages to it. They can't enjoy the present, much less look forward to the future.

Most of us have met people who like to get their baggage out every time someone's around and then talk about it for hours. I have known people who don't appear to have any baggage or, at least, cannot define the bags they have. Yet, for some reason, they need to act like they have a lot of baggage when asked, "How are you?" In more extreme cases, people allow their baggage to become a part of their lives. They hold onto it as if they would not know who they are without it.

So what do we do when the baggage and burdens of life — real or imaginary — weigh us down to the point we are overwhelmed and exhausted?

Jesus offers a simple answer to our dilemma, "Come to Me all who labor and are heavily laden, and I will give you rest…For My yoke is easy to bear, and the burden I give you is light" (Matthew 11:28). Jesus is saying that anyone who is weighted down by the baggage of their life can come to Him and He will provide them with rest.

The concept for these photographs was to have Jesus in settings and locations that appeared to be the from the first century when Jesus lived. Then I would add contemporary people and elements to each setting to visually connect Jesus' time in history with ours. I wanted the images to make the point that Jesus' messages and teachings—spoken over 2000 years ago—were also meant for the present and for those who will live in times beyond ours.

So Jesus invites us to come to Him if we are weighed down by the baggage of our lives and He will give us rest from our burdens. Then He explains, "For My yoke is easy and the burden I give you is light" (Matthew 11:28).

It would be easier for us to understand Jesus' comment, "His yoke is easy," if we lived in biblical times or in a country where oxen are still used to pull carts with heavy loads. The yoke is a device, usually made of wood, that goes over the necks of a pair of animals, keeping them together so they can pull in unison. Its basic design has not changed for thousands of years.

A stronger and well-trained ox is often paired with a weaker, untrained ox. The stronger ox forces the untrained ox to follow the master's commands. The stronger ox also shoulders more weight, making the load lighter for the weaker ox. In this instance, the yoke's burden is considered light for the stronger ox compared to the weaker ox, and the amount of effort required by the weaker ox is less.

The Gospels writers had no idea that their words would be read thousands of years later when few of us would know anything about oxen and yokes!

Jesus' statement about the yoke makes two points: First, He says that we are to come to Him when we need rest from the weight of the burdens we are carrying. Why? Because it is easy for Him to carry them which also makes the burden lighter to us. Second, being yoked to Him keeps us on course while we grow spiritually stronger as we learn from Him.

Who wouldn't want a lighter load in life? Who would not want someone else to take the weight of their burdens? As noted, burdens, like baggage, come in all shapes and sizes. Some of our issues are heavier than others. Although we may have collected some baggage through no fault of our own, each of us carries or has carried baggage that could have been avoided.

As an example, let's say you have a car. It's not the newest model, but it is not old. Outside of the model year, it looks like it's new. It runs perfectly and, even more, it's paid off! You own it! No car payment!

Then you hear that the luxury car dealers are having big sales and offering exceptional value for trade-ins. Oh, the status and joy of driving a new luxury car plus they are offering excellent financing, too! You can only imagine the feeling you will get owning one, especially when you hand the keys to the valet and he says, "Nice car!" The temptation is just too great! "Where do I sign?"

Six months later, you realize that your new car does the same thing as your previous car — it delivers you safely from point A to point B (though it is fun to have a new car). However, when you get right down to it, the most significant difference between this new model and the older one is that you now have a whopping monthly payment you didn't have before. There is also a rumor that your company is downsizing and your job is not secure!

The purchase of the new car you wanted, but really didn't need, has changed from "Oh, what a feeling!" to feelings of anxiety. You have created unnecessary baggage you now have to carry when it could have been avoided! Your muscles are beginning to grow weary!

Although Jesus will graciously offer rest when we are heavily laden by the weight of our burdens, let's not break His back by adding additional baggage through personal desires, unaffordable lifestyles and lack of discipline. In following Christ, we cannot follow our own inclinations and the world's way at the same time.

Instead of coming to Jesus only at those times when our baggage gets too heavy — *when I am heavy laden* — Jesus desires that we stay yoked to Him for all time, allowing Him to do the heavy lifting as needed. At the same time, yoked to Him, He keeps us moving forward on the path that God wants us to follow.

Yoked with Jesus, we will experience peace and contentment that comes as we live without unnecessary baggage. Plus, we will be free to enjoy the scenery along the way.

"Come to Me all who labor and are heavily laden, and I will give you rest." Accept this invitation and He will surely lighten the load.

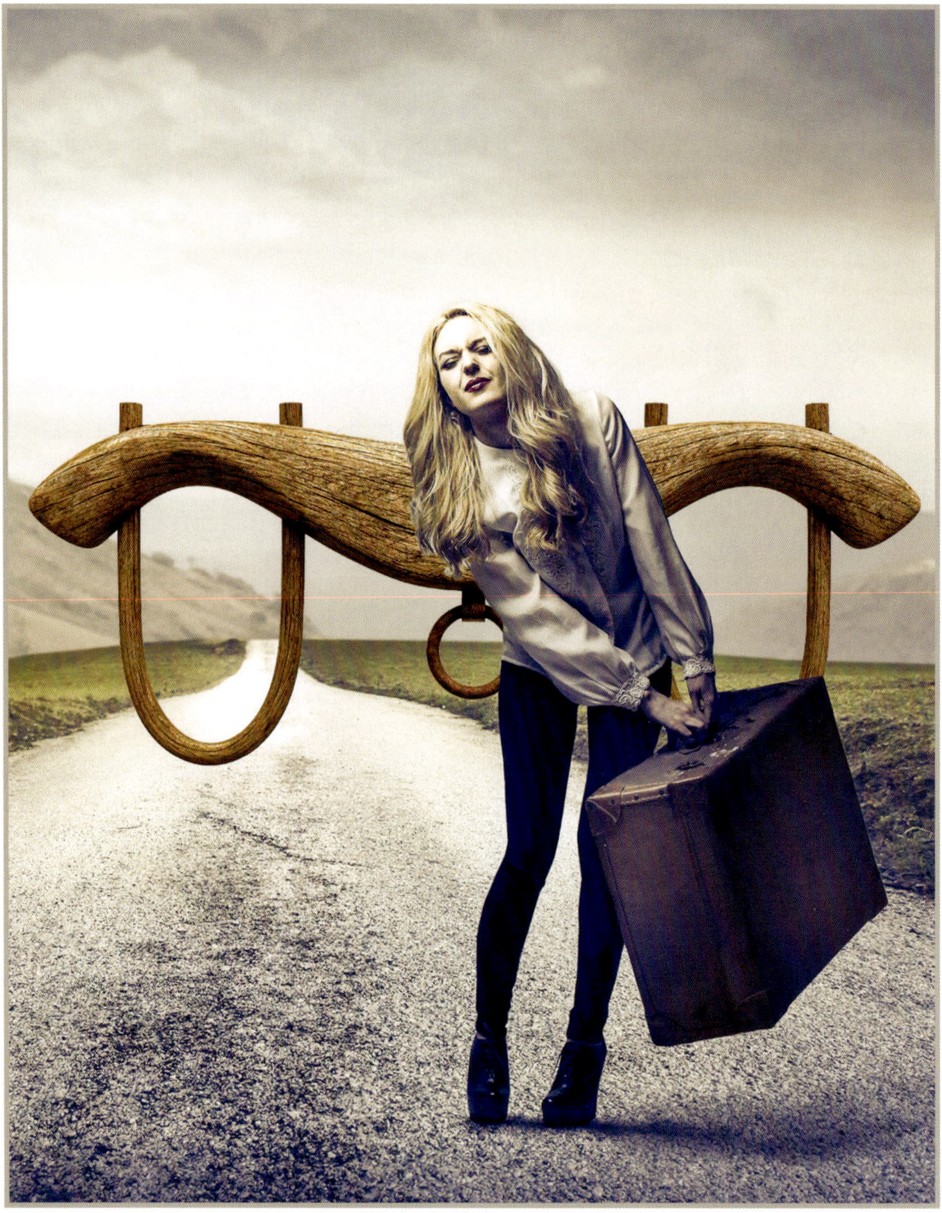

His yoke will lighten the load of your burdens.

Thoughts to Ponder

View film at ▶ journeyswiththemessiah.org

- The Urban Dictionary defines baggage as an issue regarding a person's past that can affect their current disposition. Consider baggage that may be interfering with your life or the lives of those around you. (Examples might include low self-esteem, lack of motivation, or willingness to go into debt and stay in it.) What remedy does Jesus offer?
- Are you able to work through difficulties and move on or do you allow them to linger, becoming emotional baggage that keeps you from enjoying the present moment? What remedy does Jesus offer?
- Recall if or when you have created unnecessary burdens through poor decisions and lack of discipline. The example provided was a new luxury car that was "wanted" but not actually "needed." What remedy does Jesus offer?
- "Come to Me all who labor and are heavily laden, and I will give you rest...For My yoke is easy to bear, and the burden I give you is light" (Matthew 11:28). This verse states Jesus' offer of His supernatural remedy for "the heavy baggage of life's burdens that weigh you down...past, present and future?
- Imagine your life "yoked" to Jesus, whereby He lightens the load of life's burdens by bearing most of them or all of them when necessary.

A Step Away

Heaven or Hell? Where Does God Draw the Line?

View film at ▶ journeyswiththemessiah.org

While sharing my faith with someone who was not a believer in Jesus, they asked, "If my God is so loving and kind, why would He allow some people to go to Heaven, while sending others to Hell?" It's a good question, but there is an answer!

A Step Away was created to depict the eternal separation that can exist between God and man because of man's sinful nature as opposed to the holiness of God.

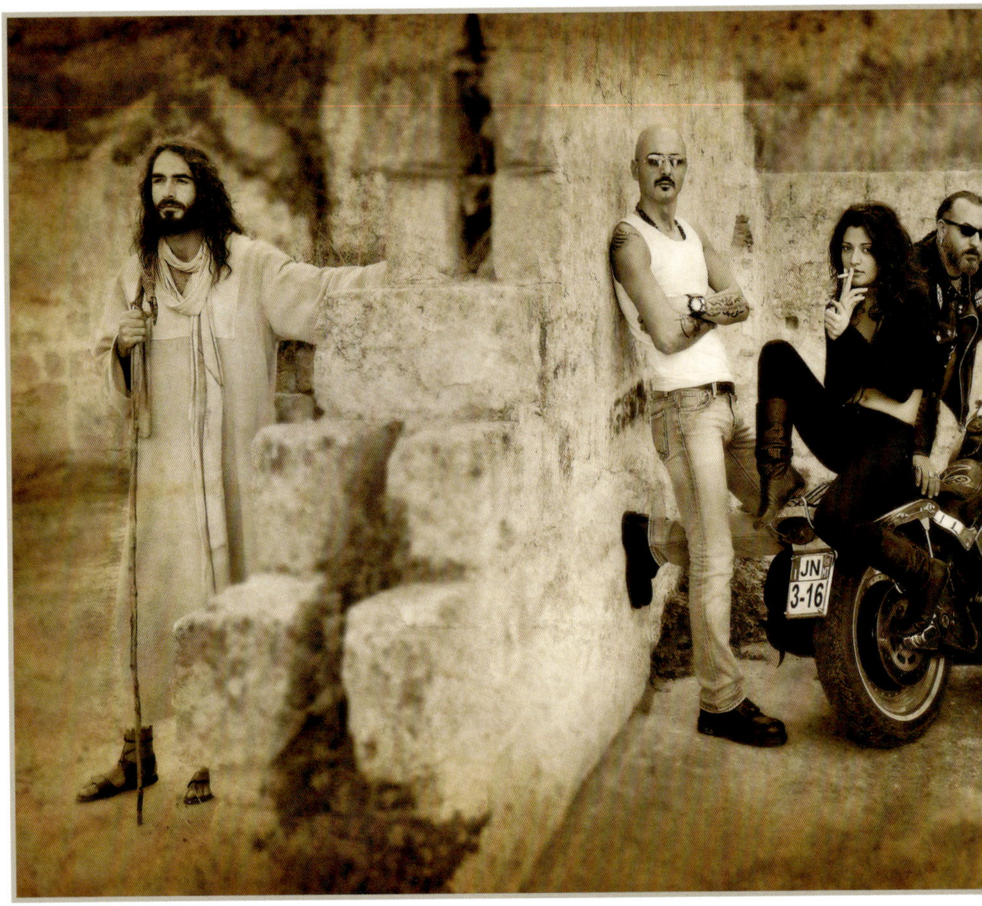

Holy means perfect or pure; it means flawless. It's a difficult concept to imagine because perfection does not exist in our world. We may say things like, "I took a perfect vacation" or "we own the perfect home," but those are just expressions of ideals. Nothing in this world is perfect. Everything, including everyone, falls short. Perfection exists only in a perfect world. It exists only in God's world.

On the other hand, God has to be perfect or the universe He created would have been imperfect or flawed. Think about that! A perfect world cannot be created by a less-than-perfect Creator? Plus, who would want a less-than-perfect God or want to worship one?

Jesus provided us with an example of God's nature when he said, "A good tree cannot bear bad fruit, and a bad tree cannot bear good fruit" (Matthew 7:18). Stated another way, Jesus was saying that a good tree can produce only good fruit and thus, God, who is holy and perfect, can create only good fruit or make only good and perfect things.

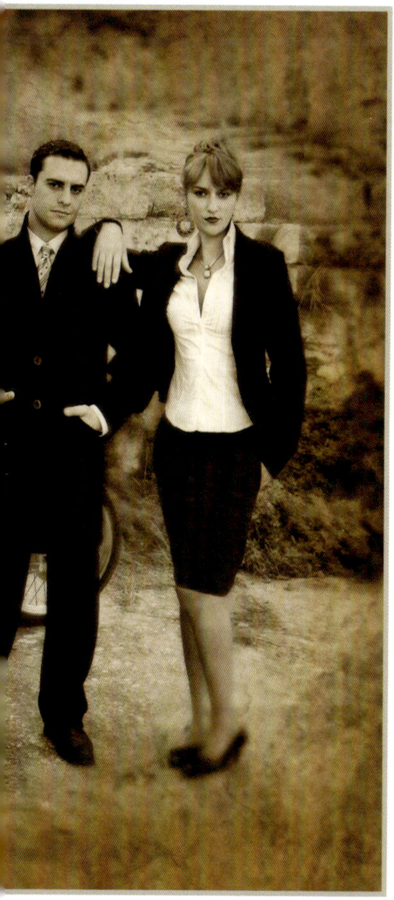

So, when God created the world, everything was perfect and nothing existed that was not perfect. Everything worked perfectly according to God's perfect design for the world and His perfect plan for mankind.

God's Holy nature also makes Him incompatible with anyone or anything that is not perfect. In other words, God cannot allow anyone into His presence that is not Holy as He is Holy — perfect as He is perfect.

Since God can create only perfect things, His plan for mankind was also perfect. Thus, if we choose to follow any plan (like our own) instead of God's plan for us, we are choosing to follow a flawed or imperfect plan. The only possible outcome is that we will be flawed or less than perfect, which makes us incompatible with Holy God and unable to be in His presence in Eternity.

Such was the case with Adam and Eve, the first man and woman created by God. You may know their Garden of Eden story as told in the Book of Genesis. God told Adam and Eve that they could eat from any tree in the Garden except one. He warned them that, if they ate from it, they would die (Genesis 2:16-17). They were disobedient to His command and ate from it anyway.

God's plans are the only perfect plans. By Adam and Eve's disobedience to God's command not to eat the fruit from the forbidden tree, they followed their plan instead of God's perfect plan. Thus Adam and Eve became flawed or imperfect through their disobedience to God.

Please recall that by God's own nature He cannot be in the presence of anyone or anything that is not perfect or Holy. Thus, God had to remove Adam and Eve from The Garden because they could no longer be in His presence. The scriptures state that God placed cherubim with flaming swords at the entrance to block Adam and Eve from re-entering The Garden (Genesis 3:23-24).

Adam and Eve would eventually die separated from God since eternal life exists only in the presence of God. We too will die separated from God, the only one who can give eternal life!

Returning to the question, "If God is so loving and kind, why would He allow some people to go to Heaven while letting others go to Hell?" I respond by asking, "Where should God draw the line between the people He considers good enough to go to Heaven and the people He judges as bad enough to go to Hell?"

In the image *A Step Away*, the wall between Jesus and the two groups of people represents the separation between God and man — a barrier between Holy God and imperfect man. The image invites you to consider the nicely dressed couple versus the motorcycle group as to who might be "good enough to go to Heaven" and who might be "bad enough to go to Hell." (It's a trick question!)

The Apostle Paul wrote in Romans 3:23, "For all have sinned and fall short of the glory of God." In other words, we are all flawed by the sin of disobedience to God's plans and fall short of God's perfection. "All" includes everyone, even good people like Mother Theresa, Billy Graham and The Pope.

In the Bible, disobedience is referred to as sin. I like to characterize sin as choosing our way instead of God's way; our plans instead of His. Even the smallest sin makes us imperfect, which separates us eternally from Him.

Like Adam and Eve, we will die separated from God and eternal life unless there is a way to have our sins removed, allowing us to enter His presence.

We can say we're sorry and God will forgive us, but the sins remain because of the price that must be paid for breaking God's laws. However, because sin has made us imperfect, we have nothing to offer as payment to a Holy and perfect God. Yet God did!

John 3:16 states, "For God so loved the world that He gave His only begotten Son, that whoever believes in Him should not perish but have everlasting life." God loved you and me so much that He sent His Son into the world to exchange His life for ours. He allowed Jesus to be sacrificed — to die a brutal death on a cross — so that you and I might be cleansed of sin and restored to Holiness; that we may live forever in Eternity with Him.

John the Baptist said of Jesus, "Behold! The Lamb of God, who takes away the sins of the world." (John 1:29) Jesus came to take away our sins, erasing them forever, tearing down the wall that separates us from God in Eternity. That's some kind of crazy love!

There was a time when I was too proud to understand that I was a sinner; that I was flawed by my disobedience to God's plan as I went my own way following my own desires. I knew I was bad, but in my arrogance I still thought I was good enough to go to Heaven. It was not until I was given the gift to understand that God is Holy and as long as I am not, I cannot live in His presence in Heaven after my time ends on earth.

Oswald Chambers states it this way: "I cannot save and sanctify myself; I cannot make atonement for sin; I cannot redeem the world; I cannot right what is wrong, purify what is impure, or make holy what is unholy. That is all the sovereign work of God. Do I have faith in what Jesus Christ has done?"

When you look at this picture, you can see that He is only a step away. If you sense there is a wall between you and Him, I encourage you to take that step today.

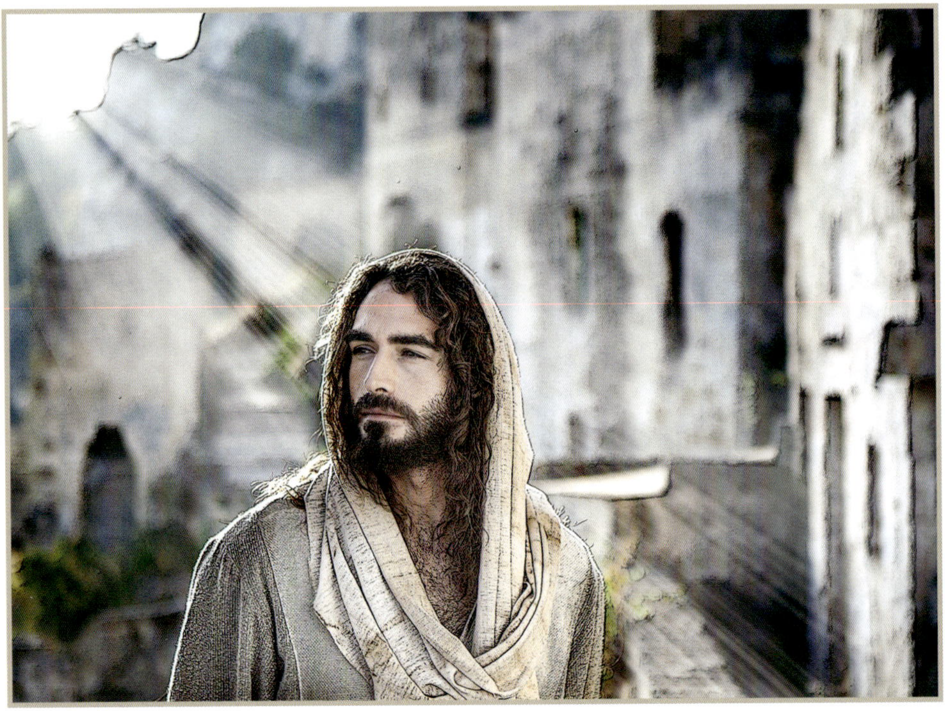

On location Sassi di Matera

Thoughts to Ponder

View film at ▶ journeyswiththemessiah.org

- To live in Eternity with God, we must be Holy as He is Holy — pure as He is pure. Even the smallest sin disqualifies us. Romans 3:23 states that we have all sinned [by disobeying God's commands/directions] and have fallen short of His Holiness. Instead of salvation through grace, pretend that God judges us on the scale of "good enough for heaven or bad enough for Hell." Where would you place yourself on God's scale and why?

- If God is so loving, why would He allow some people to go to Heaven while others go Hell? If asked, can you answer the question?

- "A good tree cannot bear bad fruit, and a bad tree cannot bear good fruit" (Matthew 7:18). Jesus is saying that a good tree can produce only good fruit. Picture your life as a "fruit market" and take inventory of the types of fruits you need more of and the ones you need to eliminate.

- Everyone is aware of big sins like adultery, stealing, lying, and lust. However, every sin — large or small — begins with disobedience to God's authority and commands. Consider a sin in your life (now or in the past) and see if you can trace it back to a specific disobedience to God's directions.

- Adam and Eve were told not to eat the fruit of a specific tree as it would result in death. However, it was not the fruit that would kill them. It was disobedience that caused them to be locked out of the Garden of Eden, separated from God and His eternal Tree of Life. When we are saved through Christ, we will not be separated from God in Eternity. Yet, our daily sins of disobedience can still create daily walls of separation when we do not repent.

- Have you heard of a King falling on his sword, sacrificing himself to save his subjects? That would be some kind of crazy love! It's what Jesus did when God sent Him into the world to save us, not by falling on a sword, but being nailed to a cross! Take time to consider what Jesus did. He gave up His perfect life in payment for our imperfect lives flawed by sins of disobedience.

5

As for Others

Our Beliefs Illustrated through Actions

View film at ▶ journeyswiththemessiah.org

Have you heard the expression "walking the talk?" It means performing actions that are consistent with what one claims they believe. Saying we believe in something — like saying we are Christians — is not validated until our claim is reflected in the way we live out our faith.

The image *As for Others* was inspired by the concept of walking the talk as it was

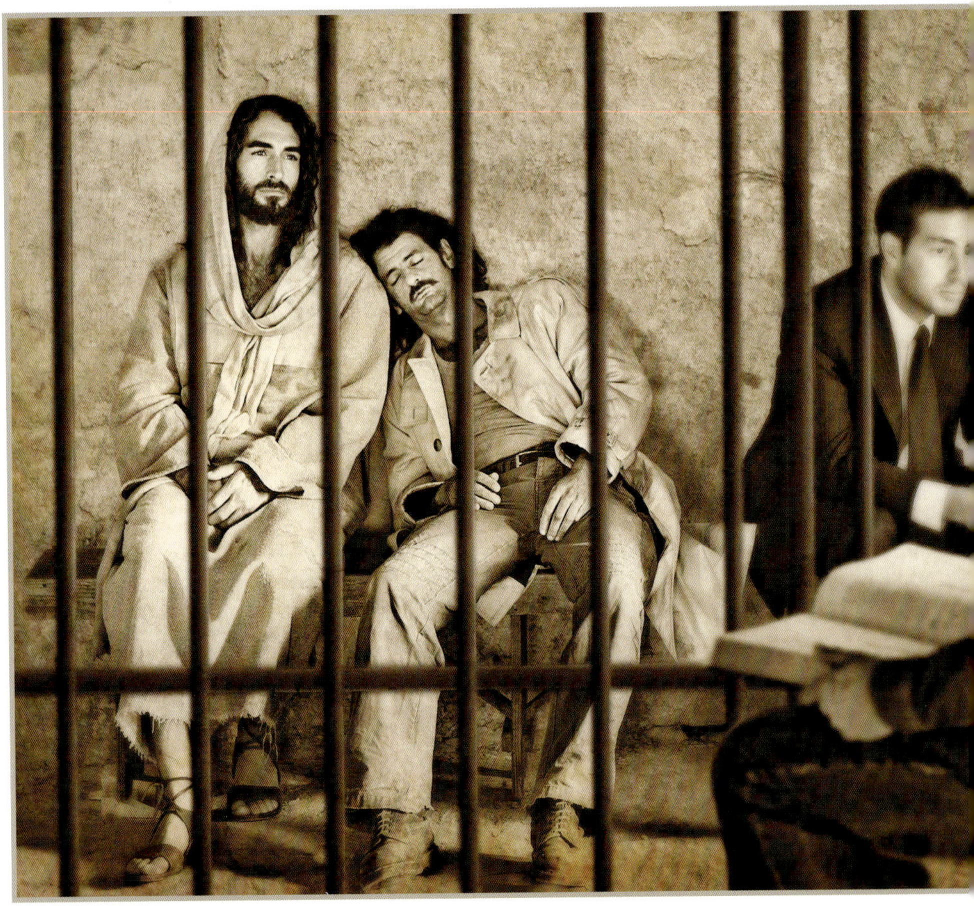

illustrated in a story Jesus shared with His disciples 2,000 years ago. Jesus was teaching His disciples about how things would be in His eternal Kingdom after His death. In reference to Himself, He said that The King would sit on His glorious throne and gather everyone around Him — people from all nations, all races, all walks of life — regardless of how they had lived their lives. Then He said that The King would separate the people as a shepherd separates his sheep from his goats, placing the righteous on the right (Matthew 25:31-32).

So, imagine this setting: We are all gathered together in Eternity with Jesus who stands before us and separates us into two groups. He places "the righteous" on the right and tells them they are blessed. Then He invites them to *take their inheritance which is The Kingdom of God that has been prepared for them since the world was created* (Matthew 25:32-34).

Okay, I think we're clear on that part — the righteous are on the right. The question is, "Who are these people and what makes them righteous?"

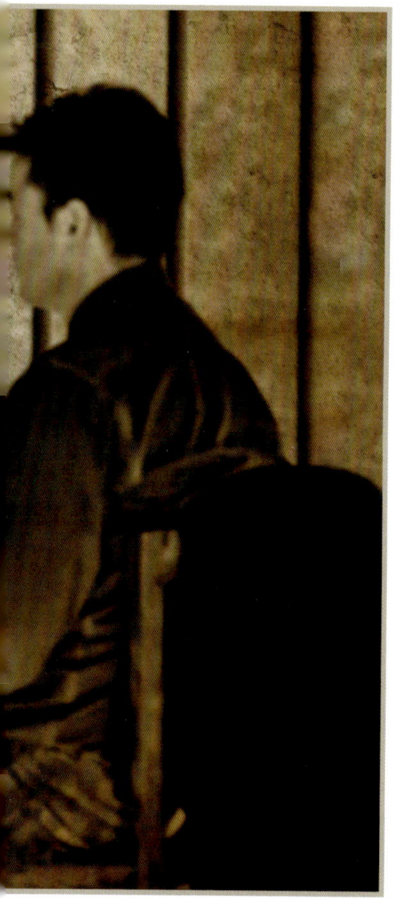

Jesus answers this way: "For I was hungry and you gave me something to eat, I was thirsty and you gave me something to drink, I was a stranger and you invited me in, I needed clothes and you clothed me, I was sick and you looked after me, I was in prison and you came to visit me" (Matthew 25:35-36).

Well, you can only imagine that everyone is perplexed by what The King has just said. So we speak up: "Excuse me Lord, but when did we see you hungry and feed you? Can you remind us about the time you were thirsty and we gave you something to drink? We can't say that we recall a time when you were a stranger and we invited you into our homes! Did you say we took you shopping when you needed some clothes? We know we would remember visiting you in prison because you were never in prison. What's up with all this?" (Matthew 25:37-39). Jesus says that The King will answer their questions by saying, "Truly I tell you, any of these [kind things] you did for any of these brothers and sisters of mine, you also did for me" (Matthew 25:40).

Jesus was instructing his disciples, and us, that when we show kindness to anyone, it is the same as showing kindness to Him. He was also making the point that the people who do this will be known as "the righteous," and they will inherit The Kingdom and live eternal life in Heaven with Him.

Love one another is the dominating theme in Jesus' teachings and the subject we wanted to share in our images. Jesus' statement, "I was in prison and you came to visit Me," inspired our photograph of Jesus behind prison bars.

The Jewish leaders of that time, the Pharisees, tested Jesus by asking him, "Which is the greatest [of the] commandments?" (Matthew 22:36).

Jesus answered them by combining the Ten Commandments into just two commandments: "Love the Lord your God with all your heart and with all your soul and with all your mind. This is the first and greatest commandment." Then he said that the second greatest commandment was just like the first, "Love your neighbor as yourself" (Matthew 22:37-39).

In essence, Jesus was saying that if you are loving God, then you will show love to your neighbors and if you are showing love to your neighbors, then you are loving God. Jesus said that people who follow these commandments will be known as "the righteous" and will inherit the Kingdom of Heaven.

This is a beautiful passage and an excellent analogy for understanding that "righteous people" love God and love their neighbors as they love themselves. Their inheritance will be an eternal life in Heaven with God. Yet the story did not end there! The King divided the people into two groups and we have talked only about the "people on the right."

As the scripture continues, "To those on His left he will say, 'Depart from Me, you who are cursed into the eternal fire prepared for the devil and his angels. For I was hungry and you gave Me nothing to eat, I was thirsty and you gave Me nothing to drink, I was a stranger and you did not invite Me in, I needed clothes and you did not clothe Me, I was sick and in prison and you did not look after Me" (Matthew 25:41-43).

Okay, let's review to make sure we understand all of this:

Those who love God with all their heart, soul, and mind will show that love by loving their neighbors as they love themselves. So, if you love God, you will show love to your neighbors and if you show love to your neighbors, you show love to God. You can't do one without doing the other. Jesus said these people will be called "the righteous" and they will inherit the eternal Kingdom of God, meaning they will live an eternal life in Heaven. However, Jesus says that "all others will go away to eternal punishment!" (Matthew 25:46). "Depart from Me, you who are cursed into the eternal fire prepared for the devil and his angels" (Matthew 25:41).

I wish there was another way to interpret Jesus' words, but I'm afraid there's not! This scripture shows the difference between those who are truly committed to be on Christ's side and those who just say they are with Him. He is clear about the two options available!

Please do not misinterpret this scripture to mean that we can work our way into Heaven by doing good deeds for our neighbors. As stated in Ephesians 2:8-9, "For by grace you have been saved through faith…not a result of works." We must understand that there is a spiritual transformation that arouses us to love others as we love ourselves. It occurs when we are born again into a totally new life with Jesus as our Lord.

While it is good that Jesus has presented these options to us, let's not dwell on the second option — the one regarding His warning about eternal punishment. It's crucial that we know about it, but let's focus on the positive message about how we can be assured that we will be "placed on the right, called righteous and inherit the Kingdom."

When asked "who can be saved," Jesus told His disciples, "With man this is impossible, but with God all things are possible" (Matthew 19:26). It is only through His Holy Spirit working in and through us that we are capable of loving our neighbors as ourselves.

If Jesus is your Lord and Savior, perhaps this is a good time to restate your belief and rededicate your life to Him. If He is not, perhaps you will consider Him by exploring His words and the abundance of evidence that clearly points to Him as the Messiah, the Son of God. Maybe you will desire to accept His gift of salvation and eternal life provided to you through His sacrificial death.

When Jesus is our Lord and Savior, we will want to spend quality time with Him, hearing His story and learning about His Father's love for all of His children. We are transformed as God replaces our old desires with His perfect desires. Then He synchronizes them with actions as we begin to "walk the talk" of our faith.

Eventually, when our numbered days come to an end on earth and we are ushered off to eternal life, we will be recognized as one of "the righteous." Jesus will place us on the right and invite us to inherit The Kingdom that He personally created for each of us before the beginning of the world, and…we will be blessed!

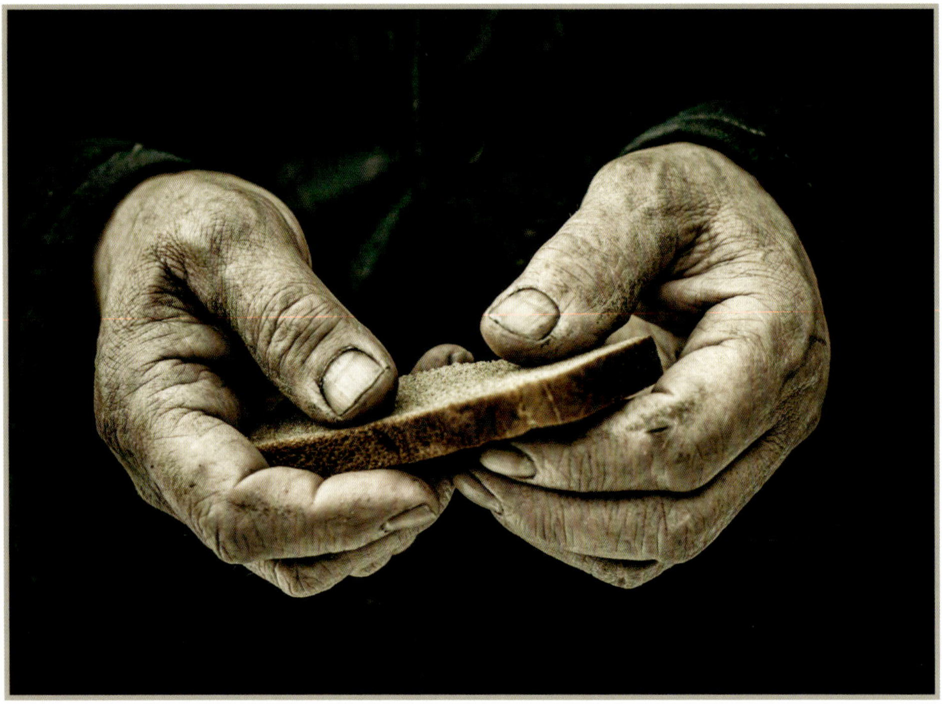

"I was hungry and you gave me something to eat."

Thoughts to Ponder

View film at ▶ journeyswiththemessiah.org

- The Book of Acts reveals that before Christians began to call themselves Christians, they called themselves "the Way," as Jesus said He was "the way" in John 14:6. Thus, a Christian follows in the way of Jesus. Ponder your life, asking Him to guide you in new ways to better follow His way. Tell Him you want to "walk the talk" of your belief in Him.

- Although we cannot work our way to Heaven, "works" are an excellent barometer for indicating how we are "'walking the talk" of our Christian belief. Based on Jesus' answer in Matthew 25:35-36, (Pg.33), what are a few of the things "the righteous" do? Which of these are part of your Christian walk?

- Jesus said that loving our neighbors was the same as loving God. Providing food, water and shelter to those in need plus visiting the sick and people in prison was the same as if we had done these things for Him (Matthew 22:37-39). If you inventory your life or interviewed those who witness your actions, are you showing your love for God through loving others?

- Jesus does not say that we can inherit the Kingdom through works but shows that "the righteous" (those on the right) have characteristics different from those on the left: They love others! They show their love by doing for others. Consider these characteristics. Are they familiar?

- When you wander from His way to go your own way, do you notice that your desire to love others gives way to focusing only on your own needs and love for yourself? How do we change directions? (Hint: "With God, all things are possible.")

6

Can't Take It with You

A Lesson in Retained Earnings

View film at ▶ journeyswiththemessiah.org

The inspiration for this image came from a story I read about the American business magnate, John D. Rockefeller. So the story goes, at a news conference held after his death in 1937, a reporter asked Rockefeller's attorney, "How much wealth did he leave behind?"

The attorney thought for a moment and then responded, "He left it all!"

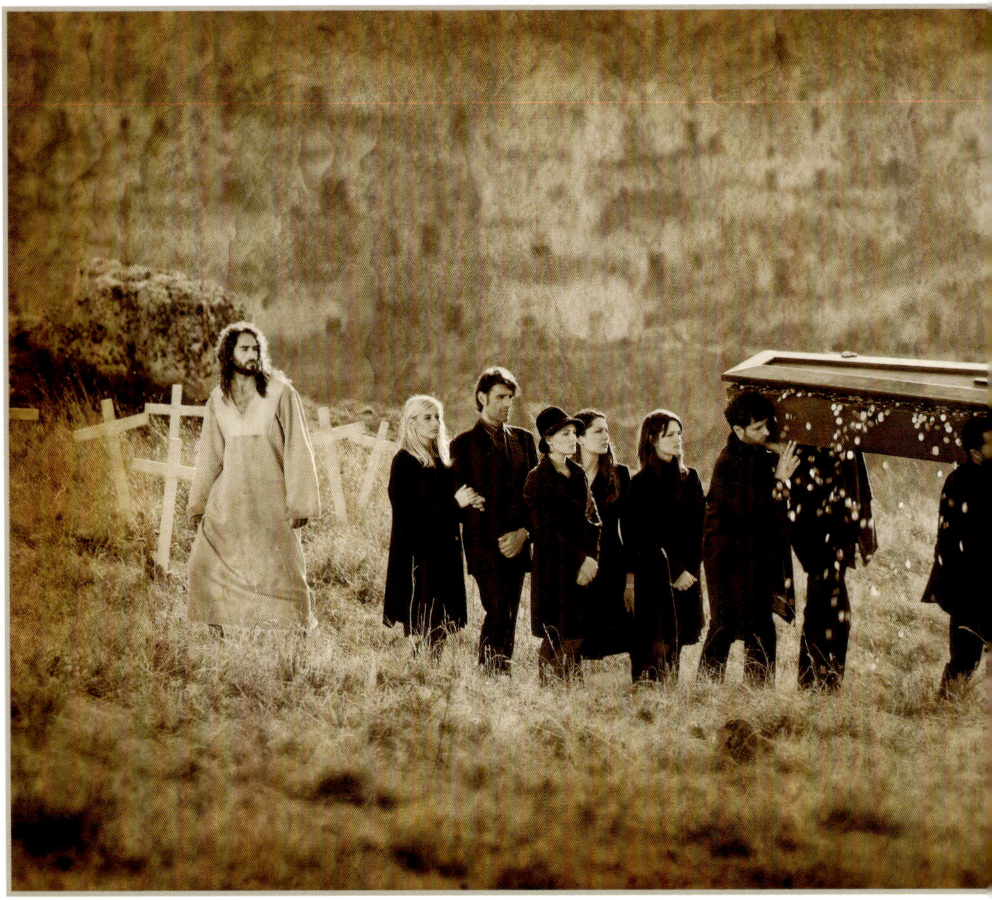

Most everyone has heard that the only things certain in life are death and taxes. Well, there is something else that is certain: Whatever physical treasures you have collected on earth, when you die, you're not going to take them with you!

The world's way of pursuing riches is by grasping and hoarding. God's way is by letting go and giving. That's why Jesus talked more about money and possessions than He spoke of Heaven and Hell.

I felt it was important to create an image depicting at least one of His teachings on the crucial topic of money and possessions; a photograph that would catch people's attention—creating curiosity that would entice them to read the message.

We chose Matera, Italy for our backdrop as its appearance is how people might imagine Jerusalem 2,000 years ago when Jesus lived. My concept for *Can't Take it with You* included a funeral procession of modern-day people carrying a casket. The casket would have gold coins pouring out of it as a way to suggest that the deceased was trying to take his wealth with him to the grave.

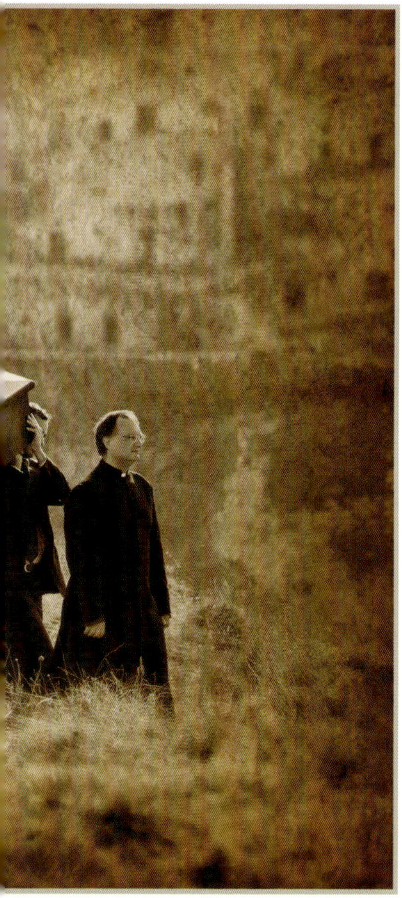

Someone taking their money to their grave is not as far fetched as we might think. King Tut and other Egyptian Pharaohs buried a lot of their wealth with them, much of it in the form of gold. Though I have not heard of people doing that in modern times, people become so attached to their wealth that they try to control its disposition after death by leaving wills stating who gets what and when and even setting timelines for its distribution.

Jesus is against accumulating wealth to the point that one would consider burying it with them. Here is what He said about it, "Do not store up for yourself treasures [wealth] on earth" (Matthew 6:19).

Don't store up? What does He mean? Is Jesus saying that we should not plan for the future or put a little money away for a rainy day and retirement? No, I don't think that's what He is saying. I believe Jesus is saying do not hoard! Do not store up for yourself more than you can practically use. Really? Do we do that?

Jesus told a story about a rich man who planned to tear down his barns to build bigger ones to store his wealth. God called him a fool, saying that he would die that very night (Luke 12:18 -20). Jesus was saying that the rich man would never get to enjoy his stored up wealth.

That's a great story but very few of us are rich, so this story doesn't apply to us, right? Hoarding, or storing up more than we can practically use, is done by more than just rich men and sadly, applies to most everyone — rich or poor. If you don't believe me, go take a tour of your closet!

I went to my closet and found sixteen pairs of shoes. I need a variety of shoes, but there were at least eight pairs I never wear. (Oops...forgot to count the golf shoes and cowboy boots!) I have thirty shirts. I wear a third of them. I am embarrassed that I discovered seventeen pairs of jeans, a dozen shorts, and fifteen dress slacks. Since we live in Southwest Florida, I wear shorts more than eighty percent of the time!

My wife and I moved recently to find that we had stored up far more than we could practically use. We gave away half of everything we owned and we still have too much. Over the years, we have had to clean it, insure it, move it and store it, which has amounted to a lot of wasted expense — money that could have been used for better purposes.

Though we never considered it to be that big of a deal, Jesus says it's a real big deal! While we hoard, people in need go without! This has to be the reason Jesus said "Do not store up!" He is saying don't accumulate and hoard your wealth, which includes everything that is more than we can practically use.

Jesus is concerned about the spiritual condition of our souls caused by hoarding. He says, "Wherever your treasure is, there your heart will be also" (Matthew 6:21). He means that if my heart is into storing up more than I can practically use, then my heart is in the wrong place. As an old friend would say, "You've come down with a serious case of poverty consciousness!" She defined it as being fooled into thinking that there is not enough and I must get my disproportionate share. Many people do this no matter the cost.

Hoarding creates a dilemma: It keeps my focus on me rather than on others. When my focus is on myself, I am looking in the direction that Jesus said will never bring the joy I seek. In fact, here is precisely the way He said it, "If your first concern is to look after yourself, you'll never find yourself" (Matthew 10:38-39 MSG). And shortly after that, He said, "What good is it for someone to gain the whole world, yet forfeit their soul" (Matthew 16:26)?

In Psalm 39:6, King David offers words of wisdom about storing up, "Remind me that my days are numbered…that all our busy rushing ends in nothing as we store up wealth, not knowing who will spend it."

David's words can be used to describe the rich man in Jesus' story (the one who was building bigger barns to store his wealth). He didn't know he was about to die or who would spend his money after he was gone. 1 Timothy 6:7 states, "We brought nothing into the world, and we can take nothing out of it."

Yet, there is a way we can enjoy our wealth without storing it up now, without hoarding it from others. Jesus said we can take it with us by sending it ahead! After He said, "Do not store up treasures and wealth on earth," He said store it up in Heaven where it will not rot, deteriorate, or be stolen (Matthew 6:20). And just how do we do that? We do it by letting go and giving!

If you want to be rich in eternal life in Heaven after your time is over here, then take inventory of all you have stored up and, if it is more than you can practically use, start giving it to those who are in need. This includes everything — closets, attics, garages and warehouses, plus saving accounts and 401Ks. God also offers a plan that allows us to multiply our rewards in Heaven. It's called "sacrificial giving." It's characterized by giving more than we can practically use and giving things we would rather keep.

Giving from your overflow is a good thing to do, but it's easy to do because it doesn't involve sacrifice. (I donated over 50% of my clothes but it didn't hurt because I had so many!) Sacrificial giving is when your gift may—or will—leave you with a shortfall. However, in either case, God loves the one who gives cheerfully (2 Corinthians 9:7).

Storing up treasures in Heaven means giving away more of our earthly treasures now. Yet, to give more away now requires more faith in Him. At first, it might seem like a radical idea, but Jesus offers us the gift of living a radically different life.

So start storing up treasures in Heaven. Besides, you can't take it with you!

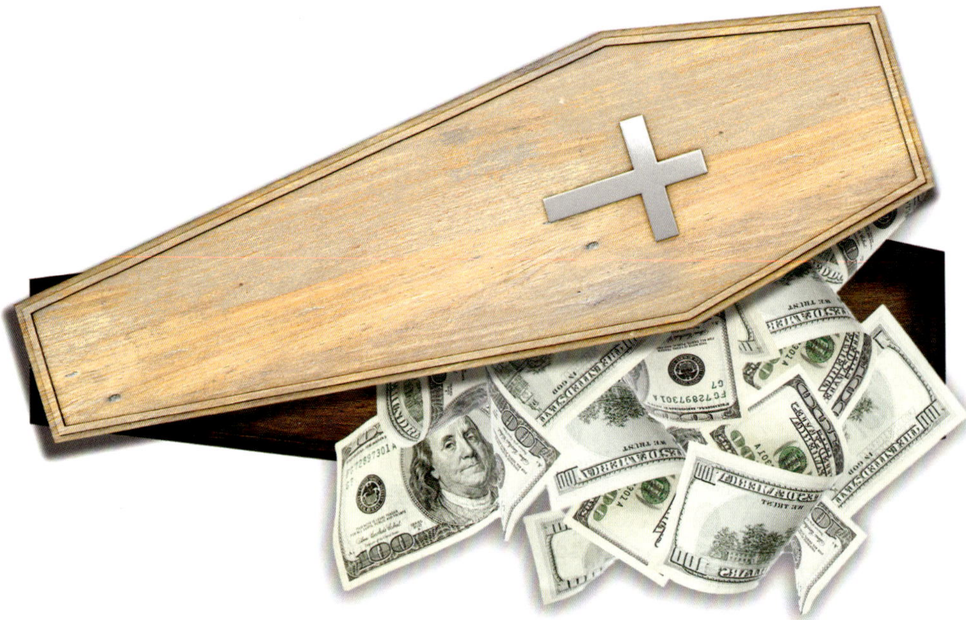

Thoughts to Ponder

View film at ▶ journeyswiththemessiah.org

- Two ways to pursue riches: The world's way of "grasping and hoarding." God's way of "letting go and giving." Only as we understand "the true riches" that God wants us to pursue will we be able to acknowledge why His way is better! Consider the "riches" you are pursuing?

- John D. Rockefeller, the wealthiest man who ever lived, did not take anything with him when he died. Midway through his career, he began giving away vast sums and spent his retirement giving away most of his money. He was a devoted religious man who read the Bible, basing his philosophy of giving on biblical principles, in particular Luke 6:38, "Give, and it will be given to you. A good measure, pressed down, shaken together and running over, will be poured into your lap. For with the measure you use, it will be measured to you."

- "Do not store up for yourself treasures [wealth] on earth" (Matthew 6:19) means do not hoard by storing up more than we can practically use. Yet, everyone hoards at some level. Perhaps you can ponder adopting a Non-Hoarding Plan. Begin with the attic and work your way to the basement and garage. Eliminate anything more than you can practically use. (Hire some high school or college kids to help. Some ministries will come to your home, pick it up and turn it into money for those in need.) Inventory your finances. Calculate a liberal amount for yourself for now and the future. Consider some for your heirs if you like. With all your needs covered, consider giving away the amount in access of the amount you can practically use.

- The exercise in the paragraph above is designed for "giving from your abundance or overflow." It should cause you no discomfort because you won't miss it. However, "sacrificial giving" is when your gift may, or will, leave you with a shortfall. Sacrificial giving is when you give money (and possessions) you would rather keep in exchange for helping someone in need. Jesus calls this "Storing up in Heaven," where it will not rot, deteriorate, or be stolen (Matthew 6:20).

7

Compassion

There May Be More to the Story

View film at ▶ journeyswiththemessiah.org

Have you ever come to the wrong conclusion about something or someone because you didn't know all the facts? President John F. Kennedy said, "We enjoy the comfort of opinion without having the discomfort of thought."

The image *Compassion* was inspired by the story of the "Woman at the Well," one of the most well-known biblical stories from the Apostle John's account of Jesus' life (John 4:4-26). The story took place while Jesus and his disciples were traveling through Samaria.

During that time in history, Israel was divided into two regions. The northern province was Galilee and the southern province was Judea with the holy city of Jerusalem. The two regions were separated by the territory of Samaria.

Samaria once belonged to the Israelites, who lived in Galilee and Judea. After most of the Israelites (also known as Hebrews or Jews) had been taken into captivity in Assyria, the King of Assyria sent non-Jewish people to live in the region. The remaining Israelites in Samaria intermarried with these foreigners and adopted many of their religious customs, including the worshipping of idols (2 Kings 17). Thus, Samaritans were generally considered half-breeds and were universally despised by the Jews for their idolatrous practices.

Although the Jews generally avoided the Samaritans, sometimes they needed to travel through Samaria to shorten the trip between Galilee and Judea. Jesus and several of his disciples were taking this shorter route as they headed back to Galilee (John 4:4).

It was close to noon when they arrived in the town of Sychar. Jesus sat down by a well while the disciples went to buy food. A Samaritan woman came to the well to draw water and Jesus asked her if she would give him a drink. The woman was surprised and asked Jesus why he would speak to her since he was a Jew and she was a Samaritan, and so a conversation began (John 4:6-9).

Jesus told her that if she knew the gift of God and who she was talking to, she could ask Him and He would give her "living water" (John 4:10). He explained that

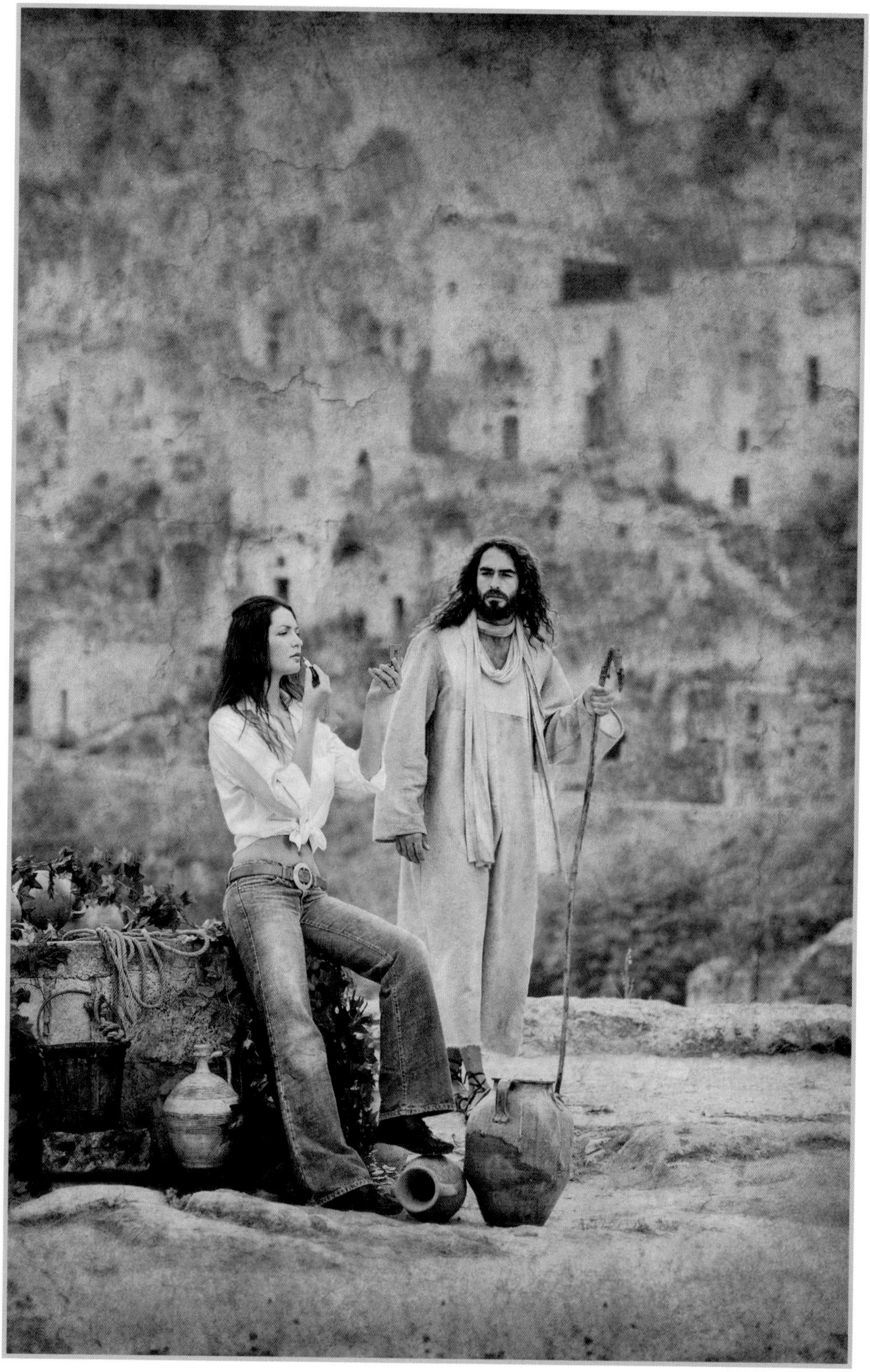

this "living water," unlike the water from the well, would allow her to never thirst again; that it would become a spring in her that would well up into eternal life (John 4:13-14).

Jesus was using water as a metaphor to describe a spiritual condition of the heart that would occur through Him, but she thought He was talking in literal terms. So she asked Him to give her some of the water so she would not thirst again, and so she would not have to keep returning to the well for water (John 4:15).

Jesus told her to go back and get her husband, but she replied that she had no husband. The story gets even more interesting! Jesus told her that He knew she did not have a husband. In fact, He knew that she had been married five times, and she was not married to the man with whom she was living (John 4:16-18).

When I first heard this story, I immediately formed an opinion: She was a prostitute or at least a woman who had been "intimate" with other partners. In fact, throughout history this passage of scripture has been used to illustrate an immoral woman whose life was changed by Jesus. Perhaps we have judged her character as "immoral" without knowing all we should know about her. Maybe we need more information.

For example, it might be helpful for us to know why the Samaritan woman was at the well by herself in the middle of the day, when most women went to the well together in the morning. And, why had she been married five times and was not married to the man with whom she was living?

Neb Haden is a professor, scholar and friend. In his book, "When the Good News Gets Even Better," he explains that we would have a better understanding of the Gospels if we could see them through the eyes of a Jew who lived in the first century. He says that the most likely reason that the woman was at the well in the middle of the day, married five times and living with a man to whom she was not married was because she was barren — she could not have children!

In biblical times, women who could not produce children were of little value by most men's standards. So, if she could not have children, it's likely that after she got married and could not have a child, her husband would divorce her. In those days, men could divorce their wives for almost any reason, and not being able to have children would be a good one. So, she would marry again and would be divorced again for the same reason.

Most women had no way of supporting themselves. If they did not have their father's home to return to, they would be left on the street, and some of them were forced to become prostitutes as a matter of survival.

In this particular case, the Samaritan woman obviously had to lean on the help of a man by living with him. Under such an arrangement, she would not have been in a position to give him an ultimatum about marriage. If in fact she is barren, it would explain the multiple marriages and why she was alone at the well in the middle of the day.

Just imagine the stigma her situation would have placed on her. The other women would have shunned her for living with another man. And, because she could not have children, they may have been so callous as to say that she was not in favor of God. Proverbs 18:2 says, "Fools find no pleasure in understanding, but delight in airing their own opinions."

Fortunately, Jesus did not see her in the same way others may have. Regardless of her embarrassing and difficult situation, Jesus saw her as a woman scarred by her past; a woman whose circumstancess may have caused her to lose hope. In our photograph depicting this story, we set the scene so that she is viewed from "the side of our contempt," while Jesus approaches her from the "the side of His compassion."

Jesus said, "Do not judge or you too will be judged" (Matthew 7: 1). This does not mean that we are to ignore or deny truth. It means we should know the facts and circumstances of an issue before we blurt out our personal opinion of them. Jesus continued, "For in the same way you judge others, you will be judged" (Matthew 7:2).

Christian theologian Thomas B. Smedes wrote, "Any lazy or biased fool can have opinions, but making judgments is the hard work of responsible and compassionate people." And, the Apostle Paul adds, "When we point out the sin of others while we commit the same sin, we condemn ourselves" (Romans 2:1).

Until we have walked in another person's shoes, we don't know their story and, until someone has walked in our shoes, they don't know ours. Like the woman at the well, we seldom know the circumstances surrounding another person's past. Even if they are sinners, Jesus said that anyone who is without sin should be the one who casts the first stone (John 8:7). I can assure you that will not be me!

Perhaps it will be wise of us to put down our stones of opinions and judgments of others and live our lives as examples of Jesus — with hearts of compassion. The chances are, we just don't know all the facts!

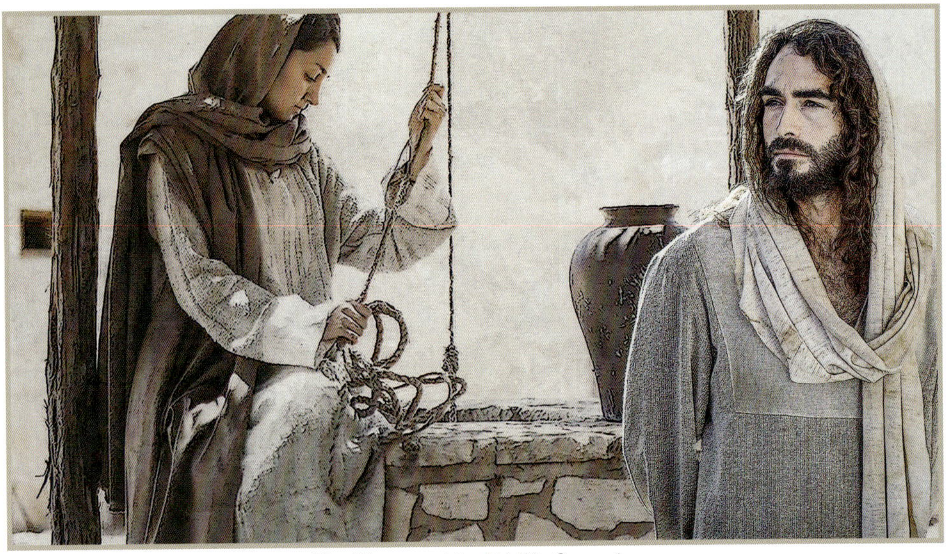

The Woman at the Well in Samaria

Thoughts to Ponder

View film at ▶ journeyswiththemessiah.org

- In the biblical sense, compassion goes beyond feelings of sympathy and empathy for someone who is suffering to the feeling that we are compelled to reduce their suffering with a desire to alleviate it. Jesus is the most remarkable example of someone with genuine compassion. In Matthew 22:39, He provided a simple statement to show us how we can have compassion: "You shall love your neighbor as yourself." Consider times you have shown compassion. Is there an opportunity awaiting you this week?

- The story of the "Woman at the Well" can remind us of our lack of compassion when we judge others without knowing the facts of their circumstances. We often draw conclusions based on the way a person looks or dresses, the car they drive, where they live or how they talk without knowing the person or their circumstances. If we took the time to know them, we might find them to be delightful! Take time to observe people who create a negative emotion in you and then imagine the circumstances of their lives (past and present) that may be causing great suffering to them. Imagine the feeling you will have as you show them compassion.

- "Do not judge" does not mean we must ignore the obvious truth of a particular situation. Yet Jesus cautions us that we will be judged [by God] in the same manner we judge others. Thomas Smedes says that judging is [and must be] the hard work of compassionate people. Note the word "compassionate." In Romans 2:1, Paul says, "When we point out the sin of others while we commit the same sin, we condemn ourselves." Thus, until we know the circumstances surrounding someone's life, "do not judge" should be the course of action we should follow.

8

Daily Bread

Living Today, Secure in Tomorrow

View film at ▶ journeyswiththemessiah.org

In the Fall of 2008, the stock markets around the world began to decline rapidly. Like many people, I panicked as I watched my life savings evaporating before my eyes. My sixtieth birthday had arrived earlier that year and now, after a long and successful career as a fashion photographer, every dollar I had saved — including the money set aside for this project—was disappearing at an alarming rate. It would eventually be gone, and I was at a loss as to what to do!

I spent most of 2008 planning these images, including trips to the ancient town of Matera, Italy, the backdrop for our pictures. By the fall, when we arrived back in Italy to begin production, the world's markets had officially crashed!

The photograph *Daily Bread* was inspired by the 2008 financial disaster and a lesson I learned from *The Training of the Twelve* by A. B. Bruce. This 1871 discipleship classic provides insight into Jesus' life, especially on how he taught His disciples, including teaching them to pray.

According to Luke's Gospel, Jesus had just returned from praying alone when one of the disciples asked Him, "Teach us to pray as John the Baptist taught his disciples" (Luke 11:1). Jesus responded by giving them a model prayer that would be simple and brief, yet comprehensive. It was actually intended to be more of an outline to guide their prayers until the time that they could pray on their own.

The content of this prayer, as recorded in Matthew and Luke's Gospels, became so beloved by Christians that these scriptures eventually became known as *The Lord's Prayer.* Over time, it became a corporate or group prayer and is recited in unison millions upon millions of times every year throughout the world.

There were six requests or petitions that Jesus suggested could be included in the disciples' prayers. The first three referred to God's glory and the last three to man's needs. In the three requests for man's needs, Jesus suggested they pray, "Give us this day our daily bread" (Luke 11:3). In essence, when we pray this part of the prayer, we ask God to provide for all of our needs, day-by-day.

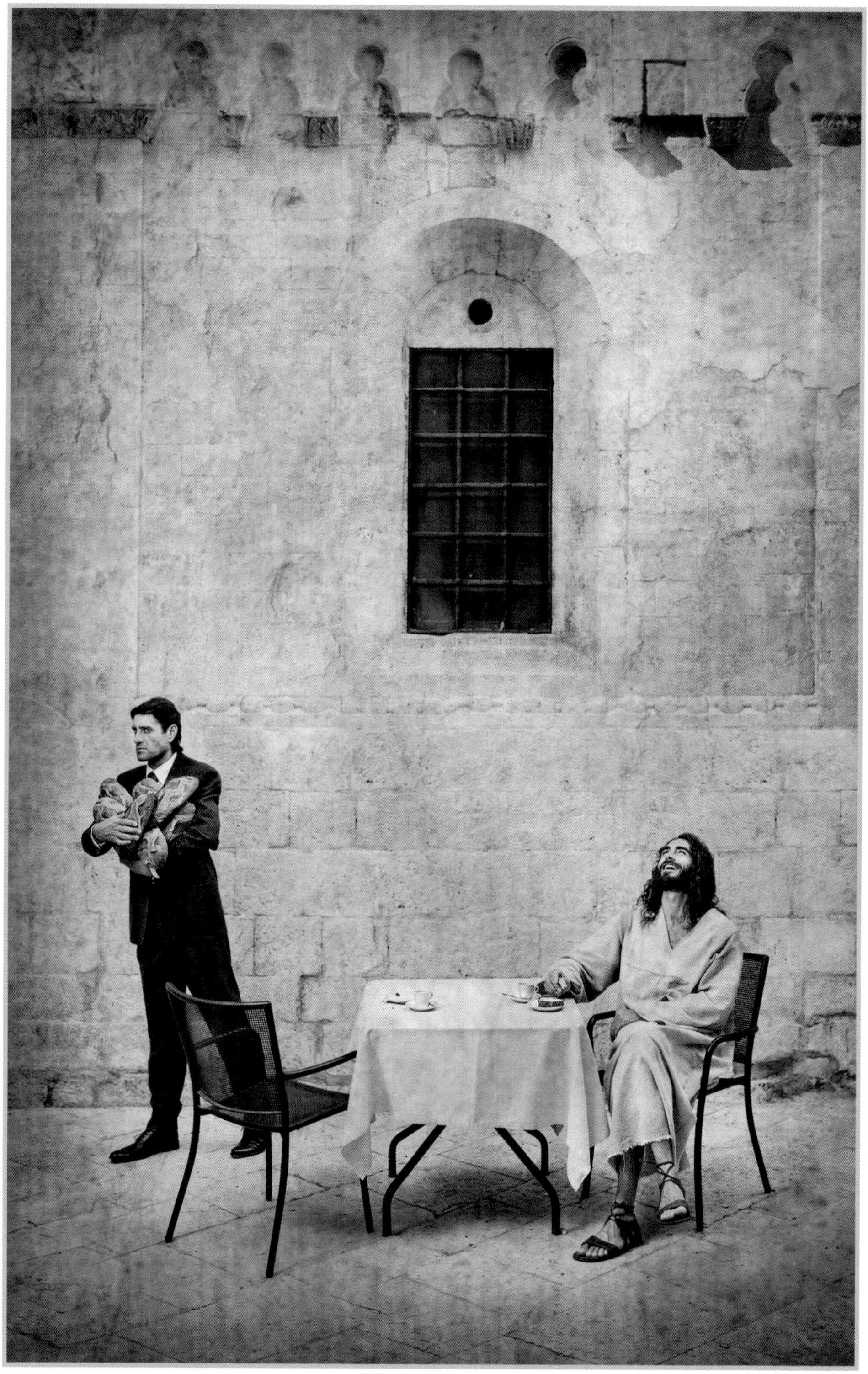

In light of the economic collapse around me, Jesus' prayer instructions to His disciples was a discovery for me. Despite Jesus' promise that God would provide for my needs, I did not trust that He would! Not only did I want my bread for today, I also wanted my bread for tomorrow and the next day and the next. Plus, I wanted to know that "retirement bread" had been set aside for me and that there would be stockpiles of it!

While waiting for our crew to finish preparing the set for this photograph, I went to Sergio (our actor portraying Jesus) and asked, "Suppose you were Jesus, and you were witnessing this scene of the man walking off with all of the bread, what would you do?" He replied, "I'd probably laugh at Him!"

I agreed and asked him to laugh at the foolishness of the man walking away with all of the bread while I captured the image. If you look closely at the picture, you see that Jesus has one small piece of bread while the businessman has seven loaves, representing the days of the week. Jesus — with just one piece of bread — is laughing while the businessman with seven loaves looks unhappy.

The image invite us to ask ourselves, "How much of our lives do we spend worrying about tomorrow and tomorrow's bread or tomorrow's needs?" Most of us do, so don't feel you are alone! Yet, are we willing to have today's happiness depend on having tomorrow's bread...today?

Financial issues are the leading cause of stress for Americans. I imagine it's the same worldwide. A large percentage of visits to primary care doctors originate with anxiety that is driven by money and finances. Under stress, our bodies can experience high blood pressure, increased risk of heart disease and sleep issues to just name a few. Plus, money-related stress knows no boundaries; it's an issue across all income levels.

I recently found a letter I had written to myself during a period in which I made and accumulated the most money I had ever had. Yet, the letter revealed my deep concerns about not having enough. How foolish I was in retrospect!

Jesus had full knowledge of all of these things and, in Matthew 6:25, He wrote a prescription for us: ***"Do not worry!"*** It wasn't just a casual suggestion, it was a command, ***"Do not worry!"***

Jesus knows that when we worry about the future, it takes us away from today. However, today is the only day where He can meet us to meet our needs because tomorrow doesn't exist yet, and for many it will not. As stated by American author, Leo Buscaglia, "The only thing worry can achieve is robbing us of tomorrow's joy."

During His *Sermon on the Mount*, Jesus offered an alternative to worry. He said that since God is already aware of all of our needs and will provide for them according to His will, we should spend our time seeking Him and His righteousness instead of worrying (Matthew 6:33).

Daily Bread hangs in my office. When I feel anxious about my needs and not having enough, I can turn to it and almost hear Jesus saying, "Come back, Michael. Get a cup of coffee and a piece of bread and then sit down and enjoy spending time with me. I know my plans for you and they're good."

When we spend time with our Lord, we are supernaturally released from the anxiety of believing we need tomorrow's bread today. We are reminded that peace comes when we are content in knowing that our needs are met today and there's no need to worry about tomorrow.

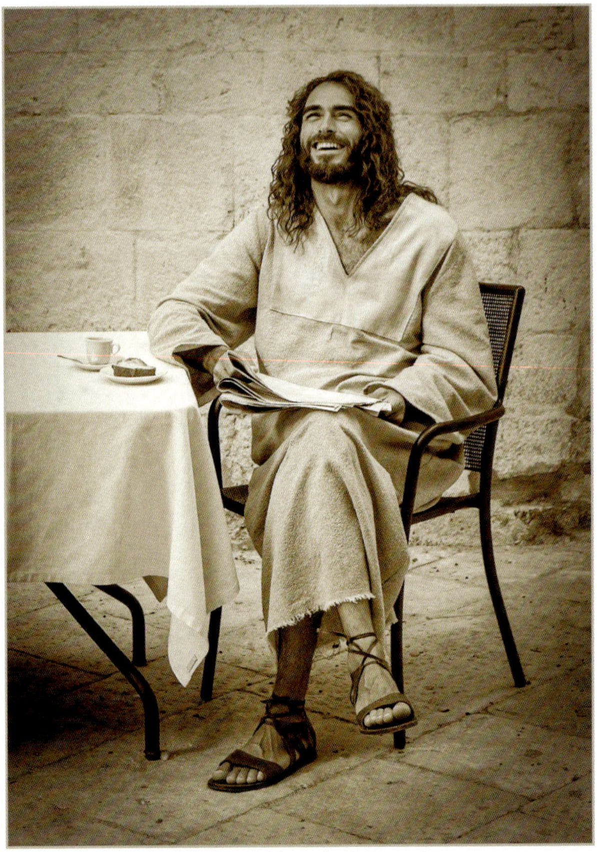

Content with today's bread.

Thoughts to Ponder

View film at ▶ journeyswiththemessiah.org

- The inspiration for the image *Daily Bread* came to me as I began to worry about this project's ballooning cost. It is not ironic that this occurred while I was studying the Lord's Prayer. Most of us have recited this prayer in unison as far back as we can remember, but do we pray the words or just say them? Let's not forget that it was Jesus who gave these words to us! Take a moment to understand the prayers six petitions and then consider praying it as a personal prayer.

- Having "our daily bread" can be a source of contentment. It can also be a source of anxiety and worry if we leap ahead to wanting tomorrow's bread today! Jesus said that we are to pray, "Give us this day our daily bread," not give us this day tomorrow's bread! Learning that my prayer is a petition to God to "provide for me today" helps me stay in the moment. Besides, tomorrow does not exist yet and may not!

- Jesus command "Do not worry!" in Matthew 6:25 could be used as a prefix to many things about which we worry. For instance, "Do not worry today about tomorrow's groceries" or "Do not worry today about my job tomorrow." The Lord's Prayer doesn't say, "Give us this day our daily bread while I worry about bread for tomorrow." Imagine sitting at a banquet table with Jesus. Now, close your eyes as you hear yourself thanking Him as He passes His heavenly bread to you. Feel the emotion! Would you dare ruin this moment by saying, "This is great bread Jesus, but will we have food for tomorrow?"

- Jesus knows that our circumstances of having enough or not having enough are in constant flux. Having faith in His provision — that He will give us day by day the bread we need — leads us to contentment. Worrying about tomorrow's bread today replaces the "bread of joy" with the "bread of anxiety." Turn back to the picture of *Daily Bread*. Which of these breads — *the bread of joy* or *the bread of anxiety* do you think is on Jesus' plate? Which do you want on yours?

www.desiringgod.org/messages/our-deepest-prayer-hallowed-be-your-name
www.tji.org/ Download Chapter 6 of A.B. Bruce's "Training of the Twelve."

9

Denial

If Only Three Was the Limit

View film at ▶ journeyswiththemessiah.org

In the excitement of a moment, have you ever said that you would do something or made a promise that, when the time came, you could not keep?

The image *Denial* was inspired by a promise the disciple Peter made to Jesus. It is one of the most well-known stories of the Bible and is recorded in all four gospels of Matthew, Mark, Luke and John.

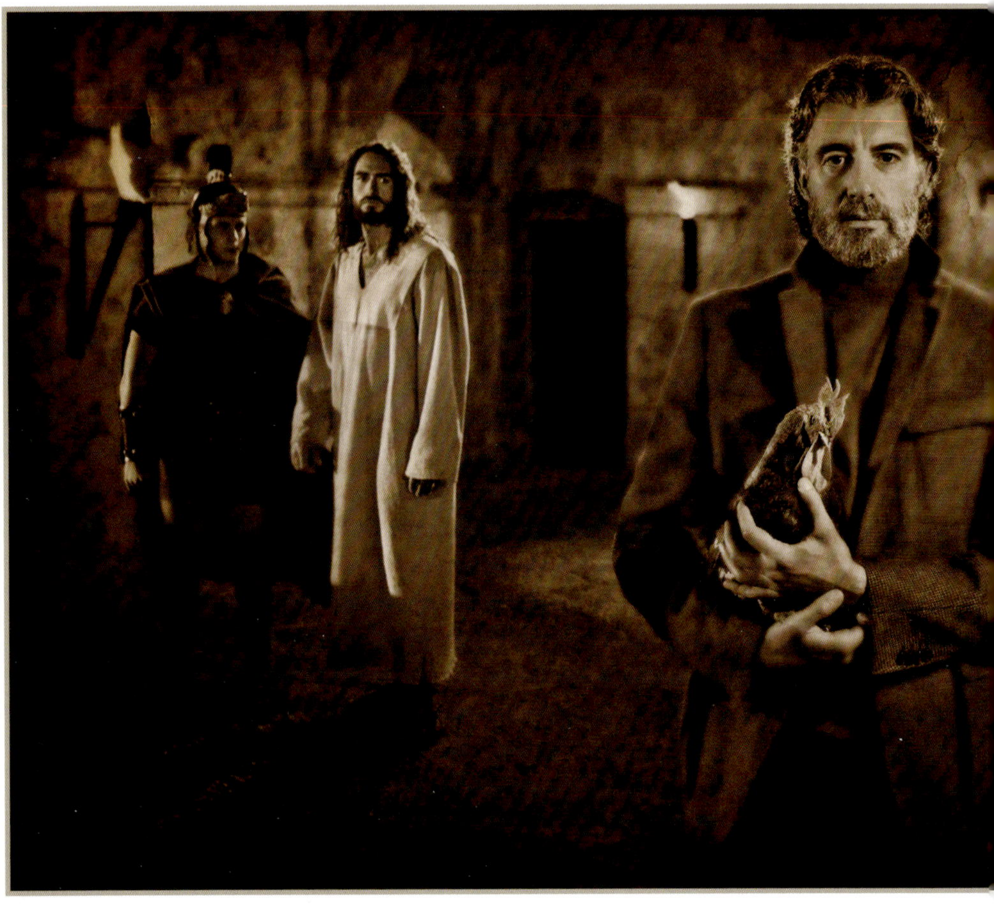

In the Book of John, the story starts just after sunset in an upper room of a home in Jerusalem. Jesus gathered there with His disciples to share the traditional Passover meal. Passover was an annual event held by the Jewish people to celebrate their ancestors' miraculous release from captivity in Egypt 1300 years before. It was also the evening Jesus would be arrested — an arrest that would lead to His crucifixion the following day.

During the evening, Jesus told the disciples many things about God's eternal Kingdom. He talked about His divine mission to bring salvation to all who believed in Him. He spoke of what was about to happen to Him and what lay ahead for them. He prayed for them and for all believers. He said that one of them — one of His trusted disciples — would betray Him that night. He also announced that He would be with them for only a little longer, adding that where He was going they could not come (John 13:33).

This vague statement prompted the disciple, Simon Peter, to ask Jesus, "Lord, where are you going?" Jesus replied, "Where I'm going, you can't follow now, but you will follow later." Peter responded by asking Jesus why he couldn't follow Him now (John 13:36-37).

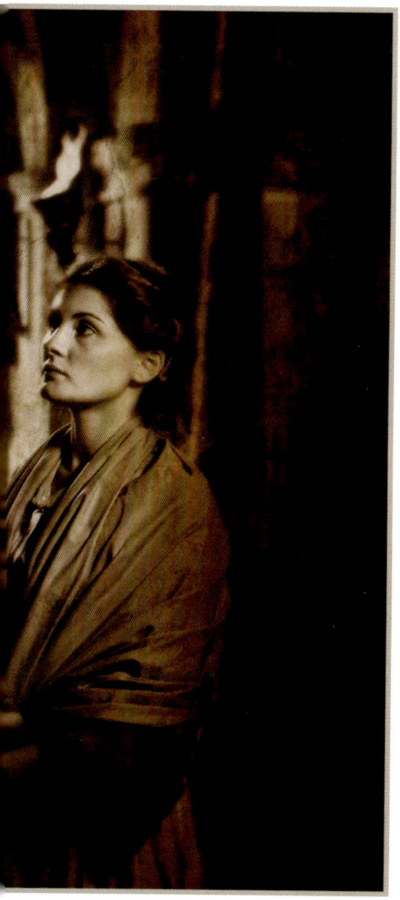

The things Jesus said and did that evening — like uncharacteristically washing the disciple's feet — had to be overwhelming to them. In the passion of the moment, the disciple Peter made a promise, a promise for which he had not considered the cost or whether he could live up to it when the time came. Peter boldly stated to Jesus, "I will lay down my life for you!" (John 13:37).

Lay down your life? Such an act would require bravery on a super-hero level, like today's Secret Service agents assigned to guard the President or like the bodyguards of dignitaries and celebrities. Such people are supposed to "protect at all costs." Yet, when faced with danger, no one really knows how they will respond until that moment arrives, especially when it means putting their life on the line.

Peter wanted to believe that he would lay down his life for Jesus. He just didn't know his bold promise would be challenged so soon...in just hours to be specific.

When Jesus heard Peter's declaration, he looked at him and asked, "Will you really lay down your life for me?" Then He told Peter that before the night was over, he would have disowned Him three times (John 13:38). Taken into the context of what was about to happen, Jesus was saying that before the night was over when the rooster crowed the next morning, Peter would have denied Jesus three times.

Later that evening, Jesus went to pray in the Garden of Gethsemane. It was there that He was arrested after being betrayed by his friend and disciple, Judas (John 18:2). After his arrest — which led to a brief scuffle with a detachment of soldiers — He was taken by guards to the home of Annas, the father-in-law of Caiaphas, the high priest (John 18:12-13). Peter and another disciple followed the soldiers and Jewish leaders. According to John's account, the other disciple with Peter knew the high priest and went into the courtyard while Peter waited outside (John 18:15).

There was a girl there who asked Peter if he was one of the disciples. I'm sure that Peter surprised himself when he responded, "I am not!" (John 18:17). On two other occasions before morning, when asked if he knew Jesus, his response was the same — he was not one of the disciples and did not know Jesus. (John 18: 25, 26)

Why did Peter end up denying Jesus after being so confident that he would lay down his life for Him? The most obvious reason has to be "fear." Jesus had just been arrested and taken to be interrogated by people with unlimited authority — so much power that in only a few hours, they would have him put to death without cause and even without a trial.

Just a short time before, when the soldiers came to arrest Jesus, John's Gospel reports that Peter drew his sword and cut off the ear of the high priest's servant named Malchus. (John 18:10). It would be quite reasonable to assume that Peter followed Jesus to the high priest's palace without expecting to be recognized in the darkness of night. He had to have been caught off guard when he was recognized as one of the disciples who had been with Jesus earlier.

Considering these circumstances, do you think we should extend a little grace to Peter for not admitting he knew Jesus? After all, what would he say, "Yeah, sure, I know Jesus. I'm the disciple who just cut off the high priest's servant's ear!"

Do you recall any times in your life when you were unexpectedly asked a question, even an innocent one, and for some reason you responded with a lie? It's human nature to commit to more than we can handle or live up to. We all fall short on some of our promises. As it says in Matthew's Gospel, "Our spirits are willing, but our flesh is so weak" (Matthew 26:41). In our spiritual hearts we want to stand firm and do the right things, but our physical bodies are just too weak. The Apostle Paul writes, "For I have the desire to do what is good, but I cannot carry it out" (Romans 7:18). Have you ever felt that way? I know I have!

Peter's story of denying that he knew Jesus, after saying that he wouldn't deny Him even to the point of dying with Him, paints a rather negative picture of Peter. However, as we continue to read the Book of John, we find a beautiful story of redemption. Peter had great remorse for his failure to stand strong on that night and the scriptures tell us that, when the rooster crowed and Peter remembered what Jesus had said about denying Him, he wept bitterly (Luke 22:61-62).

Yet the rooster's crowing actually marked the beginning of a new day in Peter's life. Jesus forgave him (John 21:15-19) and through this trial Peter was made stronger, allowing him to encourage the other disciples. Three years later he preached a sermon in which 3,000 people were converted in one day to become followers of Jesus (Acts 2:41).

Peter became a pillar of the church's strength in Jerusalem by laying the foundations whereby, over the next 2,000 years, two billion people profess the name of Jesus Christ. His writings give strength to all of us who are followers of Jesus.

Accepting Jesus as the Lord and Savior of our lives marks a new day for us, too. Like Peter, we are forgiven for all of our denials and unkept promises. Through Jesus Christ, our weaknesses are made strong.

Jesus called Peter — and He calls us — to live radically different lives that are too difficult to live on our own. Then, He says that we are not to worry for He will live them for us and through us when we invite Him to be the Lord of our life.

Peter stumbled on that one night. Yet, in the end when he told Jesus that he would die for Him, it turned out that he kept his promise! Peter was martyred for standing firm in his belief. According to tradition, it is reported that he was crucified upside down rather than ever deny his Savior again.

Though few of us will ever be martyred for standing up for our faith, the rooster's crowing awakens us to a new day — a day in which we are forgiven and our weaknesses are made strong to proclaim the good news of Jesus Christ.

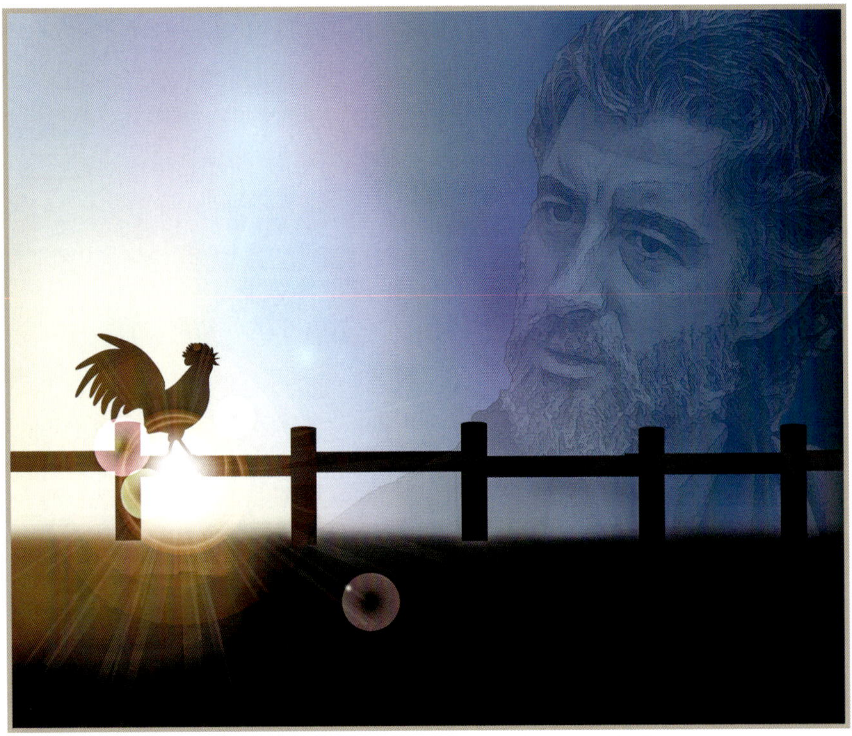

The rooster's crowing awakens us to a new day!

Thoughts to Ponder

View film at ▶ journeyswiththemessiah.org

- Like the disciple Peter, we all have made promises we couldn't keep. Since we began this project, we have had the painful experiences of many unkept promises made to us. Yet, eventually they required me to look inward to my own unkept promises — even small things like not calling someone when I promised, showing up late to an appointment, or saying I would mail something to someone and never getting around to it. Ask God to walk with you down memory lane to reveal any unkept promises.

- On your walk down memory lane (assuming God revealed an unkept promise), try to recall the circumstances under which you made the promise, why you didn't keep it, and if you can do something about it now.

- Consider the circumstances that caused Peter to deny Jesus. Jesus would have been crucified even if Peter had not denied Him. Peter was concerned he would be crucified too! Under these circumstances, should Peter have kept his promise?

- Although Peter denied Jesus three times, Peter eventually made good on his promise that he would lay down his life for Jesus. Knowing that Jesus is the Messiah and that because of Him your spirit cannot be killed, do you think that you would be able to lay down your life for Him?

10

Embrace

A Savior for All

View film at ▶ journeyswiththemessiah.org

Christians believe there is no other way to Heaven and eternal life except through belief in Jesus Christ. Assuming this belief is true, what happens after death for the people of all other religions?

In 2019, the world's population was around 7.5 billion people. Christians represented the largest segment at about 30%. Consequently, that means that 70% of the world's people are not Christian.

In the Apostle John's account of Jesus' life, Jesus stated, "No one comes to the Father except through Me" (John 14:6). Christians understand this statement to mean that only those who accept Jesus as their Lord and Savior will go to eternal life in Heaven after death (John 3:16). Assuming that we have interpreted Jesus' statement correctly, eternal life in the presence of God is impossible for those who embrace other religions.

This is quite a bold statement, and one that non-Christians probably find offensive! Yet, I'm reminded that it was Jesus who made this statement and He never shied away from the truth!

Wait just a second! Doesn't the Bible teach that Jesus came as Savior of the world, for all people and all nations? If so, it appears there is a severe dilemma for 70% of the world. What is God's plan for the two-thirds of the world's population that are not Christians?

As I planned the images for Journeys with the Messiah, the question of God's plan for non-Christians was on my mind. I wondered if Christians have a pious view of themselves. Do we think, "I'm going to Heaven and the rest of you non-believers are going to Hell?" I also wondered how would Jesus have acted when He was in the presence of people from other beliefs?"

On a scouting trip through the ancient streets of Matera, Italy, I thought about how I would convey this idea. Eventually, I decided to show Jesus in a group photo with His friends. The image required people from several nationalities dressed to

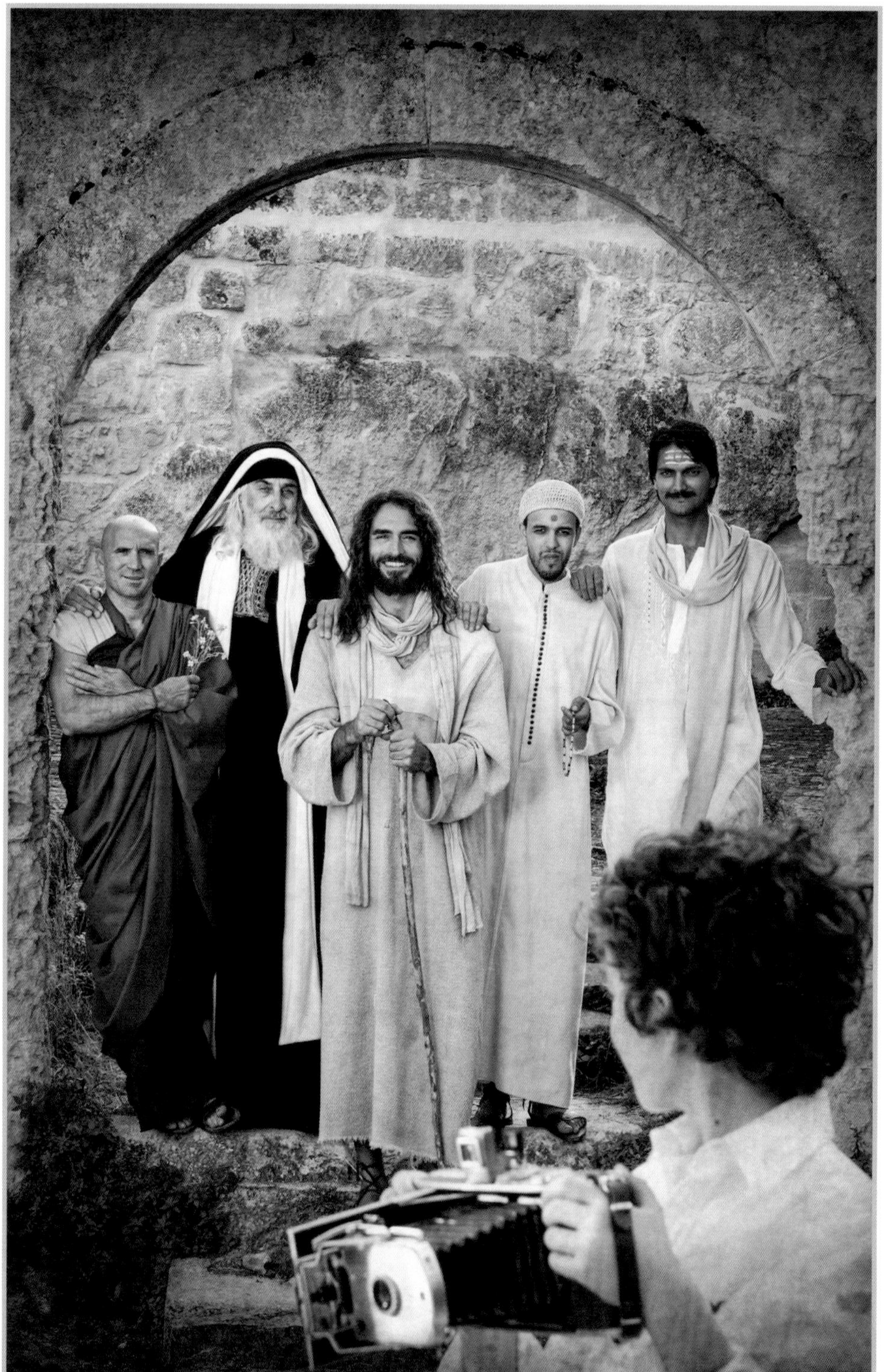

represent other religions. It would also depict that Jesus would not have shunned His friends because He disagreed with them. After all, He befriended tax collectors and prostitutes as well!

Our scene for this photograph would include Jesus with people who professed faith in other religions — Buddhists, Hindus, Muslims, and Jews. The photograph would depict Jesus embracing them as friends, regardless of their beliefs. (Note: Islam did not exist until almost 500 years after Jesus. However, I felt it essential to have Muslims represented in the photograph.)

There were several ideas I planned to evolve with the creation of this image. I wanted it to convey that Jesus did not come to start a religion, He came to start a revolution — a revolutionary new way of living through understanding God's plan for mankind. He came to testify to the truth of His Father and to teach and show us how to follow God's plan of hope through salvation. Jesus wants us to experience the joy of The Kingdom now, while He guides us back to his Father in Heaven and eternal life with Him. He came to share these truths with all people of all nations.

If there is no other way to Heaven and eternal life except through Jesus, then what are God's intentions for people who are not Christians? Does God have a plan for them. Will they have an opportunity to accept or deny Jesus as their Lord and Savior? The answer to my question is that He does have a plan!

For each of us who have accepted God's gift of salvation through the death and resurrection of Jesus, our part in His plan has been written clearly in all four gospels of Matthew, Mark, Luke, and John. We have been instructed to go into the world, go to all nations and tell them the good news of Jesus Christ and the hope we have found in Him (Matthew 28:19-20). "Go to all nations" also means "go to all religions." Christians refer to these instructions as The Great Commission.

Jesus' instructions "to go into the world and tell everyone" indicates that we have been chosen for God's A-Team. Our assignment is to deliver the Gospel message to the world. It's important to note that God does not have a B-Team standing by to back us up if we fail. Failure is not optional! We are God's last line of defense!

Jesus' instructions do not include "go sell them, coerce them or beat them into submission." We are simply told to "go tell them" — to tell everyone! The Apostle Peter adds that we should always be prepared to give a reason to anyone who asks why we have hope in Jesus and we are reminded to do this with gentleness and respect (1 Peter 3:15).

To follow Jesus' instructions requires that we take time to draw closer to Him by learning what we believe as Christians compared to what other religions believe.

This will provide a solid foundation for us, including why Jesus said (and we believe), "There is no other way to The Father in Heaven and eternal life except through Him" (John 14:6). Knowing this and embracing it in our hearts, minds and souls will allow our faith to become streams of living water as we share it with others.

Unfortunately, I'm sad to report that the A-Team is not as big as the percentage of Christians in the world. Many people fall into the Christian segment in name only, with no affiliation beyond it. They live the secular lifestyle of most non-Christians. They do not attend church, read the Bible or pray. Some have a church but are not engaged in their faith. Others, who believe that they are Christians, do not even understand what is required to be saved. So it is likely there are many unsaved people in our churches today.

So, the percentage of dedicated followers available to tell all nations about Jesus is much smaller than the 30% of the population counted as Christians. It appears we must go beyond "telling all nations" to "telling all Christians" who are Christians in name only but not yet true followers of Christ!

When we allow our faith to shine before others, we can ignite or reignite the fire in the hearts of those who say they are Christians but do not truly understand or enjoy what that means. And, when we are reaching out to people of other religions, we must learn to embrace them as Jesus did or they will never be open to hear about our faith!

While we are looking outward to others, perhaps we should reflect inward to ourselves. How are we personally responding to God's call? Are we Christians by default of the family into which we have been born? Do we believe we are Christians because we go to church? Or, are we truly engaged in knowing Jesus as active followers because our hearts are on fire for the one who laid down His life for us?

If you are married or have experienced a long-term relationship or friendship, please recall that the relationship did not happen overnight. Relationships take time. You do not know a person by just reading their biography. You must spend time with them, getting to know them to the point that you become comfortable sharing your joys as well as your heartbreaks.

It's the same with Jesus. You know Him by spending time with Him and learning about His life through the scriptures and through all that has been shared about Him through the two thousand years since He walked in Galilee and Judea. The more you know Him, the more you will want to know Him. Then, you will want to share Him with others because you have discovered He is just so fascinating!

Did you know that more has been written about Jesus Christ than any other subject in all of history?

In the final analysis, we need to go into the world and embrace all nations in the name of Jesus Christ. Yet, we also need to go across the street to embrace our neighbors and into our workplace — even to our church — to embrace the people there. Remember, we are God's last line of defense. If we do not tell them, who will?

When I arrive in Heaven, my biggest concern is hearing someone outside the gates saying, "I can't believe you knew and didn't tell me!" Yet I love the idea of walking through the gates to have someone tug on my sleeve and say, "I'm here because you told me about Him."

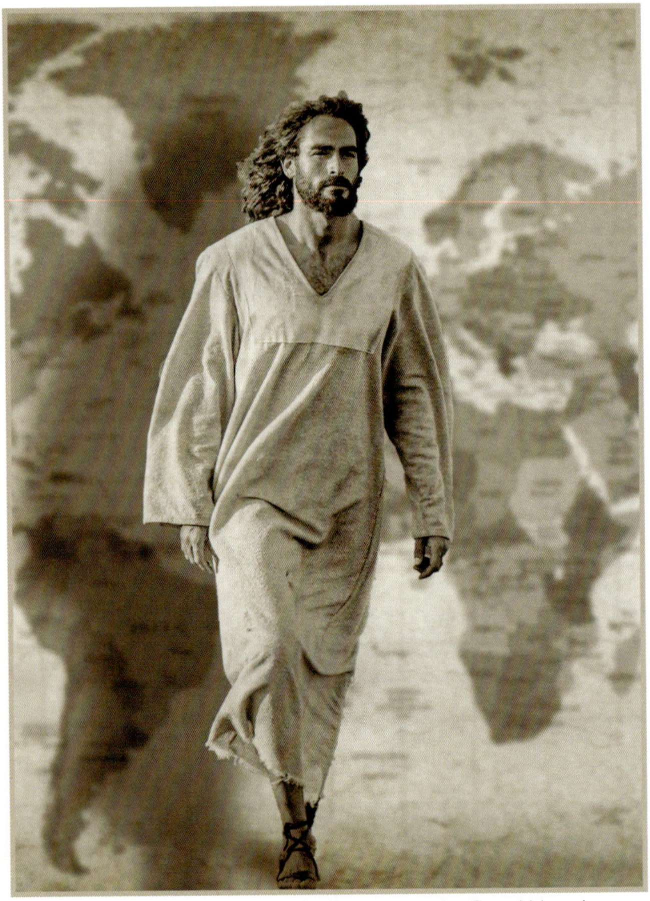

Go into all the world and tell everyone the Good News!

Thoughts to Ponder

View film at ▶ journeyswiththemessiah.org

- Do you believe Jesus' statement that "No one comes to the Father except through me," meaning that no one can have eternal life in Heaven except through salvation through Him? If yes, can you explain to someone why Jesus is the only way (not just why you think He is the only way)?
- Thirty percent of the world's population say they are Christians. However, many of them are Christians in name only. They do not follow Jesus or understand what is required to be saved. It's a dilemma since they may be traveling through life with false security. What can you do to help them?
- Take time to ponder what it means to you to be a follower of Jesus Christ. Can you point to specific changes it has made in your life? Do you believe that you make a positive difference in the world because Christ is in you? How?
- Christians believe that Jesus is the only way to eternal life with the Father in Heaven, yet 70% of the world's population are not Christians. Does God have a separate plan of salvation for them? Is it different from ours?
- God's plan is to tell the world the Good News of Jesus through us! The Great Commission is Jesus' instruction for us to spread the gospel to all the nations of the world. Do you believe that people have come to Christ through your desire and willingness to share the gospel? Do you know people who have been saved because of your witness to them? Do you know of anyone specifically who may be left behind if you don't tell them?

11

End of the Road

The Future Looks Bright Ahead

View film at ▶ journeyswiththemessiah.org

One of the simplest, most engaging and non-threatening questions I ask people who have yet to hear or accept Jesus' offer of eternal life is this: "What if I could show you that when your life comes to the end of the road, it doesn't have to be the end of the road?"

Years ago,the embers from my childhood with Jesus were passionately reignited

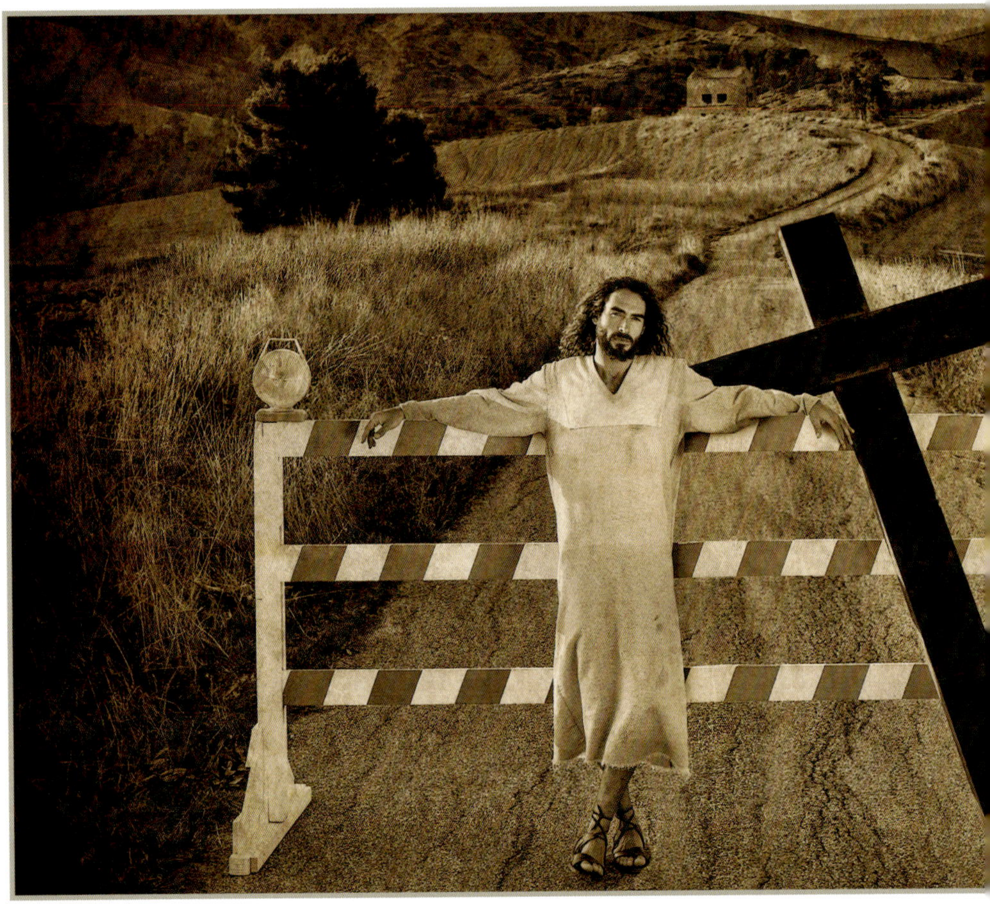

in adulthood, and I wanted people to see and understand Jesus from the exciting perspective with which as I was seeing Him? As a photographer and creative director of fashion advertising I thought, "Maybe I could show them pictures illustrating what I wanted to share. I could produce photographs to depict Jesus' messages and teachings from a fresh and inviting point of view."

Jesus' gift of Heaven and eternal life was His message that intrigued me the most. In my notes, I had written, "Life does not have to end at death!" Then next to it, I wrote, "The end of the road doesn't have to be the end of the road." I wanted to create a photograph to depict this message? A year later, we photographed *End of the Road* on a beautiful country road on the outskirts of Matera, Italy.

Assuming you have been introduced to Jesus, do you recall some of the things that first attracted you to Him? One of the first many things that attracted me was His promise that He could deliver peace into the jet-setting chaos of my life. To have peace in my life was very appealing at that time.

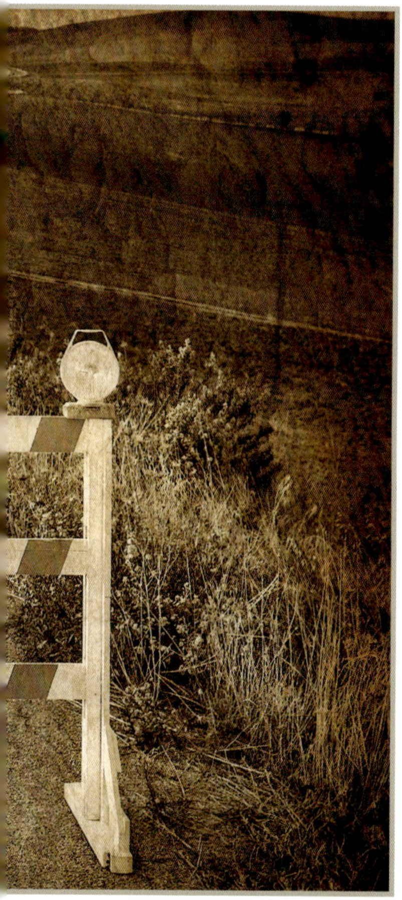

As I learned about Him — who He was 2,000 years ago and who He could be in my life today — I began to understand that the peace He offered, and I desired, would come as the result of something else. It would come in knowing that, when my life came to the end of its road, I would live an eternal life in Heaven with Him. Now, let me attempt an analogy of what I just said.

Imagine you have arrived on the first day of school or college. You are met by the Dean of Academics who presents you with your graduation diploma, noting you received "A"s in all of your courses. Imagine the feelings of freedom and confidence you would have as you realized that study would not be required in order for you to graduate. Instead, you could learn simply for the joy of learning!

God offers a similar graduation opportunity to all of us. We receive it on the day we accept Jesus, acknowledging that He has already planned and paved the road that leads to eternal life after our lives come to an end on earth. His gift allows us to be joyful and grateful as we freely roam the halls of our "earthly university" until graduation day delivers us into Eternity with Him.

Although we know that our earthly death is inevitable, it is challenging to grasp the reality of it while we are still young. My mom died at 98, but even in her early 90s, she said she didn't think about it often, even though she knew it was getting nearer.

God's promise in Psalm 139 is that He has numbered the days of our lives and Jesus says, "Therefore keep watch, because you do not know on what day your Lord will come." Although this verse, Matthew 24:42, is spoken in regard to Jesus' eventual return, it reiterates that we have no way of knowing how many days we have or how many we have left. It reminds us to enjoy today as if today is our last on earth.

The Bible's central theme is of a loving God who wants each of us to live in Eternity with Him when our time ends here. The Old Testament books reveal the "what, why and how" of God and tells us of a coming Messiah — an anointed or chosen one — who will come to save us from eternal death. The New Testament marks the Messiah's arrival and unveils God's plan for His Son to lead us home to Eternity with Him.

Although most people have heard of Heaven, why is it we seem to know so little about it since it is a significant tenant of the Christian faith? My childhood impressions of Heaven were from paintings and artists' depictions of angels sitting on white billowy clouds playing their harps! Honestly, it appeared to be very boring and definitely not inviting!

In Randy Alcorn's book *Heaven,* he writes that the evidence contained throughout the Bible points to an eternal life that will be very much like our physical lives now. Randy says the Bible reveals a world where people work, not for a paycheck, but simply because they enjoy working; that Heaven will be a place where the lion chases the lamb, not for a meal, but merely because they're having fun. Plus, the trials and tribulations that cause anxiety, fear, jealousy, hatred, sickness and death will be replaced with love, joy, peace and abundance. There will be no more tears nor death! Can you imagine a world like that?

Randy's book helped me find peace about my future in Heaven, realizing the good times I've known here will be replaced with better ones there. And, it's quite comforting to know that the road that will take me there has already been paved by Jesus and He has paid my toll.

Learning about Heaven helps us to focus on our eternal future, which in turn makes it easier to navigate the streets of this world. You've heard the expression, "It's not about the destination; it's about the journey!" In God's world, it's about both — the journey on earth and the destination of eternal life in Heaven.

Throughout the history of Christianity, God's story has not always been presented from a positive perspective. This has resulted in many people being pushed away from God's message of love rather than being drawn to Him. I know because I was one of them! Yet, the story of Jesus is a story of love. It is the story of a Father who loved us so much that He sent His Son to bring us home, despite knowing His Son's life would have to be sacrificed to complete our journey.

The image *End of the Road* depicts an engaging question: If life can continue in Eternity as I have described here, would you want it? If the end of the road does not have to end at death, would you choose to go on? For many, this is an offer that's too good to be true. Others fear that it comes at a price. "What's it going to cost me?" they say. "What do I have to give up?"

Yet a relationship with Jesus has never been about what we give up, it's about what we get because of what He gave up. It's a relationship of transformation in which the desires of God supernaturally become our desires as they replace the world's desires. God transforms our character to become more like Jesus. So, knowing Jesus is not about what we do, it's about what He does. We don't invite Him on a journey — He invites us!

There are times when the road to Eternity will be challenging and often for reasons we do not understand. Yet, during these times, God is building our character even at the cost of our comfort. So, if life is not great at the moment, spending time with Jesus may not immediately change your circumstances. However, He will provide something better — His supernatural peace! Jesus assures us that what we are experiencing now is only temporary, this is just a season. Heaven promises better!

On the other hand, if life is going great for you, coming to know Him will make it even greater. A life that may be defined by success but is shallow on meaning, will transition into one defined by significance. Work takes on new meaning when it's for His Kingdom. The best is still yet to come!

So how do you have this relationship with Him? You could say something like,

> *"Lord, I don't know the way, I have lost my way, or I think I know the way, but I believe you have a better way. I have arrived at this crossroad in my life where I confess that you are Lord. I believe Jesus is your Son who died on a cross for my sins and You raised Him back to life to show the world that there is eternal life in Heaven with you and I want to know You."*

When you come to the end of the road, the bottom line is this:

> *If you lived your life following God's plan and you die to find none of what has been said here is true — the end of the road is just that, the end of your life — you will have lived a very good life and lost nothing. However, if you live your life without Him and die to find it was all true, you will have lost everything!*

Your part is to make the commitment, then walk with Him as He molds your life with the plan He has always had for you.

Please don't take the detour!

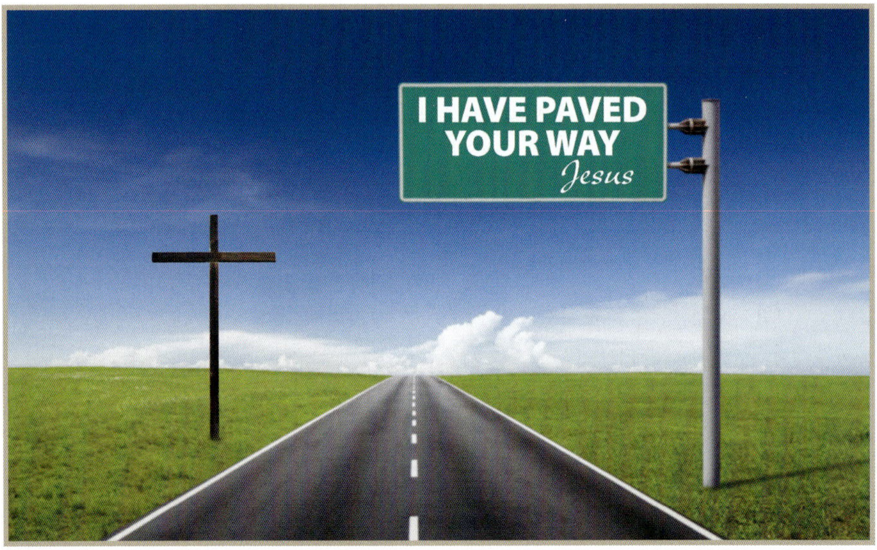

The way has been paved to Eternity for you.

Thoughts to Ponder

View film at ▶ journeyswiththemessiah.org

- When your life ends on earth, are you sure confident that it will continue forever in Eternity with God in Heaven? How do you know?
- Psalm 139:16 states that God has numbered the days of our lives. Do you find comfort in knowing that God is in control and, therefore, you don't have to be?
- In his book "Heaven," Randy Alcorn writes that the Bible points to an eternal life that will be very much like the physical life we live now. Google "scenic photos," then select a beautiful scene and try to imagine how Heaven might feel where there is no pain, sickness, death, sadness and all of your needs are met.
- "Let go and let God" is a popular expression that suggests something we seldom do. Jesus said, "With man, this is impossible, but with God, all things are possible." This week, allow the impossible to be possible by just *letting go and letting God!*
- Many people fear a relationship with Jesus because they fear what they may have to give up. Yet, a relationship with Jesus is not about what we give up; it's about what we get because of what He gave up? Conisder the things you may be missing by holding back from a relationship with Him.
- Imagine your compass or GPS set so that regardless of which way you turn, you setting brings you back toward Heaven. With Heaven as your destination, see if navigation becomes easier for you in this world!
- The unique characteristic of God's peace is that it functions perfectly when all is well in your world and continues to work perfectly when the world is falling apart. It's called Perfect Peace. Try it. You'll like it!
- Sales associates sometimes have "an elevator presentation" designed to get their message across in the brief time from the closing of the elevator doors until they reopen. Try to develop a similar presentation for sharing the Gospel.

12

Faith & Trust

Faith Taken to New Heights

View film at ▶ journeyswiththemessiah.org

Faith & Trust was inspired by a story about a traveler hiking in the wilderness. His journey was interrupted when he came to the edge of a canyon. Wondering how far he might have to walk to get to the other side, he spotted a large rope stretched across the canyon and attached to where he was standing. As his eyes followed the rope across, he saw a man walking toward him while pushing a wheelbarrow.

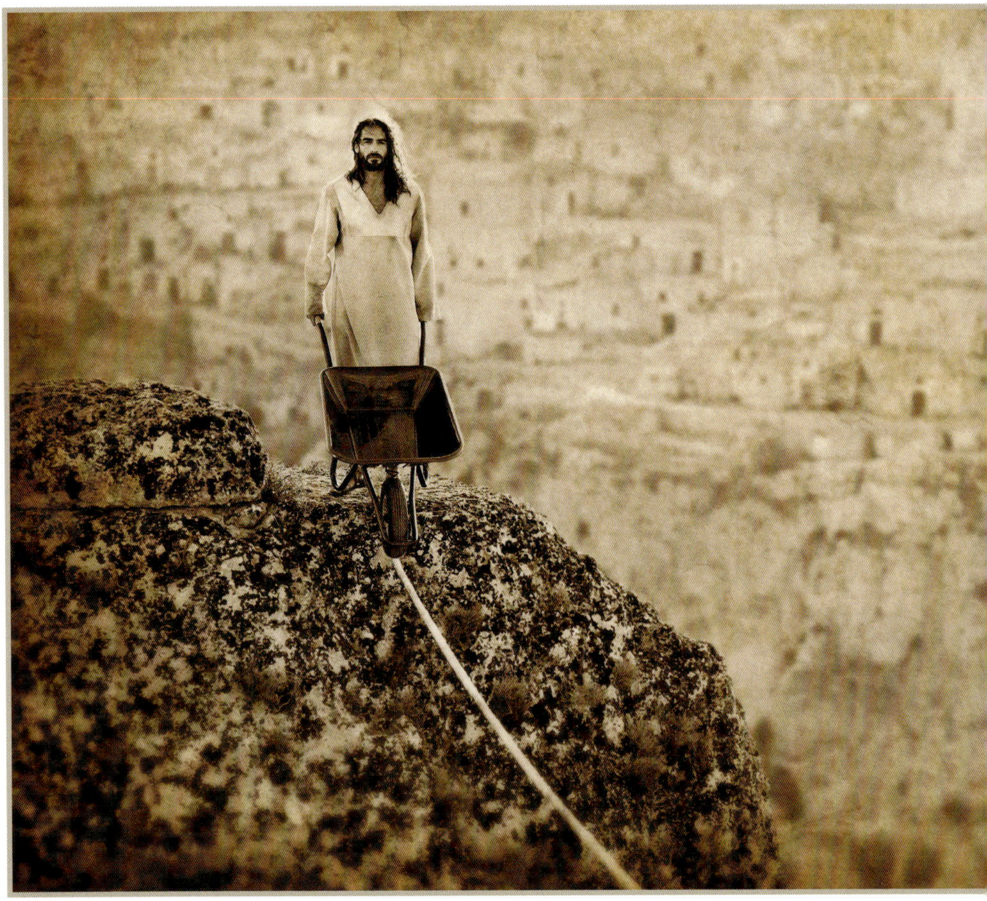

"Why, of course," the traveler replied, "You walked across the rope with such confidence."

The man on the rope asked, "Do you really believe I can do it again?"

"Oh yes, I definitely do," replied the traveler.

The man with the wheelbarrow looked at him and said, "Very good then, hop in and I'll take you across!"

When I felt God encouraging me to create this series of photographs, the man on the rope with a wheelbarrow was an idea that immediately came to mind. It would be an engaging and thought-provoking visual I could use to open conversations with others about "faith and trust."

The inspiration for these images came to me in different ways. Some were inspired by specific biblical events and Jesus' teachings, while others came from stories like the wilderness traveler. Others were inspired by Jesus' parables — simple stories He used to explain the message He wanted his audience to hear.

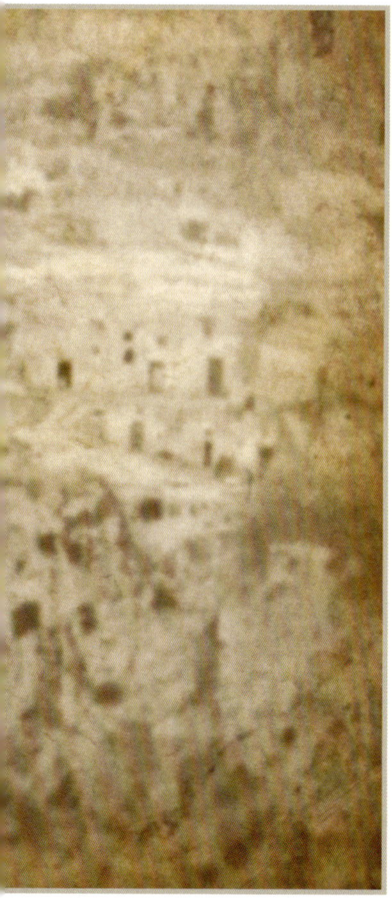

For example, in Luke's Gospel in the *Parable of the Good Samaritan*, Jesus painted a mental picture of "a man going down from Jerusalem to Jericho when he fell into the hands of robbers" (Luke 10:30). In the *Parable of the Fishing Net,* Jesus says, "The Kingdom of Heaven is like a net that was let down into the lake and caught all kinds of fish" (Matthew 13:47). It would be easy for listeners to visualize this scene since they would be familiar with catching fish with nets.

The words *faith* and *trust* are often used interchangeably. However, *faith* is defined as the substance of hope, while *trust* is a conviction based largely on evidence that is real.

In the image *Faith & Trust*, we see a picture depicting the relationship many of us have experienced with God. We say that we have faith and that we believe God can do anything. Yet, when that moment comes that our faith is challenged—when Jesus invites us to get into His wheelbarrow—the faith we thought we had fades and even disappears.

Using the definition that "faith is the substance of hope and trust is a conviction based largely on evidence that is real," look at the image of the man with the wheelbarrow and pretend that he has just extended an invitation to take you across the canyon.

If you have seen him make the trip only one time, you might need faith to get into the wheelbarrow (and maybe a sedative as well)! But, what if you had watched him go back and forth, effortlessly carrying one passenger after another, would you feel that you could trust him to take you across? Again, "trust is a conviction based largely on evidence that is real," and you now have real evidence.

The biblical definition of faith is found in Hebrews 11:1: "Faith is confidence in what we hope for and assurance about what we do not see." Combine the phrase *"confidence in hope"* with *"assurance in the unseen,"* and we can say that *"faith is trusting in something we cannot explicitly prove."*

The scriptures offer many examples of faith and trust. The blind man Bartimaeus told Jesus that he wanted to see. We can assume that he said this because he trusted Jesus to heal him...and Jesus did (Mark 10:46-52). In Luke's Gospel, we are told about a synagogue leader named Jairus who fell at Jesus' feet and begged him to heal his dying daughter. Jairus trusted that Jesus could heal her and hoped He would. Not only did Jesus heal her, but He also brought her back to life (Luke 8:41-56).

In these instances, notice that *faith and trust* required a certain level of action. Bartimaeus shouted out to Jesus and would not allow himself to be quieted by the crowd. When Jesus called him, he jumped up and came to him. And Jairus sought Jesus by falling at his feet while begging him to go to his house. *Faith and trust* are not complete without action! The world says, "I need to see first, then I will believe." Jesus says that we are to "believe first, then we will see."

The Hebrew word *"yada"* means to know; to ascertain by seeing. To have faith and trust to get into Jesus' wheelbarrow, you have to *yada* Him; you have to know Him personally. Then, **you have to take action! You have to get into the wheelbarrow!** To simply say, "I believe," and continue to stand at the edge of the canyon is to say that you really don't believe!

As most of us have experienced, life is not like a road that goes on endlessly without detours. Life is a road with a succession of canyons that must be crossed. Like the wilderness traveler, we need faith and trust to travel through life. As Rick Warren (author of *The Purpose Driven Life*) said, "If you are not in one of life's canyons or coming out of one, it's because you are about to go into one!"

Where are you on your journey? Do you stand at the edge of the canyon wishing you could get across? Or, do you have faith to get into Jesus' wheelbarrow because you yada Him; because you know Him personally and have the evidence of all the canyons of your life that He has carried you across thus far?

St. Augustine wrote, "Faith is to believe what we do not see. The reward of faith is to see what we believe." Jesus knows there will be times when we are frightened as we step into His wheelbarrow. He experienced such fear in the garden at Gethsemane on the night before He was crucified. Yet, He trusted his Father to take Him across.

A thousand years earlier, King David noted these moments in Psalm 23 when he wrote, "Even though I walk through the valley of the shadow of death, I fear no evil, for You are with me." David did not say that God would walk him into the valley of the shadow of death and leave him there. He wrote, "Even though I walk through..." and that's the key...**through**! No matter where we are in the valleys of life, it is temporary. God will not leave us, He will walk us **through** them.

That's a promise you can put in the wheelbarrow with you as He carries you across the canyons of your life!

Jesus says we must take the action faith. We must get into His wheelbarrow and then we will see!

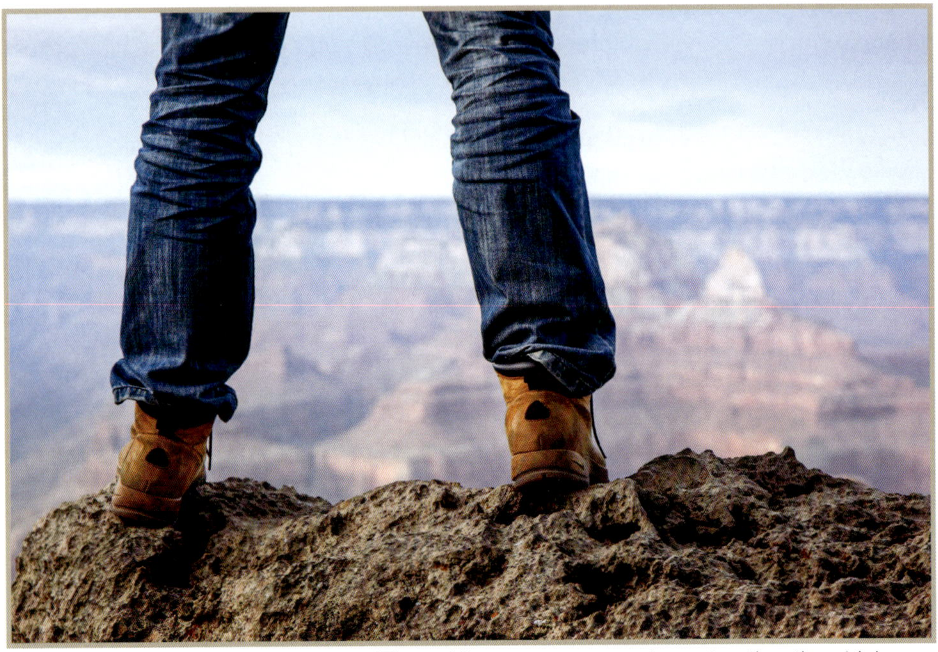

He takes us through our canyons. "Through" means we are coming out on the other side!

Thoughts to Ponder

View film at ▶ journeyswiththemessiah.org

- Gaze for a moment at the image of "Faith & Trust." Then, close your eyes and imagine yourself in the scene as Jesus invites you into His wheelbarrow for the ride across. What are you feeling? If fear, remember, this is not just anyone inviting you to trust him; it's Jesus!
- Think back to a frightening or challenging time in your life or one you face now and imagine Jesus in the scene as He reads Psalm 23. "Even though I walk through the valley of the shadow of death, I fear no evil, for I am with you." Whenever we arrive at any canyon, even the canyon of death, remember He promises to be there to take us "through" and safely across.
- I find the definition of faith more straightforward when I read it in the King James Version: "Now faith is the substance of things hoped for, the evidence of things not seen." Although I was not with God to see Him create the world, I can trust and believe that He did create it because the evidence of what He created is all around me to see.
- You can read Jesus' biography in the Bible and know a lot about Him. Yet, you cannot know Him (yada Him) personally without spending personal time with Him.James 2:14 says, "My brothers and sisters, what good is it if people say they have faith but do nothing to show it?" Faith requires action. Jesus is always available to take us safely across the canyons we encounter on our journeys. When we find ourselves standing on the edge wanting to get across, remember that faith requires action. **Get in the wheelbarrow!**

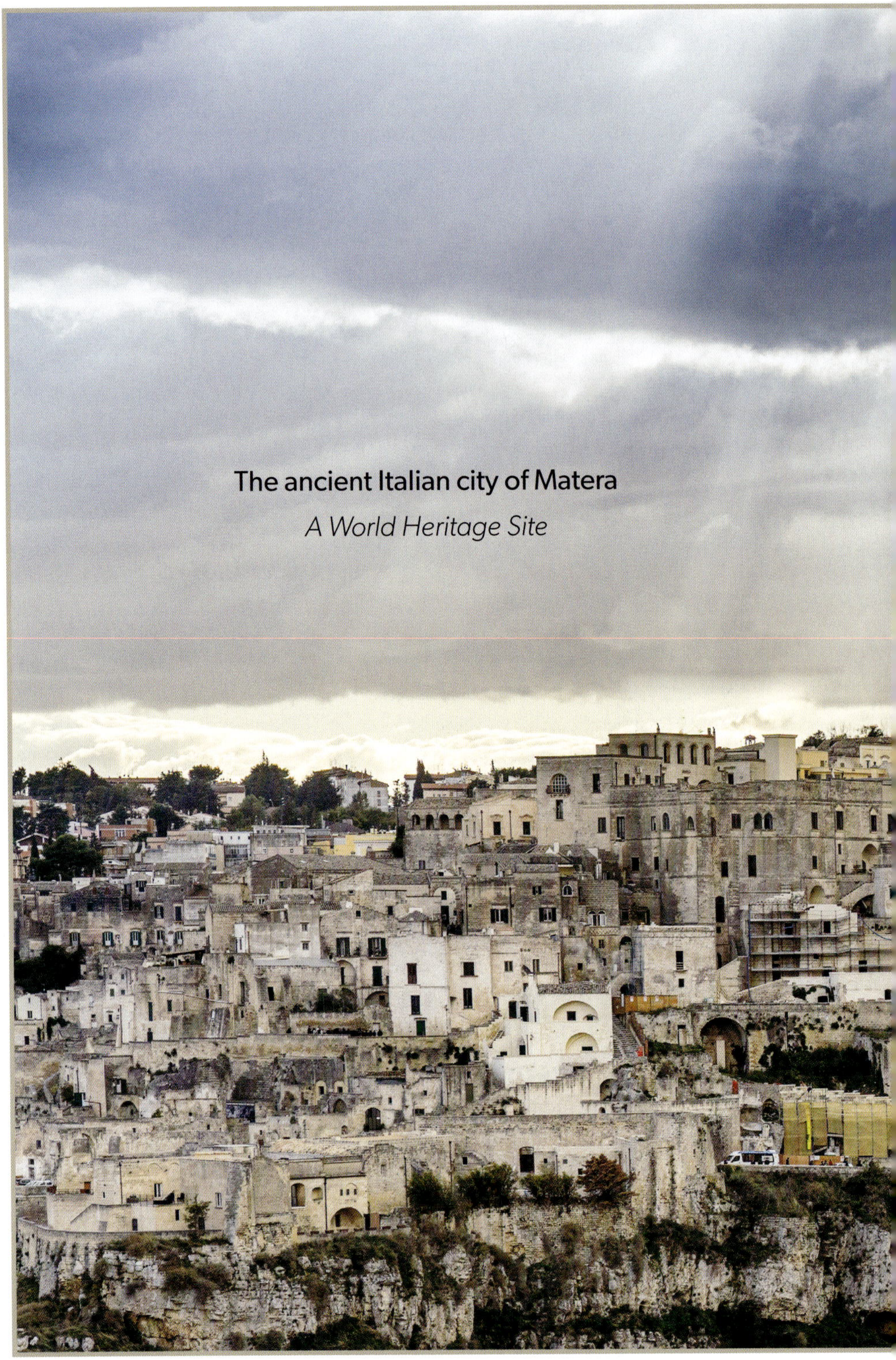

The ancient Italian city of Matera

A World Heritage Site

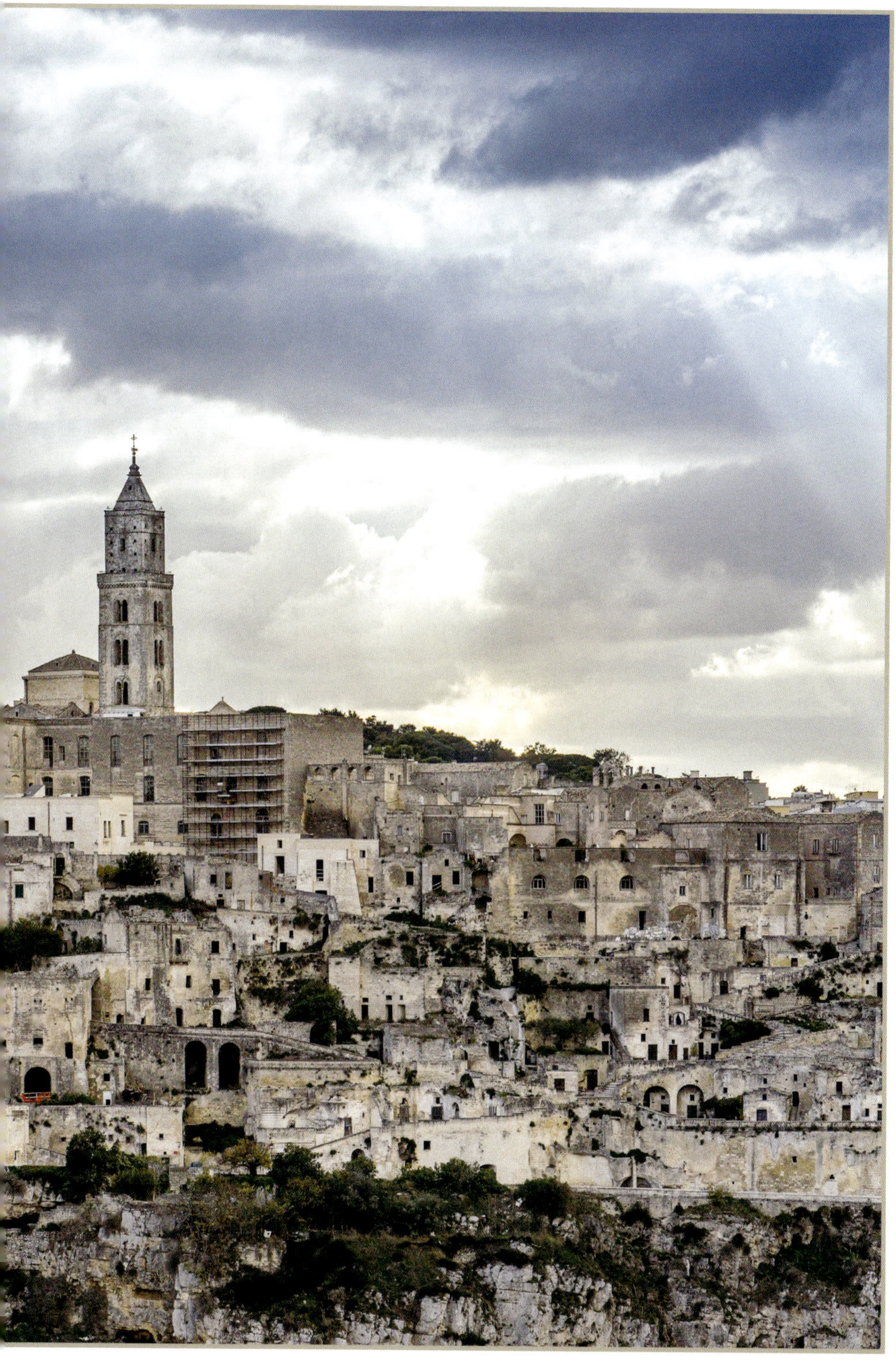

13

Gone Astray

A Shepherd to Follow Forever

View film at ▶ journeyswiththemessiah.org

Over three thousand years ago, the prophet Isaiah wrote, "We all, like sheep, have gone astray, each of us has turned to our own way" (Isaiah 53:6). Isaiah was saying that we are like sheep because we leave God's path to follow our own. If you are familiar with the characteristics of sheep behavior, you will understand why he wrote this and why it inspired me to create the image *Gone Astray.*

I grew up in a small town in Central Florida, and was involved in our church as far back as I can remember. Yet when I left for college, I was not a follower of Jesus... in fact, far from it! Other than Jesus being born in a manger, dying on a cross and being the central theme of church, I really didn't know much about Him. Then, in my early forties, as He pulled me from the dark abyss into which I had fallen, I felt it was time to investigate. I needed to know who He was and why so many people encouraged me to know Him.

As my investigation began, a friend gave me a book, *A Shepherd's Look at the 23rd Psalm* by Phillip Keller. It would take too long for me to explain the circumstances by which this book came to me. Suffice it to say that it was by the grace of God. Anyhow, it was a simple book explaining Psalm 23 from the viewpoint of a modern-day shepherd. This psalm was written by King David over 700 years before Jesus' birth. King David was once a shepherd boy.

Initially, I was somewhat insulted by Isaiah's characterization of *all of us being like sheep*. People have been called lions and tigers and said to act like baboons, but sheep, why sheep? Yet, as I read through Keller's book, I began to see that human and sheep behavior were similar in many ways. It made sense why Jesus and many biblical writers used sheep in referencing people.

As examples, sheep and humans are instinctively fearful and resist change. (I've known people who could be identified as *sheepish.*) Sheep need to be led to food and must be protected from predators. They like to gather together, but they will wander away from the flock if not continuously watched, making them even more vulnerable to predators. By nature they are followers. So a few sheep can lead the

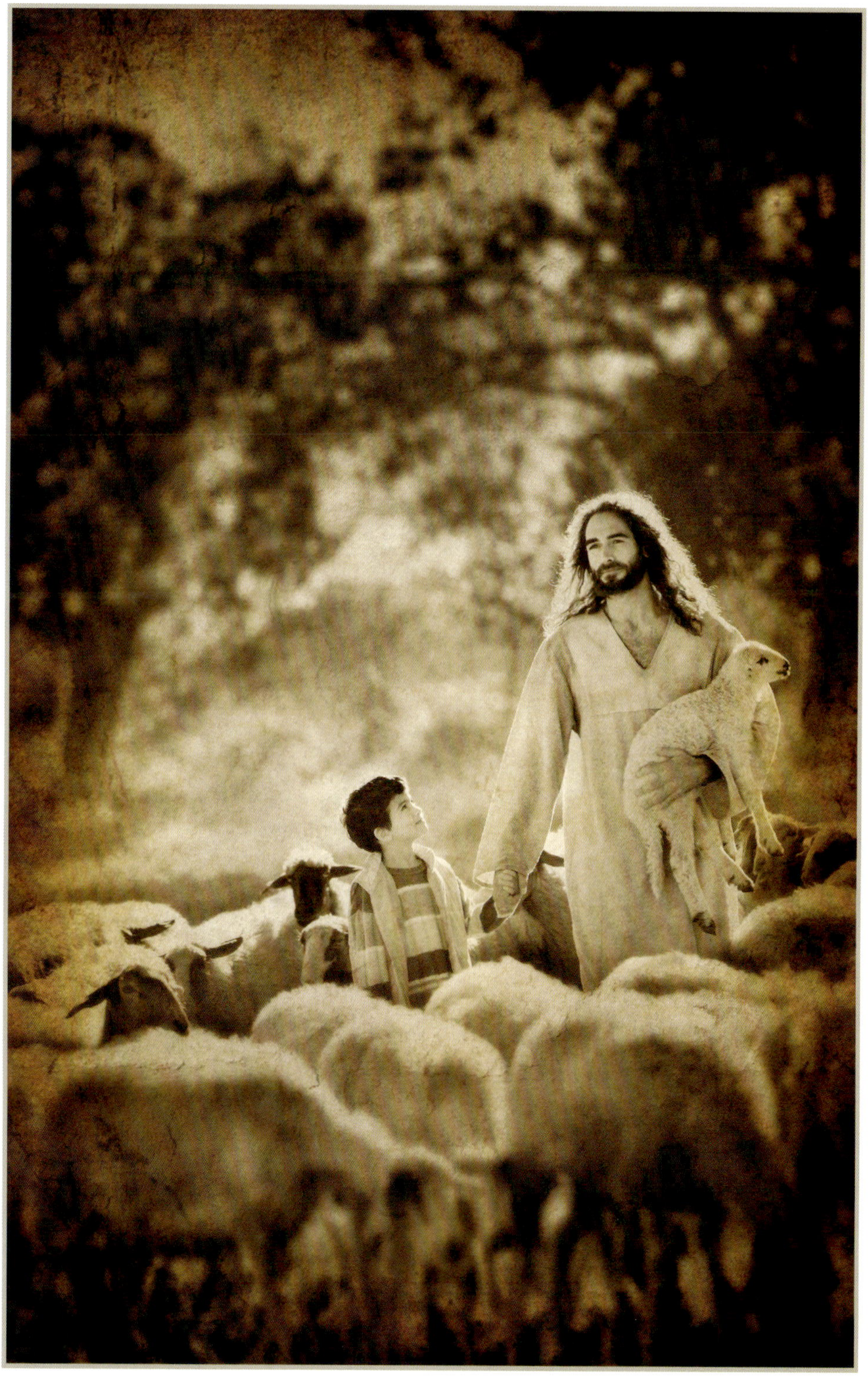

others astray, a characteristic we all have witnessed in humans.

In biblical times, sheep were a significant part of everyone's life. They were a significant food source including milk and cheese, and their wool was used for making clothing and blankets. They are referenced over 400 times in the Bible, beginning in Genesis where it is noted that Adam & Eve's son, Abel, was a keeper of sheep (Genesis 4:2). A wealthy man named Job from Uz had seven thousand sheep taken from him, but later God gave him fourteen thousand more (Job 1:3, 42:12). When Solomon dedicated his temple to God he offered a sacrifice of a 120,000 sheep (2 Chronicles 7:5). Imagine how many he actually had if he could sacrifice that many! (Historians have noted flocks in the millions.)

A small number of sheep were included along with other animals on the family farm. However, to maintain a large flock, the sheep had to be moved from pasture to pasture for fresh grass. This required a full-time worker other than the farmer. Thus, the key to a thriving flock of sheep was a good shepherd.

The shepherd's duty was to keep the flock intact and move them to fresh pastures as needed. The shepherd also protected them from predators. Shepherds would become so familiar with their flocks that they would name their sheep and call them by name. The sheep knew the shepherd's voice and would follow, but would not follow the voice of a stranger.

Jesus spoke about the shepherd in chapter ten of the Book of John. "The gatekeeper [the shepherd] opens the gate and the sheep listen to his voice. He calls his own sheep by name. Whenever he brings out his own sheep, he goes before them, and the sheep follow him, for they know his voice." Jesus said, "I am the good shepherd. The good shepherd lays down his life for the sheep" (John 10:3-5,11).

Jesus' reference to himself as the *Good Shepherd* and his use of sheep to portray how He personally cares for us, provided the inspiration for this photograph. In the photograph *Gone Astray*, the lamb in Jesus' arms represents the lamb in the *Parable of the Lost Sheep* — a story about a man who loses one of his sheep from a flock of a hundred. In the parable, the man left ninety-nine of the sheep to go find the lost one (Luke 15:3-4). Through this story, Jesus illustrates that there is no distance God will not go to find each of us...His lost sheep. Although the *Parable of the Lost Sheep* was not my primary inspiration for *Gone Astray*, it provides another example of just how much God loves us.

Returning to Isaiah 53:6 again where He writes, "We are all acting like sheep when we leave God's path to follow our own." The question we should want to ask is, "What in the world would make us do that?"

Is it human nature to think that *the grass is greener on the other side of the fence?* As long as we are thankful to God for all He provides, I think it's okay to be discontented with our circumstances (in the sense of being restless) if it drives us in a positive direction to do better or be better. However, being discontent can also push us to want things we shouldn't have.

An example of this occurs far too often in marriage, when one party leaves the other thinking there is a *greener pasture* — a more desirable person — *on the other side*. Since more that 65% of second marriages fail, the data refutes this idea. The greener grass theory often ends up wrecking the life of the "wanderer," and even more, the lives of families that get left behind. In reality, the grass is not necessarily greener on the other side of the fence, it's greener where we water it and where we spend time and effort taking care of it!

Through the prophet Jeremiah, God says that He knows the plans he has for us and they are good plans (Jeremiah 29:11). The *good plans* Jeremiah references were God's plan for Jesus, the Messiah, to descend through the Israelites' lineage 600 years later. Yet, I also believe that God is saying that He has laid out a good path for each of us. Follow Him and He will show us how to enjoy it!

So, how is it we become so misguided that we think that following our own path is somehow better than allowing Jesus to shepherd us down God's path? Are we misguided or have we not taken time to listen to God tell us about the better plan we will find on His path?

In the Old Testament book of 1 Samuel, God sent the prophet Samuel to anoint a new king from Jesse's family in Bethlehem. Samuel didn't know which of the brothers was to be king until he asked if there was another son other than the ones he had seen. There was another child, and he had been left out in the field tending to the sheep. The shepherd boy, David, was the one whom God had chosen to be King (1 Samuel 16:11).

Even after David became a famous king, he remained fond of his days as a shepherd. Midway through his life, he wrote what is known as Psalm 23, one of the most beautiful and memorable Psalms we know. In it, he shows that we can trust God to care for us in the same ways sheep rely on a good shepherd to care for them.

With Jesus as our shepherd, we don't need anything. He provides for us. He restores us when we need rest. As sovereign God, He made the way, so He knows the way. He comforts us during dark times and protects us from many things, many of which we are unaware, including ourselves! Our lives overflow with blessings, even when we think we have it tough or don't have enough. Because God is with me, I have no reason to fear, for when I die, I know that I'll be born again to live in eternity with Him.

The Twenty-Third Psalm

"The Lord is my shepherd, I lack nothing.
He makes me lie down in green pastures,
He leads me beside quiet waters,
He refreshes my soul.
He guides me along the right paths for His name's sake.
Even though I walk through the darkest valley, I will fear no evil,
for You are with me, your rod and your staff they comfort me.
You prepare a table before me in the presence of my enemies.
You anoint my head with oil; my cup overflows.
Surely your goodness and love will follow me all the days of my life,
and I will dwell in the house of the Lord forever."

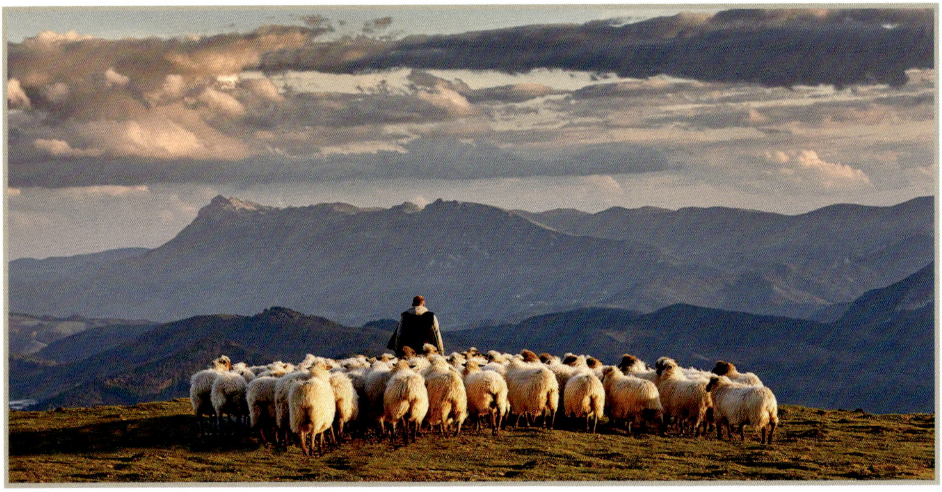

Jesus is the one who leads us back to God's path when we stray away on our own. With a Shepherd like Him, we have all we need.

Thoughts to Ponder

View film at ▶ journeyswiththemessiah.org

- Isaiah 53:6 says, "We all, like sheep, have gone astray, each of us has turned to our own way [away from God's way]." Consider Isaiah's words. Are you on God's path, off of God's path, or meandering on and off of it? Do you notice a difference in your life when you are on His path versus the times when you are not?
- People of Jesus' time understood the needs of sheep and why a good shepherd was so important. Jesus talked about himself as "The Good Shepherd" who would care for His human flock. Would you like to have a Good Shepherd who takes care of your needs while managing your life, too?
- Think of any instances in which you believed the *"grass was greener on the other side of the fence."* Which side of the fence did you settle on? Recall the circumstances and how it turned out.
- Take a walk down memory lane and consider how your life would have been different if you had always allowed Jesus to be your shepherd? Think of how it will be going forward.
- In John 14, Jesus said that the sheep knew His voice and would follow His voice but not the voice of a stranger. Do you know His voice? Do you hear Him when He speaks to you? Are you following the shepherd? Read John 15:16.

14

Holy Abundance

God's Provision Gone Awry

View film at ▶ journeyswiththemessiah.org

A couple stood on a hillside overlooking one of the world's worst slums. Overwhelmed by the poverty and despair they were witnessing in this tragic scene, they turned their faces skyward and cried out, "God, how could you let this happen?" God responded, "How could you?"

Jesus often taught using parables or simple stories to illustrate moral or spiritual lessons. In a similar way, I have created photographs as "visual parables" to invite the viewer into the simple message each image depicts. This one, *Holy Abundance,* may have made some people uncomfortable. Perhaps the message it depicts hits too close to home!

The United Nations estimates that one in every nine people in the world is suffering from chronic undernourishment. In 2016 that accounted for 795 million people or about 10% of the world's population. It's also reported that approximately 21,000 people die daily from hunger or hunger-related causes. The percentages are higher in underdeveloped countries. Yet, even in the United States, a growing share of households report what is now called "food insecurity."

Assuming these figures are accurate or even close, they add up to many hungry people and a lot of deaths that could be prevented. Although children are the most vulnerable overall, the numbers are increasing for working mothers who will forgo eating so their kids can eat. That's just heartbreaking!

It's challenging to get our minds around statistics of this magnitude. How do we begin to relate to the enormity of the problem unless we are involved in the issues surrounding it or even worse, unless we are a part of it? I am thankful that I have never known poverty or hunger. I feel confident that the majority of people reading this feel the same.

Robert Egger, the Founder of L. A. Kitchen, wrote, "A kid who is hungry cannot learn. A kid who can't learn drops out of school. A kid without an education can't get a job and help his country compete in a global economy. A kid without a job

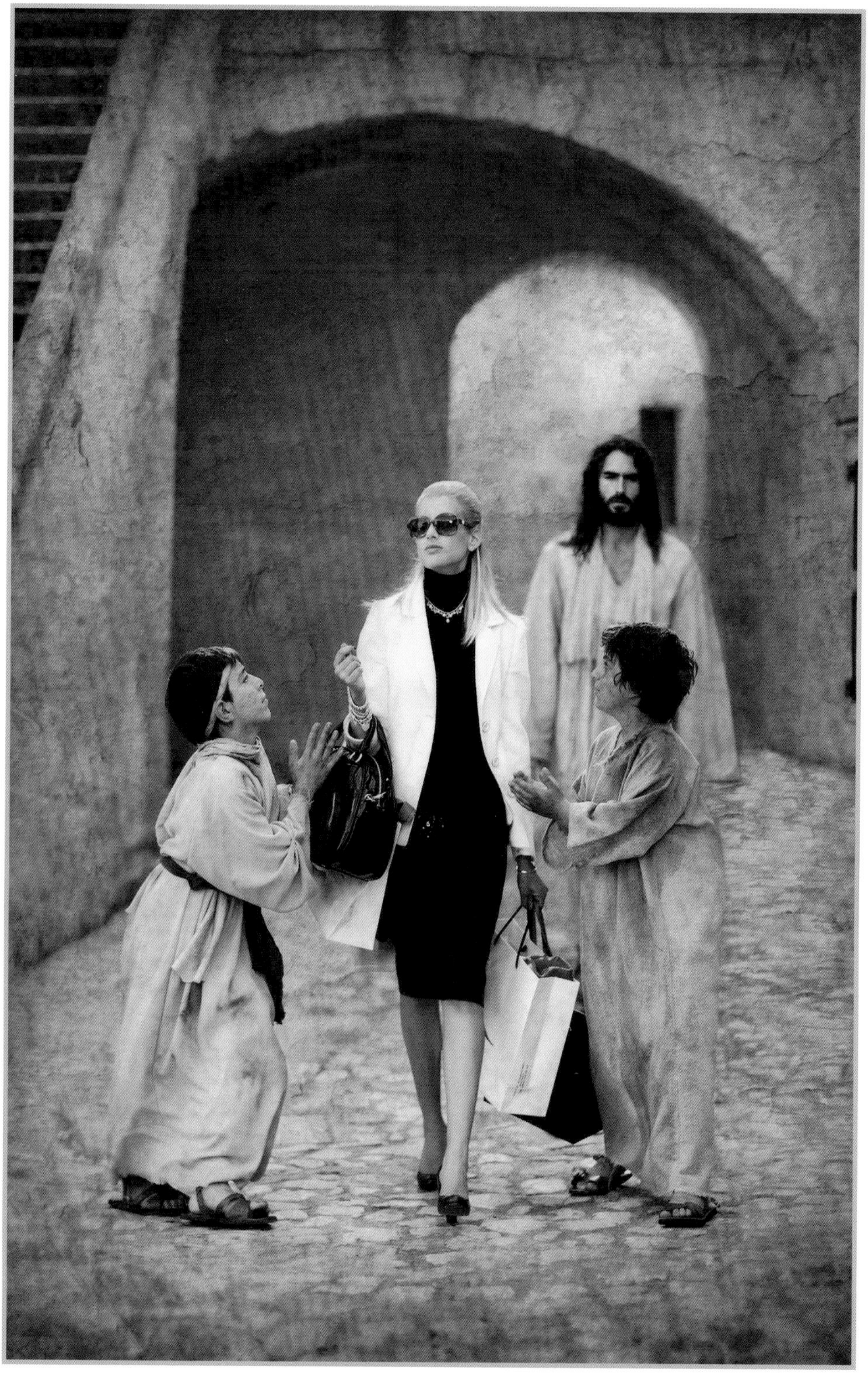

may turn to crime, get arrested and cost taxpayers $40,000 a year to sit in prison."

It appears the effects of hunger and poverty ripple out to all of us in many ways in addition to the moral issue. Since no one is entirely immune to the impact of poverty and hunger, perhaps being spared from these conditions suggests that we have been given another role to play.

While researching and developing the content for this book and the Journeys' Film Series, I read in an *Oxfam* report published in *The Guardian* that the world's eight richest billionaires control the same amount of wealth as the poorest half of the world's population. This means that the combined wealth of the world's eight wealthiest people equals the combined wealth of 3.8 billion of the poorest people. Stated differently, each of these billionaires has wealth equivalent to the combined wealth of 450 million people. (You might want to read those mind-boggling numbers again!)

Once again, that's just too big to get our minds around, so let's try bringing it down to our level. If your household income is $60,000 annually, you have 16 times the average daily allowance of 70% of the world's population who live on less than $10 per day. So, when the couple cried out to God, "How could you let this happen?" and God responded, "How could you?" it should make us pause. Actually, it should stop us dead in our tracks!

Please do not misread this as me being down on the super rich. The point I'm trying to establish is that God has made the world exceedingly abundant by providing enough for everyone! The world's poverty issue is not because of a lack of abundance. It's due to a lack of distribution! Somewhere along the way, the world has failed to understand God's plan or maybe just totally ignored it! This statement is not intended to be condemning, only instructional.

> **Jesus is a great advocate for the redistribution of wealth, but not through government-mandated redistribution, for that seldom works. Jesus advocates redistribution through sharing, whereby those who have been given much choose to share with those who are less fortunate.**

Here is how John the Baptist interpreted this concept: "Anyone who has two shirts should share with the one who has none, and anyone who has food should do the same" (Luke 3:11). This verse clearly states that for those who have more, there is a responsibility to share with those who have less. Money and possessions are not to be stored up or hoarded but shared with less fortunate people.

The First Epistle of John confirms these instructions and goes even further by questioning the condition of the heart of a person who does not embrace sharing as a part of God's economy. It says, "If anyone has material possessions and sees a brother or sister in need, but has no pity on them, how can the love of God be in that person" (1 John 3:17).

By questioning "how can the love of God be in a person who has no pity for a brother or sister in need," John is making the case that sharing is a spiritual gift and not something we do naturally. We share because God, through His love, has placed the desire in us to share with others.

Being forced or coerced to give, or giving out of guilt, is not God's desire. Instead, He desires that we are blessed by giving to others. Jesus stated God's perfect desire when He said, "It is more blessed to give than to receive" (Acts 20:35). On the occasion when He washed the feet of His disciples, Jesus told them that if they followed His example of giving to others, they would be blessed. "Now that you know these things, you will be blessed if you do them," He said. (John 13:15,17).

Furthermore, Jesus said that when we give to others we should do it in secret. He said that we are not to be like hypocrites who announce their giving by blowing trumpets on the streets so that people will see them and honor them (Matthew 6:2). (When I first learned to give, I was so proud of myself I blew the trumpets and let everyone know to whom and how much!)

Giving is always a good thing regardless of the conditions under which we give. However, Jesus warns us that in broadcasting our giving, the recognition we will receive from the crowd is the only eternal reward we will get (Matthew 6:2). He said, "Your giving should be done in secret. Then, your Father who can see what is done in secret will reward you" (Matthew 6:3-4). In other words, eternal rewards are available to us for giving to others. However, it appears that they are not available when we go around telling everyone about how much we give.

Luke's Gospel shares another great lesson about giving.

> *"Jesus looked up and saw the rich putting their gifts into the offering box, and he saw a poor widow put in two small copper coins. And he said, 'Truly, I tell you, this poor widow has put in more than all of them. For they all contributed out of their abundance, but she out of her poverty has put in all she had to live on."* (Mark 12:41-44)

I understand this scripture to mean that all giving is good, but there is a difference when we give sacrificially. **Sacrificial giving is when we give up something that we really need or want to keep, but we give it in exchange for helping someone else.**

I used to give out of my abundance. It made me feel good, but it never hurt. Today, I pay attention to the amount I give and whether it is causing me any discomfort, even a little pain. Ultimately, the more it hurts, the better it feels. No pain, no gain!

If you genuinely want the rewards of Heaven and want to store up rewards for your eternal life, then share now...and this includes more than money. God wants us to share all of our wealth and the one thing that we hold nearest and dearest is our time. It's usually more comfortable to write a check than to give our time away. Giving money may occasionally come as a sacrifice, but giving our time always does.

Jesus talked about this with His disciples when He told them, "I was a stranger and you invited Me in, I was sick and you looked after Me, I was in prison and you came to visit Me" (Matthew 25:35). Each of these actions requires the sacrifice of time.

One day I accidentally touched the call back button on my phone. It dialed the number of an elderly woman instead of who I meant to call. My first thought was, "I don't have time for this!" Instead, I gave her my name, told her I was returning her call and we ended up having a delightful conversation. At the end, she prayed for me and my wife and our ministry. I could have missed out on this!

Whether you have a little or have a lot, the message of giving is the same. "Anyone who has two shirts should share with the one who has none, and anyone who has food should do the same" (Luke 3:11).

We share because of the desire God has given to us through His love. So let's not miss out on the blessings God offers to us. Let's store up treasures for ourselves in Heaven. "For where your treasure is, their your heart will be also" (Matthew 6:20-21).

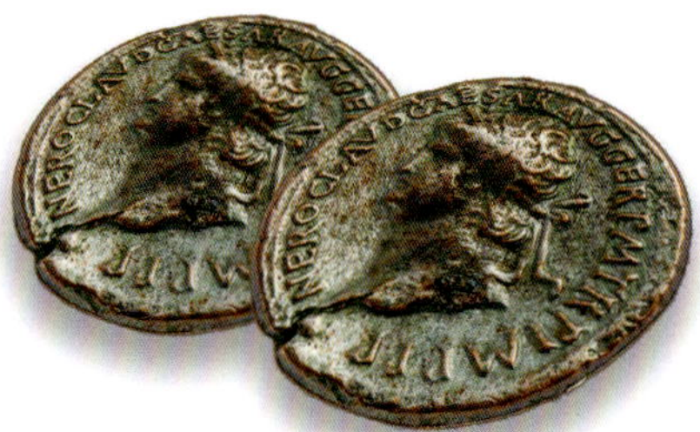

Jesus saw a poor widow put in two small copper coins. He said, "She, out of her poverty has put in all she had to live on."

Thoughts to Ponder

View film at ▶ journeyswiththemessiah.org

- At the beginning of the chapter, the couple viewing the slum cried out, "God, how could you let this happen?" Have you ever cried out at God as if He was causing the injustice in your life?
- Poverty as well as the disparity between the rich and poor is on the rise, while the increases in federal deficits are proof that taxpayers' money is not spent responsibly. Regardless of who is at fault, **the issues of poverty and disparity of wealth are issues of our hearts, not money**. If only our hearts could be fixed!
- **Poverty Consciousness: Believing there will not be enough for me!** It causes people to try to accumulate a disproportionate share for themselves. Ponder this: "Has God supplied enough for me?"

Consider each of the following paraphrased scriptures.

- Since I have two shirts, I should share with someone who has none, and because I have an abundance of food, I should do the same [often.] (Luke 3:11).
- Because I have plenty of money and many material possessions, if I see a brother or sister in need but have no pity on them, I must ask myself, "How can the love of God be in me? (1 John 3:17).
- I give anonymously because Jesus says that my giving should be done in secret; God will know and reward me for it. (Matthew 6:3-4).

  Option 1: I give from my abundance or overflow.

  Option 2: My giving is sacrificial and could or will leave me with a shortfall for myself. (Mark 12:41-44)

- Jesus said that where my treasure is, I could find my heart in the same place. (Matthew 6:20-21) **My treasure is anything that can cause my heart to be in the wrong place!**

Note: A donor-advised fund with someone like National Christian Foundation will allow you to give in secret and still get a tax deduction!

15

Life Savior

Spiritual Swimming Lessons for Life

View film at ▶ journeyswiththemessiah.org

It was a blustery afternoon when I headed out for a walk on the beach near my home in Northwest Florida. I recall small red flags strategically placed to warn beachgoers the surf was dangerous and to stay out of the water. As I approached the shore, I heard children screaming. At first I thought they were laughing and yelling while having fun in the waves, then I recognized the panic in their voices! They were screaming for help!

A disciplined person does not react to situations. Instead, they have learned to observe and gather the information that allows them to respond appropriately. Unfortunately, I learned that much later in life! So, without taking time to consider the situation, I pulled off my shirt and leaped into the water. Within a split second, the powerful current sucked me out to sea. As I looked around to get my bearings, I found I was fifty yards offshore, caught in a riptide and staring into the desperate faces of three young boys and their fathers.

Riptides, or rip currents, often occur on days when the weather is stormy. They develop when sandbars near the shore create water basins between the sandbar and the beach. When the water eventually breaks through the sandbar, it's like pulling the stopper in a bathtub—the suction drains the water through the sandbar and out to sea away from the shore. It creates a fast-moving and powerful current.

Many people drown each year when they are caught in rip currents. Most of these deaths could be prevented if people knew the simple rules of how to escape.

As I reached the children, one of the fathers pushed his child toward me. "Please save my son," he said. "I'm not going to make it." The panicked child threw his arms around my neck and his weight took us under. Though I could feel my own panic setting in, I recall thinking quite clearly, "I'm out for a walk on the beach, and in an instant, I'm staring death in the face! Is this how my life is going to end?"

So here I was caught in a riptide and believing I was about to drown when, like a neon sign lighting up in my head, I recalled how to escape a riptide:

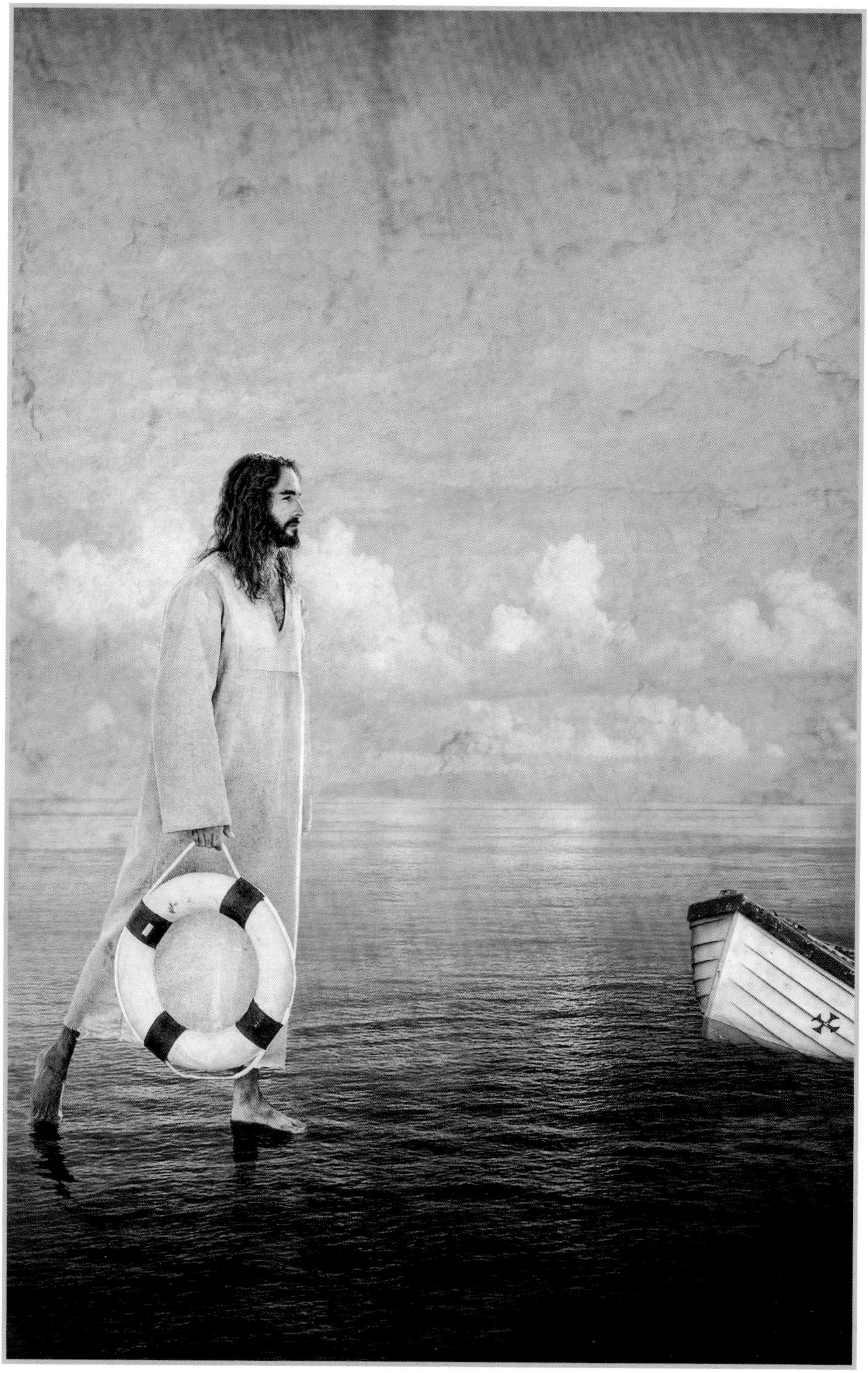

Stop struggling against the current and start swimming with it while gradually swimming toward the left or right.

Most riptides are less than thirty feet wide. Human nature makes people try to get back to the shore by fighting against the current that is pulling them out to sea. Eventually, they become exhausted and drown. On the other hand, it requires a lot of faith to swim with the current as it carries you out to sea and away from the safety of the shore.

With my sudden revelation of how to escape, I tried to convince the boys and their fathers to follow me. Yet, they were so stuck in fear they were unable to move or listen to reason. So, I allowed myself to flow with the current and slowly began swimming toward the left side.

In a short distance, I felt the current release its grip and I started circling back toward the shore. By that time, several people had waded into the surf with a rope tied to a lifesaver. They threw it to me and pulled me the rest of the way to safety.

With help from many people who had gathered on the beach, we tied together every garden hose and firehose, and every piece of rope brought to us. Then we tied it to a rubber raft which we floated out to the desperate boys and their fathers. Eventually, they were all pulled in to safety and, miraculously, no one drowned! As for me, life looked different the next day.

Since I created this collection of photographs, God has used them to open my eyes a little more each day. Projects like this will often allow us to think we are doing something for God when it is God who is doing something for us — drawing us closer to Himself.

As I planned these images, I recalled the riptide experience, which began when the little boys and their fathers were casually strolling down the beach near the water's edge. A rogue wave caught them by surprise, knocking the little boys down and the rip current quickly pulled them out to sea. The fathers jumped in to save them. That's what good fathers do!

In similar ways, isn't that how life happens? We go for a pleasant walk on the beaches of our lives and suddenly, without warning, disaster strikes. We find ourselves drowning in a sea of troubles. Like the little boys and their fathers we usually panic. We're too frightened to listen to reason, even when it will lead us to safety. Yet God sometimes asks that we let go of what feels safe for the moment so He can lead us away from a disastrous ending.

At one time or another, everyone has ignored God's red flags — flags that are screaming for us to stay away from the dangerous water in our lives ? For example, a paycheck may appear to provide security while it simultaneously drowns us in misery from a job we hate. There are people who stay in bad relationships even when they know it was a bad choice (and not God's choice) from the start. God wants to lead us away from harm to the safety of better plans He has for us.

Though life is full of trials, Jesus will rescue us from unexpected storms that threaten to drown us. Yet, He also offers free "spiritual swimming lessons" that can keep us from getting in over our heads to begin with. His lessons await us in the Bible and as we spend time with Him. The Bible is His training manual. It has directions for everything we will ever need, including how to maximize our days at the beach while learning how to avoid riptides.

Each time I look at the photograph of *Life Savior*, I am reminded of that frightening afternoon when I was caught in a riptide and thought I would die. Yet, I also recall the joy I felt when someone threw a lifesaver to me and pulled me to the safety of the shore. The events of that day also remind of a time when I was drowning from a life turned from God and the day He threw the ultimate "lifesaver" to me—

The Life Savior, Jesus Christ!

Have a great day on life's beach and be sure to take your *"Life Savior"* with you!

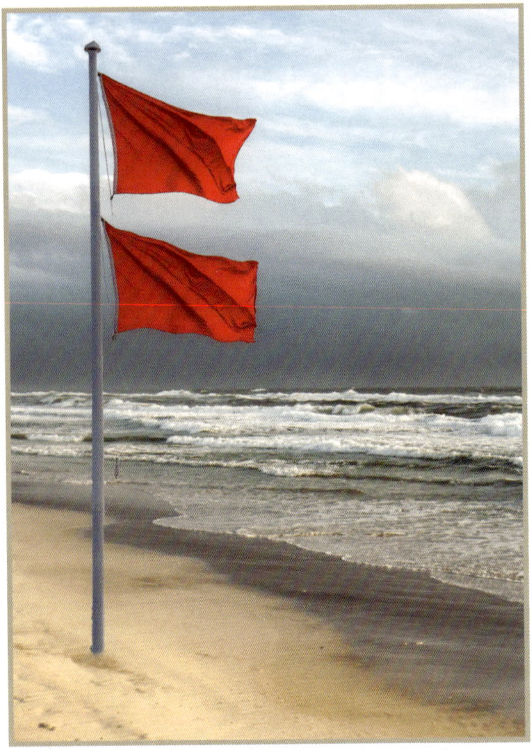

Be equally aware of God's warning signs!

Thoughts to Ponder

View film at ▶ journeyswiththemessiah.org

- At the beginning of this chapter, I talk about being caught in a riptide in the Gulf of Mexico. Recall being caught in your own physical or emotional "riptide" of circumstances. Were you shown the way to safety? By whom?
- Have you ever had a day begin perfectly only to have disaster strike without warning? Was your first reaction panic or fear? Did you turn to your own devices or seek God for His way out?
- When the little boys were knocked down by the wave and pulled out to sea by the riptide, the fathers jumped in to save them. As I said, "That's what good fathers do!" As a good father (or parent), have you or will you "jump in" to save family members who may be drowning in a life that does not include Jesus Christ?
- Do you recall a time when you ignored God's red flags warning you to stay away from life's dangerous waters? What was the outcome?
- God may require us to let go of what feels safe and secure for the moment for Him to lead us away from a disastrous ending. Has there been a job, relationship, business deal or other circumstances from which you needed to walk, but stayed because it felt or seemed safe?
- God offers free "spiritual swimming lessons" through the Bible and a host of other resources, including spending time with *The Life Savior*. Each of these are lessons that can keep us from "getting in over our heads." Consider circumstances in your life when having knowledge of "God's word" could have saved you from one of life's riptides.

16

Makeover

Let the Master Artist Shape your Life

View film at ▶ journeyswiththemessiah.org

"You are the potter, I am the clay. Mold me and make me, this is what I pray." I love these words in the song *Change My Heart, O God*. I'm sure you understand that the potter and the clay are biblical references to God and man. Thousands of years ago, the prophet Isaiah wrote, "But now, O Lord, you are our Father; we are the clay, and you are our potter; we are all the work of your hand" (Isaiah 64:8). These words form such a beautiful vision of who God is and whose we are in Him.

Do you recall the imagination you had as a child? Wonderment seemed to be everywhere and we could find pleasure in the simplest things. Our focus was usually on the present moment, although sometimes I couldn't sleep while waiting to return to the exciting things I did earlier in the day.

Somewhere along the way, many of us lost our childhood instincts of doing what we liked to do as we fell into the trap of doing what the world expected us to do. Our focus changed from the present moment to "the future" as we began designing and planning our lives for the years ahead. Whether good or bad, our plans often consumed our time, pulling us away from the present moment. We worked more, we did more and we bought more until one day, we realized we were enjoying life less!

In the story of creation in the Book of Genesis, we're told that God formed man from the dust of the ground (Genesis 2:7) The prophet Isaiah adds understanding to this by depicting God as the potter and man as the potter's clay. The prophet Jeremiah draws an even more vivid picture:

"This is the word that came to Jeremiah from the Lord: 'Go down to the potter's house, and there I will give you my message. So I went down to the potter's house and saw him working at the wheel. But the pot he was shaping from the clay was marred in his hands; so the potter formed it into another pot, shaping it as seemed best to him'" (Jeremiah 18:1-4).

When I read these verses, I made notes of them while thinking I could show their

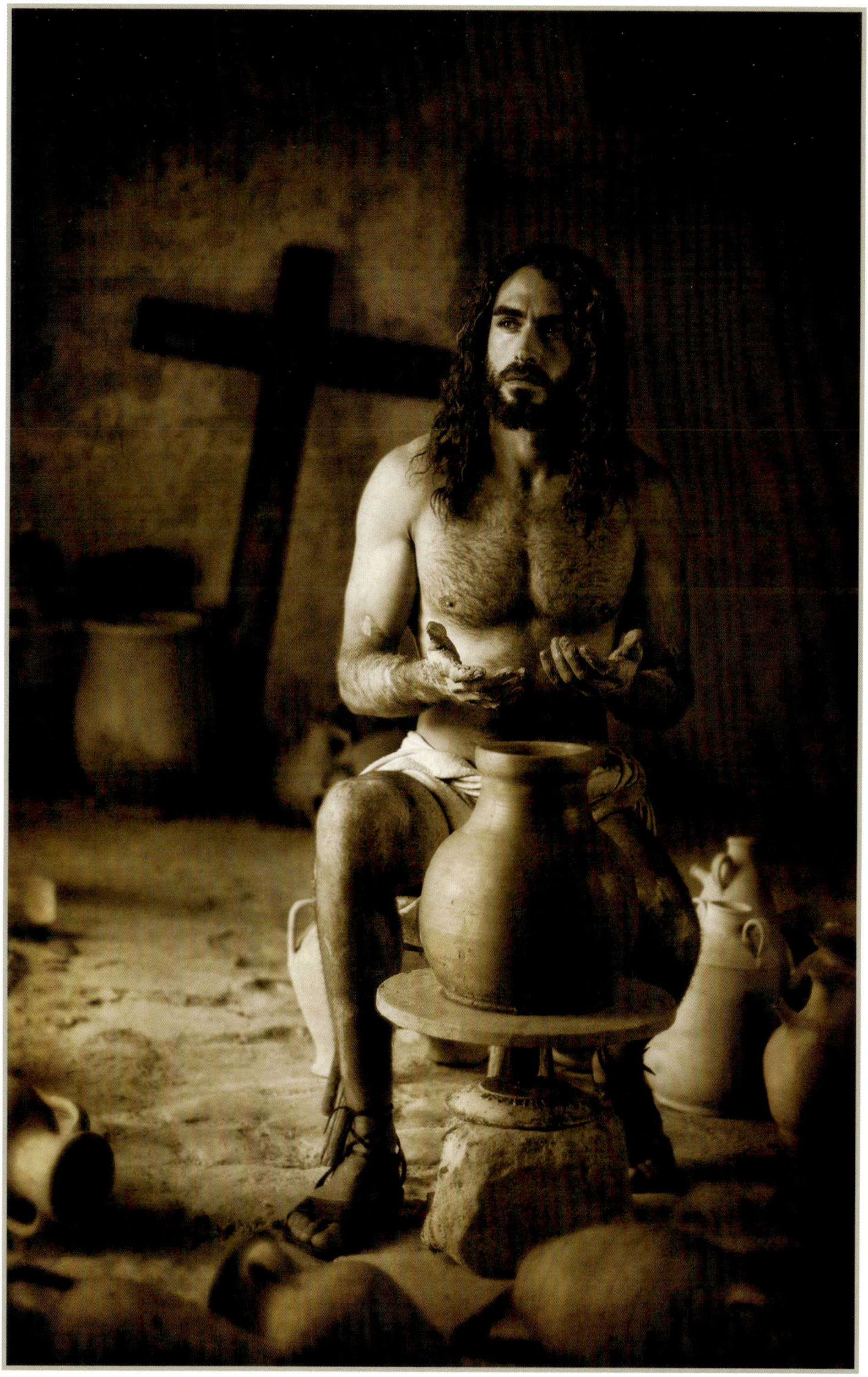

meaning and relevance by creating a photograph that depicted Jesus as the potter. It's an excellent analogy how Isaiah and Jeremiah have pictured God as the potter who has formed our lives from the dust…from the dirt of the ground (Genesis 2:7).

However, many deny God's existence by suggesting that the clay somehow jumped on the potter's wheel and formed itself. For me, it seems far more logical that a Master Artist, one with a brilliant vision, placed the clay on the wheel and as Jeremiah wrote, "With his hands, he shaped the pot the way he wanted it to be" (Jeremiah 18:4). In other words, God had already envisioned our design when He created each of us. Furthermore, according to the creation story in Genesis, "He created us in His own image" (Genesis 1:27).

This is astounding! We are created in the image of God! Would we dare be so arrogant as to consider that we could do a better job by creating ourselves? As Isaiah wrote, "Woe to the one who quarrels with his Maker…Will the clay say to the potter, 'What are you doing?'" (Isaiah 45:9).

The process of creating something from nothing, like making a beautiful piece of pottery from clay, requires time and patience. The potter must have a vision of what he wants to create and have the skill to achieve it. The clay must first be perfectly centered on the wheel. The potter must know how fast to spin it, knowing when to add pressure to the clay and when to back off. The clay must also remain pliable if it is to be shaped since the potter cannot shape clay into a beautiful piece when the clay becomes rigid.

We are the clay on the Master Potter's wheel. It takes God's supernatural vision and divine skill and patience for Him to create each of us. Just as the potter must keep the clay pliable for it to be shaped, God cannot shape our lives into the beautiful ones He planned when we are not receptive — when we resist His design by trying to shape ourselves.

I resisted God for a long as I tried to plan my life into what I thought it should be. My creation gave the perception that I was well-designed and well-crafted. Yet, without His vision, wisdom and guidance, I made many mistakes. Over time, flaws began to show, then cracks began to appear until I eventually shattered!

It must have been painful for God to watch, but He was not finished. Finally, when I realized that He, the Master Potter, had something better for my life, I surrendered my desires and failed attempts and asked Him to remold me to His desires. His design was more than I could ever conceive on my own. Mind you, I remain a work in progress. We all are!

Whether you are content with the way your life has turned out or feel like it's a shattered pot, don't worry, God is still at work. Not only can He pick up the pieces, He can remold them, shaping your life into His vision, making you into the beautiful creation He always intended you to be.

God will not be finished with any of us this side of Eternity!

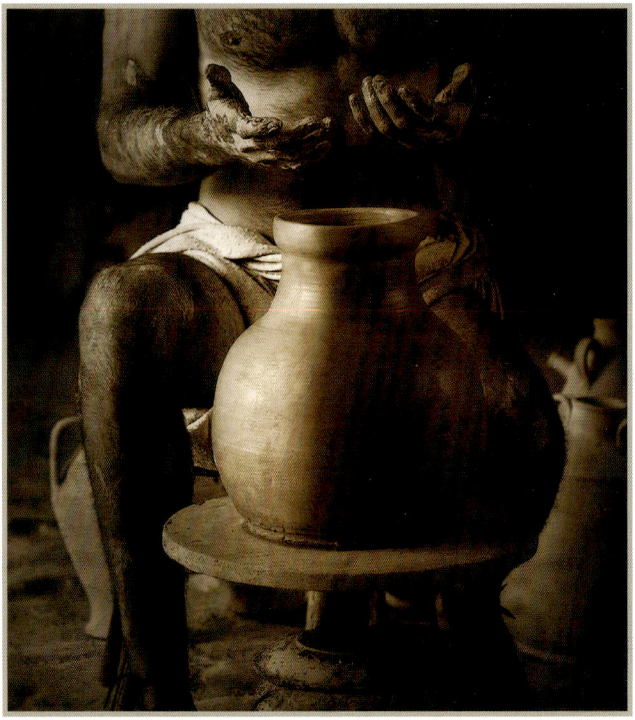

Make me and mold me to your design, Lord, not my own.

Thoughts to Ponder

View film at ▶ journeyswiththemessiah.org

- As children, we found pleasure in simple things and our focus was usually on the present moment. Where is your focus now, present or future? Do you still find joy in simple things?
- In regard to adulthood, I wrote, *"We worked more, did more and bought more until, one day, we realized we were enjoying our life less; our plans for the future pulled us away from the present moment."* If you agree with my observation and you are older like me, tell someone younger! If younger, seek the wisdom of someone older!
- Imagine God is sitting down at the potter's wheel to form your life. Jeremiah wrote, "With his hands, he shaped the pot the way he wanted it to be" (Jeremiah 18:4). Will you tell Him your plans and tell Him what to do? Will you show Him a picture of the the way you want to be or trust Him to do what He, the Master Artist, does best?
- If you have "gathered some miles" like me, do you look at your cracks (your sins) as flaws or as "character lines" that tell the story of your journey? If you see them only as flaws, may I direct you to Jesus who offers a plan to erase them!
- The human tendency is to judge God's design and, if not satisfied, try to make them into our own design. God's creations are perfect even when we can't see it.

17

Metamorphosis

Uncovering the Christ in You

View film at ▶ journeyswiththemessiah.org

Have you looked back on your life and wished you had done some things differently or made choices that would have led to better outcomes? I have! There have been times that I looked in the mirror and was disappointed with the man who was looking back. I assumed God was too!

All of God's creation is fascinating to me. The beauty of His imagination and unique

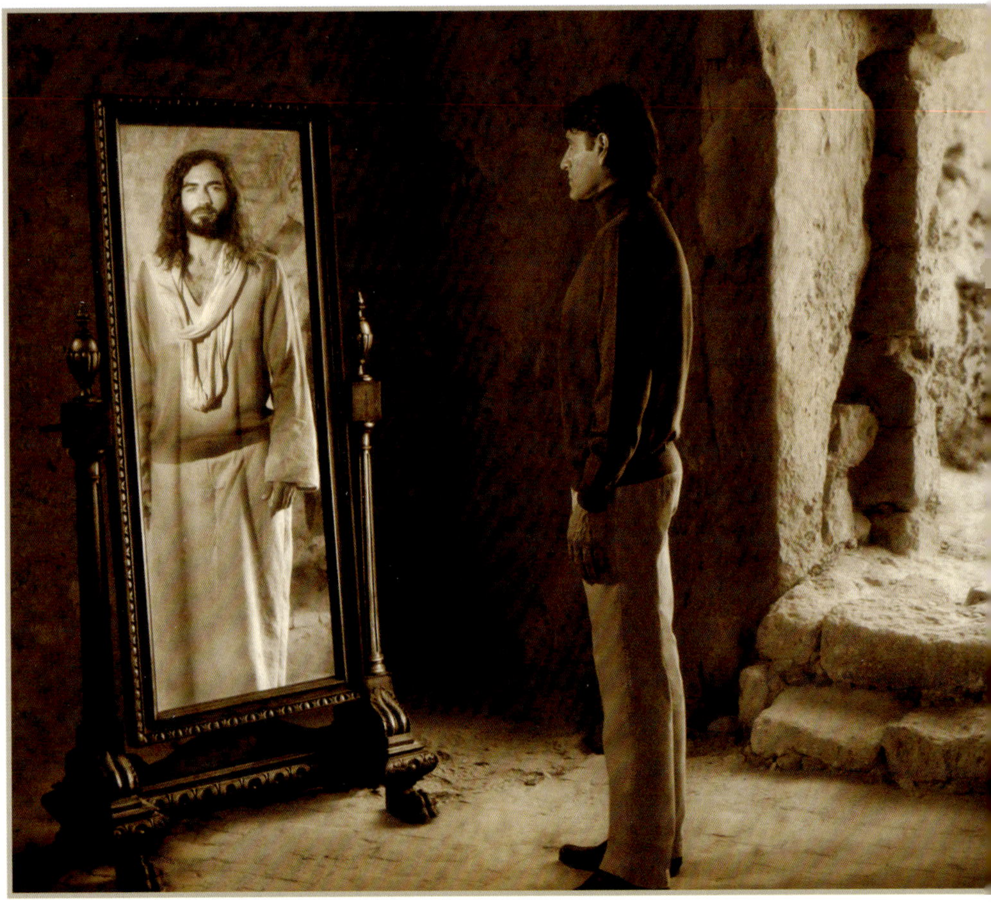

works of His hands can be found in every direction we look. Take for instance the caterpillar, an insect that hangs upside down in a tree while spinning a cocoon around itself. Then, four weeks later, the former caterpillar emerges as something completely different — a butterfly!

You have to admit that the act of a lizard suddenly changing its colors is unusual, but the transformation of a caterpillar into a butterfly...well, it is nothing short of miraculous! Here you have a six-legged crawling insect that lives in a tree and eats leaves that transforms into an insect that flies and lives on nectar. They don't just look different. They are different!

I think of the caterpillar-into-a-butterfly transformation in the same way as watching a good magician. You've seen the act when the magician puts the girl in the cage, covers the cage with a cloth and then, "Abracadabra!" He pulls back the cloth and in place of the girl is a tiger. It's really amazing! "How'd he do that!" However, the caterpillar turning into a butterfly is not magic, it's more. It's called metamorphosis and it's supernatural.

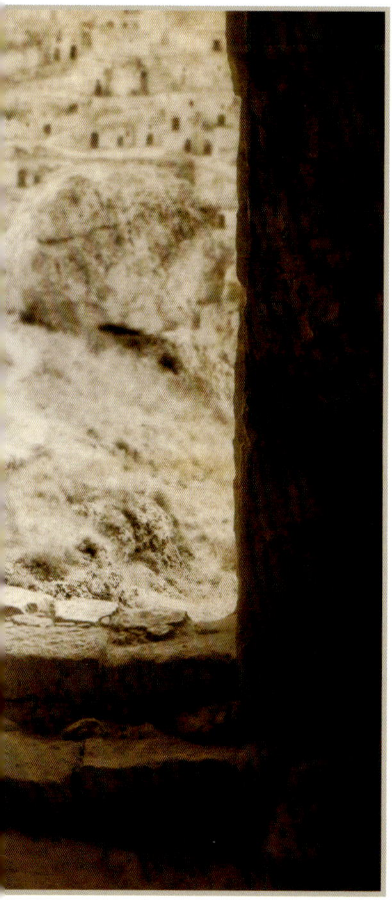

The dictionary defines the process of metamorphosis as a *change of the nature of a thing or person into a completely different one by natural or supernatural means.*

I am cautious of the rationale of anyone who observes our spectacular world and the miraculous workings of nature, and does not attribute processes like metamorphosis to the supernatural work of a Master Creator. There is just no other way to explain them.

Jesus commented about the supernatural attributes of nature in Luke's Gospel. The Pharisees (Jewish leaders) asked Jesus to rebuke his disciples for giving glory to Him. Jesus responded by saying, "If [the disciples] kept quiet, the stones would cry out" (Luke 19:40). Jesus was saying that all of creation praises God as the creator and the prophet Isaiah wrote, "The mountains and hills will burst into song before you, and all the trees of the field will clap their hands" (Isaiah 55:12). The process of metamorphosis is as if God is saying, "If you don't believe I'm the Creator, watch this!"

Church was a part of my life when I was a child. However, I was not a follower of Jesus until many years later when I began to experience Him from an expanded view that revealed to me who He was and who He could be in my life. Reading Jesus' words, and the words of others written about Him, guided me to see God's plans in practical terms and why I needed Jesus in my life.

Many resources have helped me to understand, appreciate and enjoy God's story as recorded in the Bible's unique collection of inspired writings. I have learned to look at the books of the Old and New Testaments as one continuous story. Seeing the Bible from this perspective adds to its enjoyment, especially as connections between the Old Testament and the New Testament are revealed to me.

As an example, in the Apostle Paul's First Letter to the Corinthians, he wrote, "For now we see in a mirror dimly but then face to face. Now I know in part, but then I will know fully, just as I also have been fully known" (1 Corinthians 13:12). I wanted to understand what Paul meant, so I searched the Internet to find answers regarding his statement about "seeing in a mirror dimly."

I discovered that crystal clear mirrors as we know them today did not exist in Jesus's time. The earliest mirrors were made from polished metal or even stone, but the first glass mirrors were made from tiles cut from blown glass adhered to a thin sheet of shiny metal. The tiles were slightly curved and slightly colored. It was an imprecise process that resulted in dim reflections. So, people listening to Paul would have understood his analogy, "Now we see in a mirror dimly."

The Message translates 1 Corinthians 13:12 like this: *"We don't yet see things clearly. We're squinting in a fog, peering through a mist. But it won't be long before the weather clears and the sun shines bright! We'll see it all then, see it all as clearly as God sees us, knowing him directly just as he knows us!"*

With my initial reading of this scripture, I imagined a modern-day man standing in front of a mirror. As he looks in, he sees that he is beginning to look like Jesus. I felt compelled to create a photograph depicting the message, *"A person can't spend time with Jesus without their life being supernaturally changed."* Paul talked about this kind of spiritual metamorphosis when he wrote his second letter to the Corinthians.

In his letter, he talked about Moses' face shining with God's radiant glory when he came down off of Mt. Sinai with the stone tablets on which God had written the Ten Commandments. People were afraid to come near Moses (Exodus 34:29-30), perhaps because of their sin, or maybe they feared they would die since God told Moses, "You cannot see my face and live" (Exodus 33:20). Moses responded to the crowd by putting a veil over his face (Exodus 34:33).

There is an exciting connection between this Old Testament story in Exodus (Moses putting a veil over his face) and the New Testament connection to Jesus found in 2 Corinthians. Paul explaines that we have had the veil removed from our faces because God has been revealed to us in the form of Jesus Christ. Paul continues: *"And now, as we observe God's glory as revealed in Jesus, we're being transformed into His image* (2 Corinthians 3:18). *This means that anyone who belongs to Christ has become a new person. The old life is gone; a new life has begun!* (2 Corinthians 5:17)."

Paul has just described metamorphosis, but at a level well beyond a caterpillar to a butterfly. This is supernatural metamorphosis! This is the power of God, through His Son Jesus, transforming the nature of a person into a new person. When we are the new person, people will begin to see Jesus in us and often be inspired to seek the same for themselves.

There was a time when I looked into the mirror and was not pleased with the man looking back at me. As Paul said, "I saw into a mirror, dimly" because my knowledge and understanding of God was immature and incomplete. Now I can see my own metamorphosis taking place as God transforms me into a new person, and hopefully on occasion, people will get a glimpse of Jesus in me!

As Paul wrote in 1 Corinthians, 'now I know only in part, but then I will know God fully, just as I have been fully known by Him.'

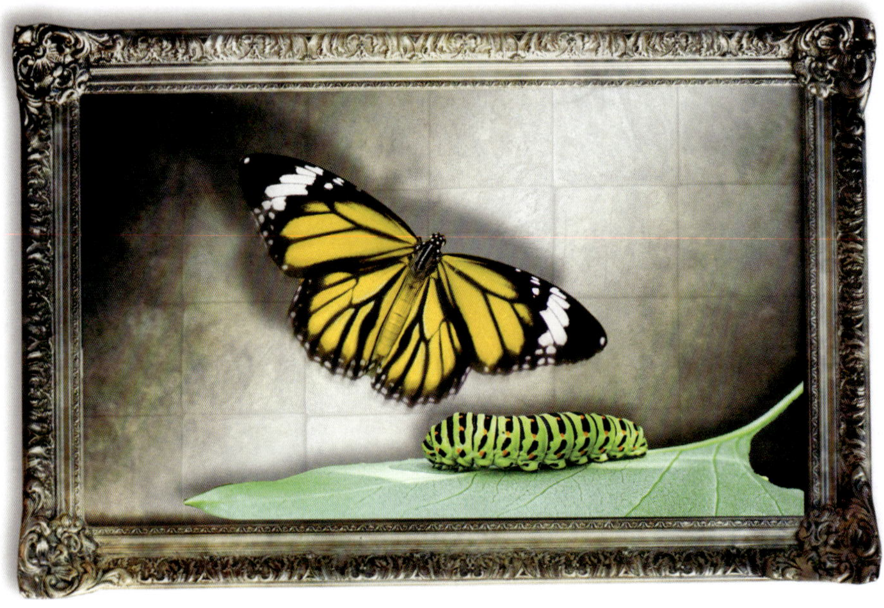

Metamorphosis is the change of the nature of a thing or person into a completely different one by natural or supernatural means.

Thoughts to Ponder

View film at ▶ journeyswiththemessiah.org

- If you are a follower of Jesus, take time to recall when you began to notice that you were changing into a new person and something better than you had been before?
- The Apostle Paul describes in 2 Corinthians 5:17 a spiritual metamorphosis that occurs when someone accepts Jesus as the Lord of their life. He writes, "The old life is gone; a new life has begun!" If this describes your life in Christ, take time to consider (maybe even write it down) who you were in the "old life" and who you are now.
- Jesus told the Pharisees that, if He were to quiet His disciples from talking about Him, the stones [all of nature] would cry out or tell about Him. Isaiah wrote, "The mountains and hills will burst into song before you..." Consider sharing your faith using a caterpillar's metamorphosis into a butterfly as an example of the spiritual change that occurs to a believer in Jesus. Use the wonder of nature to tell His story to non-believers? Maybe you could present this information on a camping trip retreat?
- In 1 Corinthians 13:12, Paul taught that before Jesus, a person's understanding of the nature of God was less clear, like looking into a dim mirror. However, in Jesus, the character of God is clearly revealed. Ponder Jesus' words, "If you have seen me, you have seen the Father!" John 14:9
- In Corinthians 3:18, Paul continues the thought above by saying, "And now, as we observe God's glory as revealed in Jesus, we're being transformed into His image." Next time you pass by a mirror, take a moment to gaze into it to see if you are being transformed to look like Him!

18

Passover

The Promise of the Last Supper

View film at ▶ journeyswiththemessiah.org

When I was a child, our family went to Sunday school and church. On one Sunday each month, a portion of the church service was set aside for what we called *Communion* or *The Lord's Supper* to honor Jesus' last supper. I recall that we lined up in the aisles to go to the altar where we were served a thin paper-like wafer that stuck to the roof of my mouth. It was followed by a thimble-size glass of grape juice that was never quite enough liquid to dislodge the wafer. The thing I remember

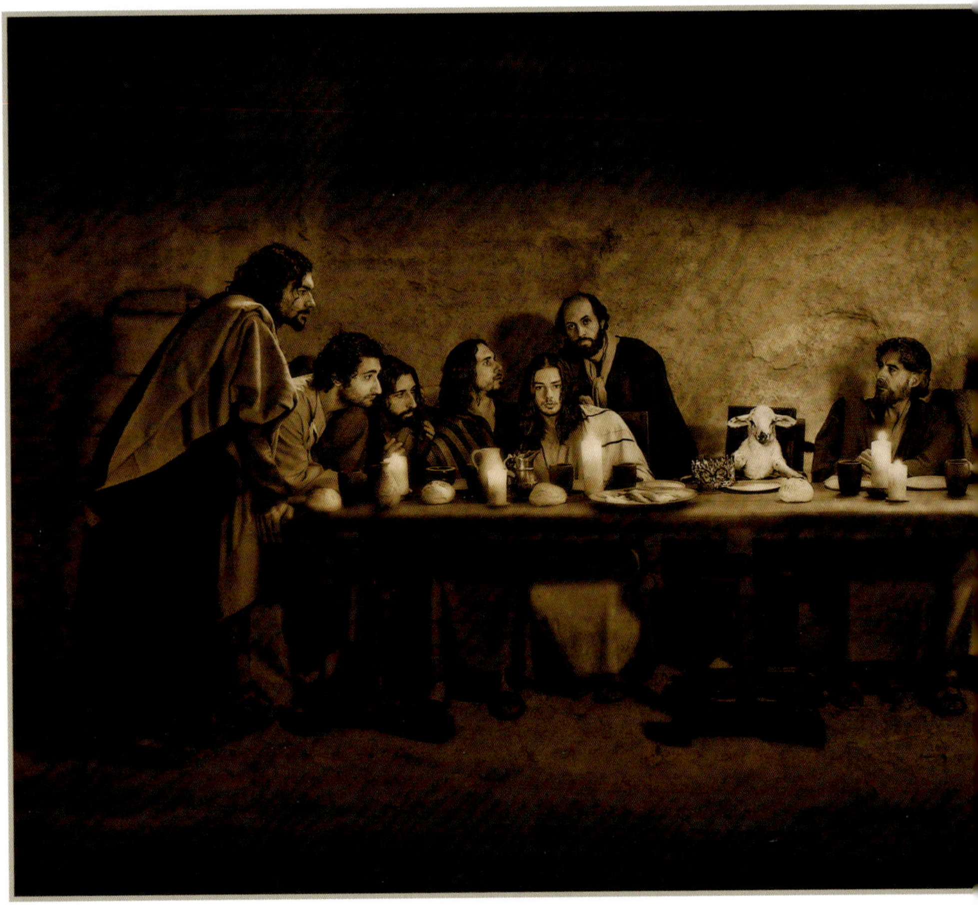

most is the service was going to run longer. I knew the story about Jesus and his disciples and the bread and the wine. Yet, as a child, I did not understand the significance of Communion or what it was about.

Many years later, I learned about the last supper Jesus had with His disciples and that He had used bread and wine (my wafer and grape juice) as symbols to represent His body and blood. Yet, it was only when I heard the story of the Jewish Passover that the dots began to connect for me.

The events of Jesus' last supper unfold on the evening before Jesus was crucified. He met with His disciples for a meal in the upper room of a private home in Jerusalem. Many people know that evening only for the part we call *The Last Supper*, but there was so much more to it. It was a very intimate evening that was filled with promises and instructions. It was the night that Jesus washed His disciples' feet as a gesture of showing His love for them. He also used the moment to teach them (and us) how to treat others.

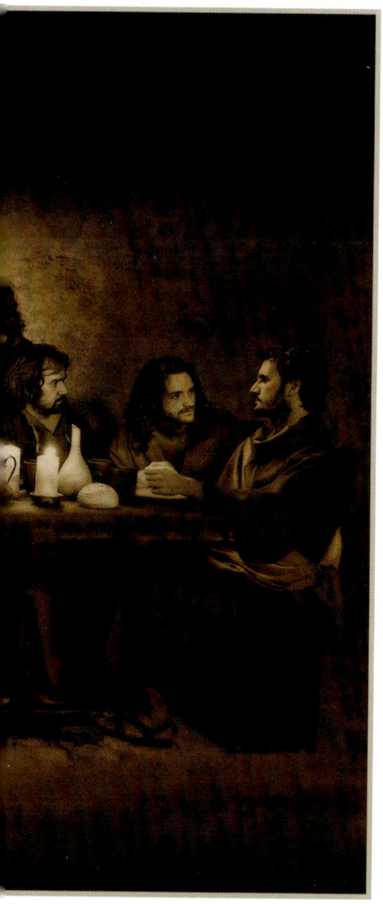

After washing the disciples' feet, Jesus asked if they understood what He had done for them. Then He said, "You call me 'Teacher' and 'Lord,' and rightly so, for that is what I am" (John 13:13). He said that He had given them an example of how they were to treat others and told them that they would be blessed when they did (John 13:14-17). Jesus was making a point that we will receive blessings when we humble ourselves by providing kindness to others.

During the evening, Jesus predicted His death and His betrayal by Judas. It was also the night that Peter said that he would follow Jesus and boldly declared, "I will lay down my life for You" (John 13:37). A few hours later, Peter would deny that he even knew Jesus — not just once, but three times! (Luke 22:54-62).

The disciples were troubled over Jesus' announcement of his pending death and confused about His predicted resurrection. From all they had witnessed, they had many reasons to believe the things He told them, but this was asking then to accept more than was possible at the time. He told them to not let their hearts be troubled. They believed in God; they could also believe in Him" (John 14:1).

Jesus described His Father's home in Eternity as one with many mansions. He said that He would be going there to prepare a place for them, and He would return to take them back home, but added, "They already knew the way" (John 14:2-4).

At this, the disciple Thomas spoke up to say that they didn't know where He was going, so how could they know the way (John 14:5). Jesus responded with what is now one of the main tenets of the Christian faith: "I am the way, and no one can come to the Father except through Me" (John 14:6).

He promised that, after He left, He would send the Holy Spirit, the Spirit of Truth, who would always advocate for them; that the Holy Spirit would live with them and in them (John 14:16-17, 16:5-9). He ended by saying that He was leaving His peace with them, a supernatural peace that the world could not give them, only He could provide (John 14:27).

Without being with the disciples that evening, it is difficult to know how much of what Jesus said was actually understood. Jesus shared so many lessons with them that evening that I encourage you to read it or reread it in John 13 thru 17.

During the meal, Jesus took the bread, broke it, and told His disciples, "Eat this, for it is My body." Then He took the wine cup and told them, "Drink this, for it is My blood poured out for you" (Matthew 26:26-28).

Imagine you were there that evening. You had followed Jesus for three years when, on this night, He tells you that the bread is His body — you are to eat it — and the wine is His blood — you are to drink it! Imagine how confusing His instructions would be. One can only imagine that Jesus' disciples had no clue what He was talking about. They would in just a few days!

From an earlier segment of these scriptures, we know that Jesus and the disciples had not just gathered together to eat. They were following the Jewish custom of the *Passover* meal. *Passover* is an annual tradition celebrating Israel's release from captivity in Egypt 1300 years before. I am surprised that I went to *Communion* for so many years without knowing the connection between the last supper of Jesus and the Israelites' exodus from captivity in Egypt.

Most Christians and Jews know this story in the Book of Exodus. It tells the story of the Israelites being held in captivity in Egypt and how God sent a series of plagues against The Pharaoh (Egypt's ruler) to prompt him to free the Israelites. The ten plagues included frogs, lice, flies, locusts, and boils. Yet, as horrifying as they were,

Pharaoh's heart grew harder with each one. Finally, God planned to send a plague that would kill the firstborn son in every home, including Pharaoh's own.

However, God told Moses (Israelites' leader) to instruct all Israelite families that on a specific night, they were to kill a young, unblemished lamb for their meal. Then they were to take blood from it and wipe or brush it on the sides and tops of their door frames. When the *Angel of Death* came that night to strike down the firstborn sons, the blood on the door frames would identify the Israelites as "God's chosen" and death would *pass over* their homes, sparing the death of their child.

I felt it was important to share this story by depicting it in an image of *The Last Supper.* I wanted my photograph to look similar to the famous painting by Leonardo di Vinci, but it needed *something more*. That *something more* turned out to be a lamb to replace Jesus at the table. God is so clever!

During their meal that evening, Jesus revealed to His disciples that just as the unblemished lamb had been slain during Passover in Egypt, He would be the new unblemished lamb that would be slain and sacrificed for all mankind. Through the blood of His sacrificial death, eternal death would "pass-over" all who believed in Him, just as death had passed over the firstborn children of the Israelites in Egypt, 1300 years before.

Three thousand years ago, God spared Israel's firstborn children through the sacrificial blood of an unblemished lamb. Two thousand years ago, God came into the world in the form of a man—Jesus—to spare us from eternal death by being the sacrificial lamb—the sacrifice by whose blood we can be saved. Jesus said, "There is no greater love than to lay down one's life for one's friends." (John 15:13). He said and then He did it!

Through Jesus sacrificial death — through His blood as the sacrificial Lamb of God —death will *passover* us as we take our last breath here on earth and our first breath in Eternity with Him.

Our image of *Passover* depicts the beautiful promise made for all who have accepted God's gift of saving grace through Jesus. It is an offer to everyone and "the gift of eternal life" to all who will receive it.

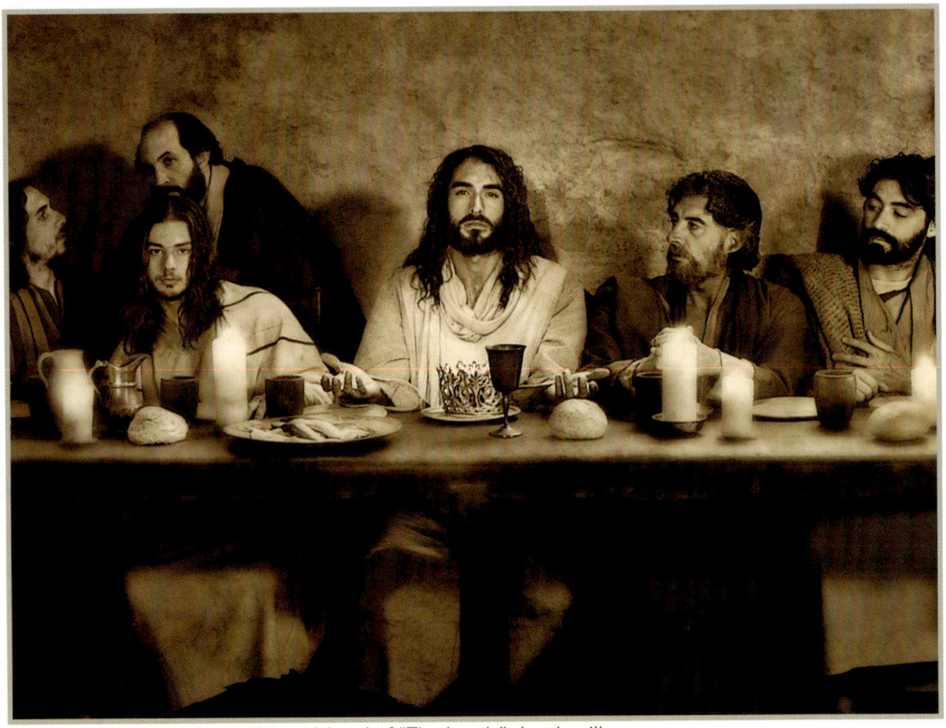

By the blood of "The Lamb" death will passover.

Thoughts to Ponder

View film at ▶ journeyswiththemessiah.org

- After washing the disciples' feet, Jesus said He had given them an example of how to treat others, adding that they would be blessed when they did the same. Thus, we are the recipients of God's blessings when we bless others. If you feel you are missing out on God's blessings, remedy the situation by blessing others!
- In John 14:16-17, Jesus told His disciples that He would ask the Father to give them another advocate, the Holy Spirit, to help them and be with them forever; that He lives with them and will be in them. I need to put signs up everywhere to remind me that I have this "advocate" who lives with me and is available 24/7.
- On the night of the Last Supper, the disciples were troubled over Jesus' announcement of His pending death. Jesus responded, "Do not let your hearts be troubled. You believe in God, believe also in me." (Easier said than done, right!) Jesus' sacrificial death as the Lamb of God means that the things of this world will one day fade away as we "*passover*" into a trouble-free and perfect eternal life with Him; that the troubles that come our way today are only temporary.
- The next time you have The Lord's Supper, perhaps you will take time to reflect on that evening 2,000 years ago when Jesus shared the bread and wine with His disciples. You can rest secure in knowing that Jesus' sacrificial death as the unblemished Lamb of God means that death will Passover all who believe in Him just as it "passed over" the firstborn children of Israel.

"Do this in remembrance of me."

19

Quandary

The Things that Hold Us Back

View film at ▶ journeyswiththemessiah.org

Have you ever felt bewildered by a decision you needed to make in a difficult situation? When I was a senior in college, what appeared to be a once-in-a-lifetime opportunity came my way. I was offered a job as a sales executive with one of the most prestigious brands in men's fashion. If I accepted the offer, it would jump-start my career in the fashion industry. However, it would also mean leaving college just short of graduation. I was in a real quandary!

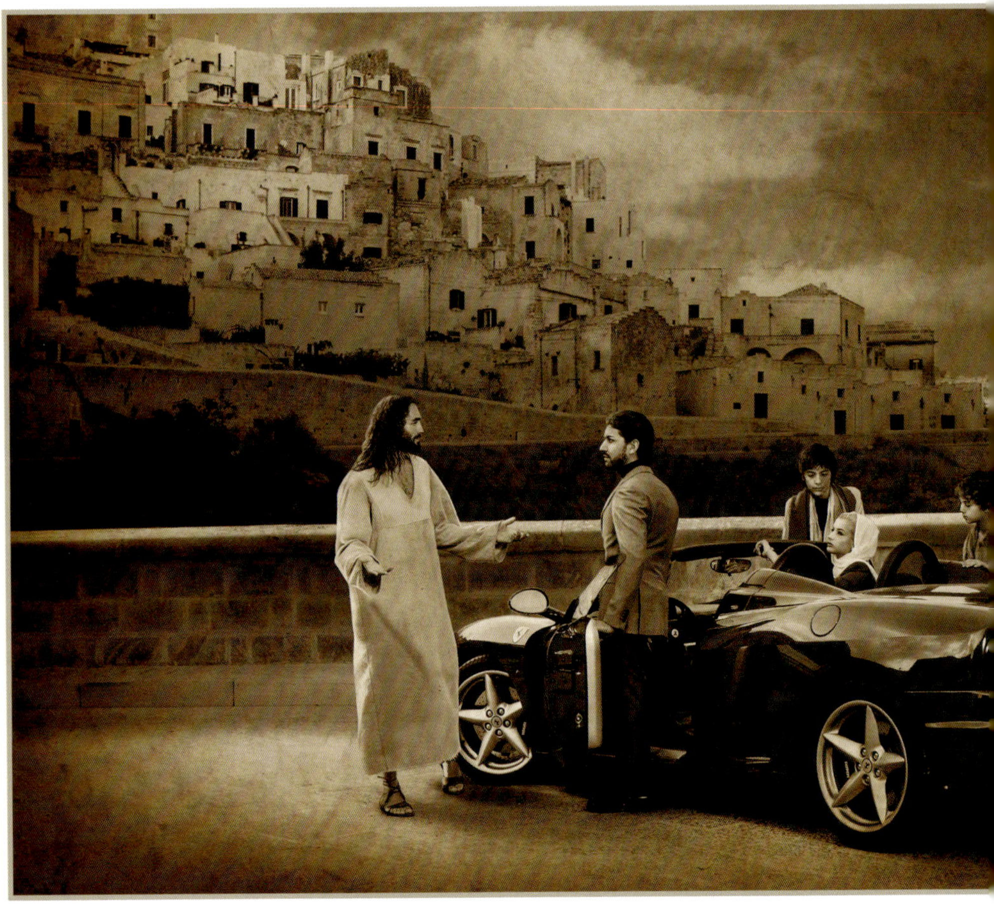

The story of the Rich Young Ruler is one of my favorite Gospel stories. Recorded in Matthew, Mark, and Luke, it tells the story of a wealthy young man who was drawn to Jesus' teaching about eternal life, but soon finds himself in a quandary. The wealthy young man approached Jesus and asked, "What good thing shall I do that I may have eternal life?" (Matthew 19:16). In short, he wanted to know how he could gain entry into Heaven.

By the tone of the young man's question, perhpas he thought there was something (as a wealthy man) he might do to assure reservations into the Kingdom of God. Perhaps he thought about it the same way we might think of slipping a nice tip to the maître d' to get us into a fine restaurant where we do not have reservations.

Jesus attempted to appease the young man by telling him, "If you want to enter into eternal life, keep the commandments" (Matthew 19:17). People of Jesus' time would most likely know that He was referring to *The Ten Commandments* found in the Book of Exodus. The young man responded by asking, "Which ones?" (Matthew 19:18).

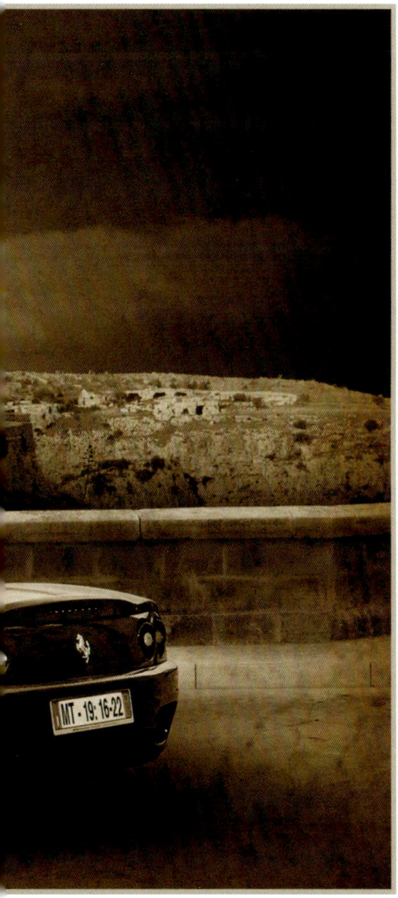

Many years went by before I considered the audacity of the young man's response, "Which ones?" Could he possibly have thought it wasn't necessary to keep all of the commandments, that some were negotiable? Maybe he felt he might be able to acquire eternal life at a bargain price. Or, perhaps he believed he really had kept all of the commandments, which is impossible for anyone to do!

So Jesus clarified his response to the young man by quoting a few of the commandments, telling him not to *murder or commit adultery, steal or bear false witness, and honor his mom and dad* (Matthew 19:18-19).

The young man seemed to be pretty sure that he was faultless when it came to keeping the commandments. He said that he had kept all of the laws since he was a boy. Yet, he must have felt some uncertainty because he asked Jesus, "What do I still lack?" (Matthew 19:20).

Suppose that Jesus had this conversation with a rich young man today in a scenario like we have depicted in our photograph. Jesus might have answered, "Okay, sell your Ferrari, your Rolex watch, and your Louis Vuitton luggage." And, as Jesus said, "If you want to be perfect, go sell all you have and give [the money] to the poor, and you will have treasure in Heaven. [Then] come follow Me" (Matthew 19:21).

Sell everything? Give the money to the poor? And then come follow You? That's a pretty tall order, Jesus!

To hear Jesus tell the wealthy young man to sell everything and give the money to the poor may cause us to think that God doesn't want us to have wealth, but that's not the case! In fact, it is just the opposite. God is the provider of everything, including money and possessions.

However, Jesus knew that our attitudes about money and possessions, and many other things, could cause us to stumble, keeping us from reaching our dreams. More importantly, it could keep us from pursuing a personal relationship with Him. For the wealthy young man, his money, which also was the source of his comforts and conveniences, became a stumbling block that kept him from pursuing his dream to follow Jesus into The Kingdom and eternal life.

God does not ask everyone to sell all of their possessions and give the money to the poor, and this scripture does not suggest that the young man could buy his way into Heaven by doing the same. Jesus knew the rich young man's wealth, and the lifestyle it purchased, had become his idols. Unless they were removed, they would keep him from following Jesus.

My success as a fashion photographer, along with the lifestyle it provided, lured me into believing I was self-sufficient like the rich young man. Why would I need Jesus? In the popular devotional, *Jesus Calling*, Sarah Young writes that "Self-sufficiency is a myth perpetuated by pride and temporary success."

The Rich Young Ruler was in a quandary and had a difficult decision to make. He could have eternal life, but he would have to let go of his false sense of self-sufficiency, which was holding him back from following Jesus. Unfortunately, money and possessions won out in the end, and as the scriptures tell us, "[The Rich Young Ruler] went away sad" (Matthew 19:22).

After this incident, Jesus told His disciples that "it was difficult for a rich man to enter the Kingdom of Heaven, "more difficult than for a camel to go through the eye of a needle" (Matthew 19:23-24). Jesus was talking about any type of wealth that becomes the focus of our lives instead of Him.

The disciples asked Him, "If a rich man cannot be saved, then who can?" Jesus replied, "With men this is impossible, but with God all things are possible" (Matthew 19:25-26).

Keeping the commandments (as the young ruler said he had) is a good practice for all of us. The commandments act as a mirror, reflecting back how we are living according to God's plan. But keeping the laws and commandments is not our ticket to Eternity, Jesus is!

We all have many quandaries of various types, yet everyone is faced with the same spiritual quandary of choosing to follow Jesus or following the world. Many people may be living with false security like the Rich Young Ruler. He thought he kept God's commands and He probably attended church and even tossed a few bucks or more into the offering plate. Perhaps he was a nice guy that everyone loved. Yet, we all should ask Jesus the same question the wealthy young man asked, "Is there still something I lack?"

We can keep some of the commandments some of the time and even be looked upon by ourselves and others as having lived a good life. Yet, only through salvation by the sacrificial death of Jesus is it possible to receive eternal life and enter His Kingdom. If we have accepted Jesus as our Savior and we allow Him to be the Lord of our lives, there is nothing we lack. The quandary is resolved as God showers us with His gift of grace. And, unlike the *Rich Young Ruler*, we're not going away sad. We're going away to live in Eternity with Him!

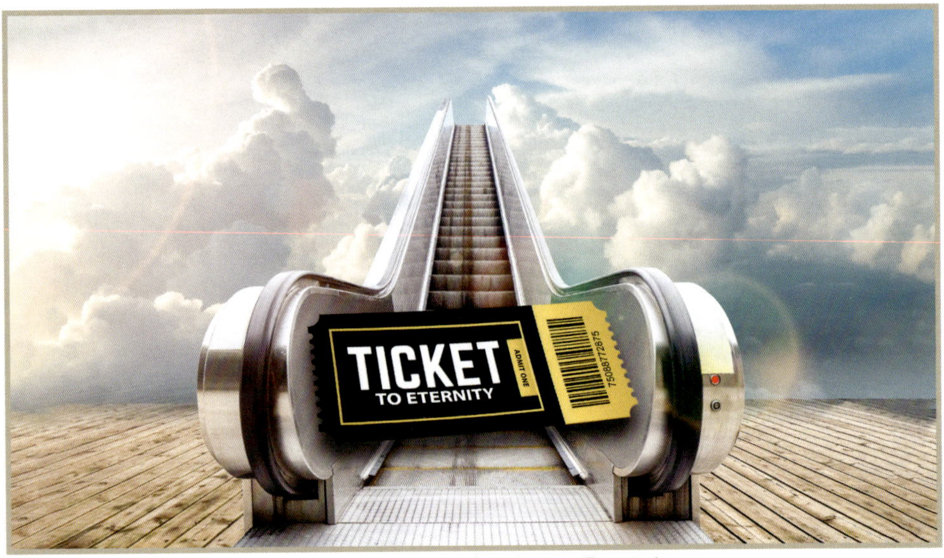

Jesus. There is no other ticket to Eternity!

Thoughts to Ponder

View film at ▶ journeyswiththemessiah.org

- When Jesus told the Rich Young Ruler to "keep the commandments," the young man responded that he had kept all of the laws since he was a boy. Review the Ten Commandments found in Exodus 20:3-17 to see which ones you have been able to keep faithfully?

- God's Commandments — His directions for our lives — show us how to live righteously with Him and others. To some people, His commands appear to be a list of "dos and don'ts." To followers of Christ, His Commandments are gifts that add to our lives, while taking nothing from them. Review them again for the gifts they are.

- When Jesus told the young ruler to follow The Commandments, the young man responded, "Which ones," as if some were of less consequence. Do we do that? Review them again and consider whether you take some more seriously than others...like keeping the sabbath holy? In following Jesus, we cannot follow our own inclinations and the world's way at the same time!

- The Rich Young Ruler seemed to be pretty sure that he was faultless when it came to keeping the commandments. Yet he must have felt uncertain because he asked Jesus, "What do I still lack?" (Matthew 19:20). Go for a walk with Jesus this week and ask Him the same question, "What do I still lack?"

- Although he told the Rich Young Ruler to sell everything and give the money to the poor, Jesus doesn't ask this of everyone. Wealth was what was keeping the young man from moving forward. What would Jesus say are the stumbling blocks that are keeping you from moving forward with your dream? What would He say is keeping you from Him?

- Jesus said that it was more difficult for a rich person to enter the kingdom of heaven than for a camel to go through the eye of a needle. What do you think Jesus meant by that?

20

Ragamuffins

Accepting a Gift with Humility

View film at ▶ journeyswiththemessiah.org

Why did God create mankind? When I ask that question, the typical reply is, "We were made for His pleasure and His glory." The source of this response is found in a phrase from Isaiah 43:7, "For I have made them for My glory."

Okay, God has made us for His glory, but why? Why would God, the creator of the universe, need us to glorify Him? For that matter, why would He need anything? He is God! So what could this mean, "Made for His pleasure and His glory?"

While planning the production for these photographs, I read Brennan Manning's book, *Ragamuffin Gospel*. Manning used the term "ragamuffins" to describe people as "children who sometimes feel bedraggled in their religious walk." Yet he also speaks about the hope we find when he writes, "When we come to God as ragamuffins and when we sit at His feet, He smiles upon us, the chosen objects of His furious love."

I was immediately drawn to Manning's idea of being "A chosen object of God's furious love" and knew we needed to create a photograph to depict God's love for us as His children.

Jesus also used children in His teaching. Matthew 18 records a time when the disciples came to Jesus and asked, "Who is the greatest in the Kingdom of Heaven?" Jesus called a little child to Him and placed the child among them and He said, "Truly I tell you, unless you change and become like little children, you will never enter the Kingdom of Heaven" (Matthew 18:1-3).

When I first read this, I assumed that the phrase "become like little children" was Jesus saying that children are innocent. After considering my time as a child and watching the children of others, I decided that innocence was probably not what He meant!

In the first century, the family did not revolve around children as it does today with gifts for every occasion, birthday parties and trips to Disney World. Children were humble and had fewer expectations than children do today. Jesus was saying that

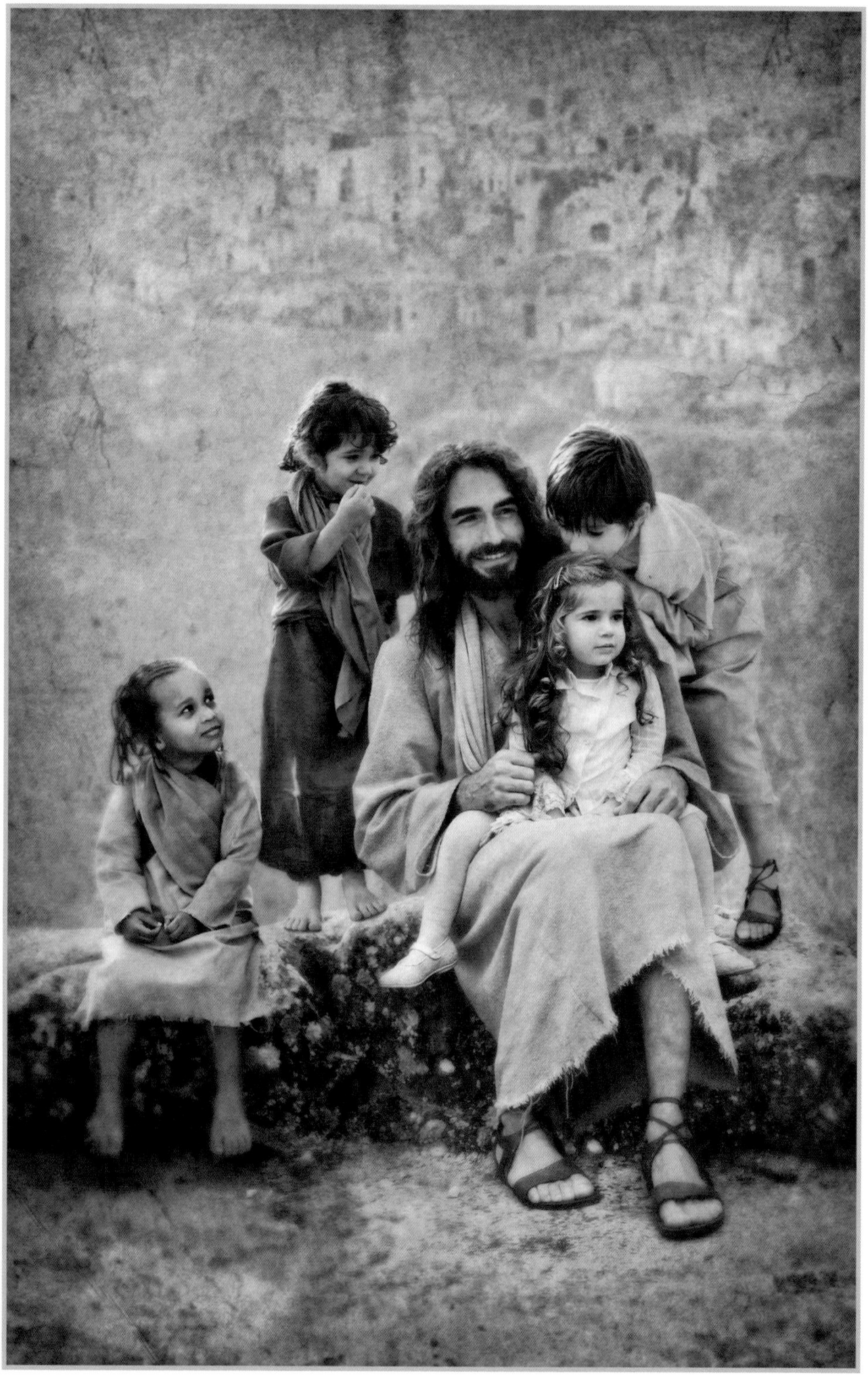

the Kingdom of Heaven will be a gift to people who, like children, are humble in knowing they are not worthy of such a blessing. He said, "Therefore, whoever takes the lowly position of this child is the greatest in the Kingdom of Heaven" (Matthew 18:4). He also referred to such people as "the poor in spirit," saying that Heaven will be theirs (Matthew 5:3). Humility is probably God's greatest gift to us ragamuffins. Yet, lack of it leads to pride, and pride makes us fall.

In an attempt to understand why God created us — since we all seem to fall by turning away from God — I turned back to the beginning of the Bible in the Garden of Eden and the creation of man. After all, if God had not created mankind, we would not need redemption from sin. With no need for salvation there would be no reason for Jesus to have died for us. For that matter, there would be no reason for Jesus at all!

Isaiah said that God "created us for His glory" and Brennan Manning says, "We are the objects of God's furious love." Yet Jesus says, "Unless we change and become like little children, we will never enter the Kingdom of Heaven." There has to be an explanation" in here somewhere!

You may have children or may be expecting one soon. Or, you may be looking forward to having a family someday. If I didn't already know the answer, I would ask, "Why would you want to bring children into this world? Don't you know the dangers that are lurking out there? Don't you know that they will face injury, sickness, even death, plus financial problems, heartbreak and more? Don't you realize that, no matter how much you do for them, care for them and love them with all your heart, they may never love you back?"

When we lose someone — a spouse through death or divorce, the death of a child or the loss of a boyfriend or girlfriend or even the loss of our pets — the pain we feel is not as much from missing the love they gave to us. The pain we feel is from no longer having them on which to pour out our love. So, whether we realize it or not, most of us have children so that we may pour our love out on them.

The Bible tells us that we are made in God's image (Genesis 1:27) and, as stated above, we have children to pour our love out on them. Therefore, since we are made in God's image, it stands to reason that God created mankind to pour out His love on us, the objects of His furious love.

Despite knowing the troubles we will face throughout our lives, God still desires to pour His love out on us. And, just as you will do for your child, God will pull out every stop to raise us to be the best we can be. He will provide for us and protect us. He will pick us up when we fall and hold us in His arms when our hearts are broken, and He will scold us when we are disobedient. As it is with your children, God will love us unconditionally even though there is no guarantee we will love Him back. Now, who wouldn't love a Father like that?

The Book of First John says, "We love because God first loved us" (1 John 4:19). So God's desire is that we take the love He first poured into us and pour it into our children and others. When we do, He basks in the glory of His creation. Isaiah was right all along, "God made us for His glory" (Isaiah 43:7). God's pleasure is in loving us and He is glorified when we love Him back through loving others.

Jesus confirmed this when responding to the question, "What is the greatest commandment?" He answered, "Love the Lord your God with all your heart and with all your soul and with all your mind." Then He said, "The Second Commandment is like the First, 'Love your neighbor as yourself'" (Mark 12:30-31). Loving God and loving others are one and the same. When we follow God's commandments to love Him and love our neighbor, we bring glory to Him.

It is essential to understand that God did not create us because He was lonely. Yet, we have to believe He wants us or He would not go to so much trouble to redeem us! That is why we break His heart when we turn from Him in disobedience or just spend no time with Him at all.

"I have loved you with an everlasting love," says the Lord (Jeremiah 31:3). An everlasting love means that we have been a part of His story from the beginning of time, and we will be part of His story until the end of time, of which there is no end. God relentlessly pursues us to bring us home one day to Eternity with Him. As Phillip Yancey wrote, "To the place we've always longed for but have never known."

In the end, it all comes down to a choice, your choice, for love cannot exist unless we are free to choose it. God chooses to love us with an everlasting love. What will we choose?

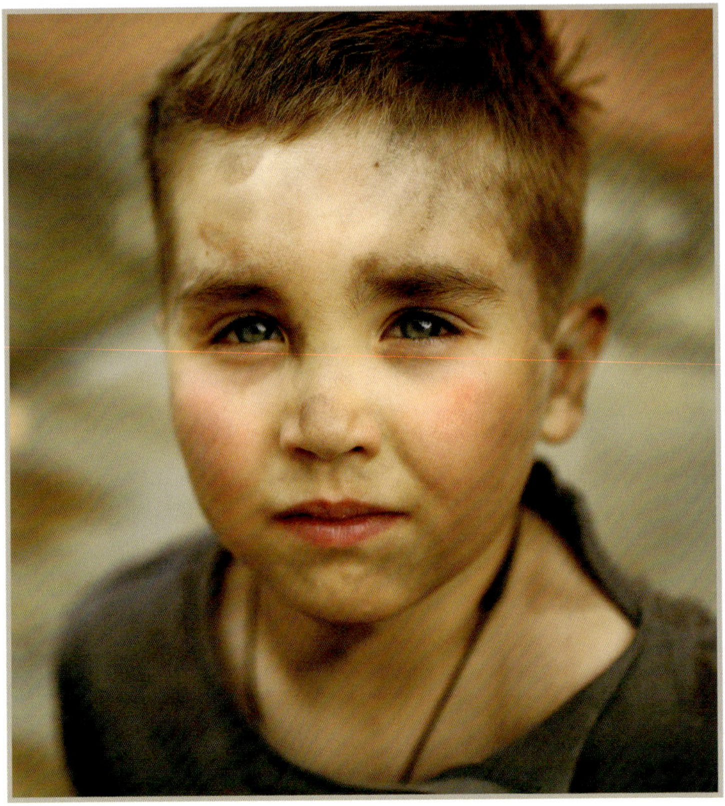

"When we sit at His feet as little children, He smiles upon us, the chosen objects of His furious love."

Thoughts to Ponder

View film at ▶ journeyswiththemessiah.org

- Isaiah 43:7 says, "I [God] have made them [mankind] for My glory." Why would God need to create us to glorify Him? He is God! He doesn't need anything!
- God says, "I have loved you with an everlasting love." I believe God created humanity to pour His love out on us, even though there was no guarantee we would love Him in return. The Book of Genesis states that we're made in the image of God. Would it not be logical that, in His image, we do the same; we have children to pour out our love on them, even though they may never love us back.
- Jesus said the greatest commandment was, "Love the Lord your God with all your heart and soul and mind." Then He said that the second greatest commandment was like the first, "Love your neighbor as yourself." If the second commandment is like the first, then loving God is the same as loving your neighbor and loving your neighbor is the same as loving God. 1 John says, "We love because God first loved us." Therefore, we can say that ***God's pleasure is in loving us and He is glorified when we love Him by loving others.***
- If God had not created you, He would have no reason to redeem you from sin and, thus, no reason for Jesus to die for you. Therefore, God had a reason for creating you despite knowing the troublesome and dangerous world you would face! Consider what His purpose was in creating you?
- Jesus said, "Unless you change and become like little children, you will never enter the Kingdom of Heaven" (Matthew 18:1-3). He meant that the Kingdom of Heaven would be a gift to people who, like children, are humble in knowing they are not worthy of such a blessing. As I review the days of my life, I am most confident that I am not worthy of such a gift!

21

Reconciled

A World in Need of a Savior

View film at ▶ journeyswiththemessiah.org

Before I became a follower of Jesus, my world revolved around me and especially my career as a fashion photographer. On the bright side, I was climbing to the top of success. On the other side, I was alone and my life lacked meaning! I met several Christians along the way who suggested, "You need Jesus in your life."

My response, "You bet! Tell me why!"

"Well, because you're a sinner," they'd say.

"Oh, you don't know the half of it," I replied, "but tell me what that has to do with needing Jesus in my life."

"Well, because He died for your sins," they responded.

"Okay," I said, "but it seems like I should be the one dying, not Him," and so the conversation went. It just seemed that no one could provide a practical explanation as to "why I needed Jesus in my life."

Throughout my youth, church was a part of our lives and I was familiar with many of the stories in the Bible and about Jesus. Unfortunately, I missed out on the significant details until much later. When the time finally came that I began searching for meaning in my life, I honestly wanted to understand who Jesus was and why people said I needed Him. As far as I knew, most of the story of Jesus was just a cleverly devised fable. If there was a legitimate explanation, it had to be more convincing than what I knew so far. I recalled Jesus saying something about, "The truth will set you free" (John 8:32), and I wanted to find the truth if it existed.

Although the New Testament books of Matthew, Mark, Luke & John contained a lot of useful information, I felt that Christianity centered around Jesus as "the fix" for something that was broken. I wanted to understand what was broken that needed to be fixed and why.

My curiosity continued to grow when friends introduced me to some great books

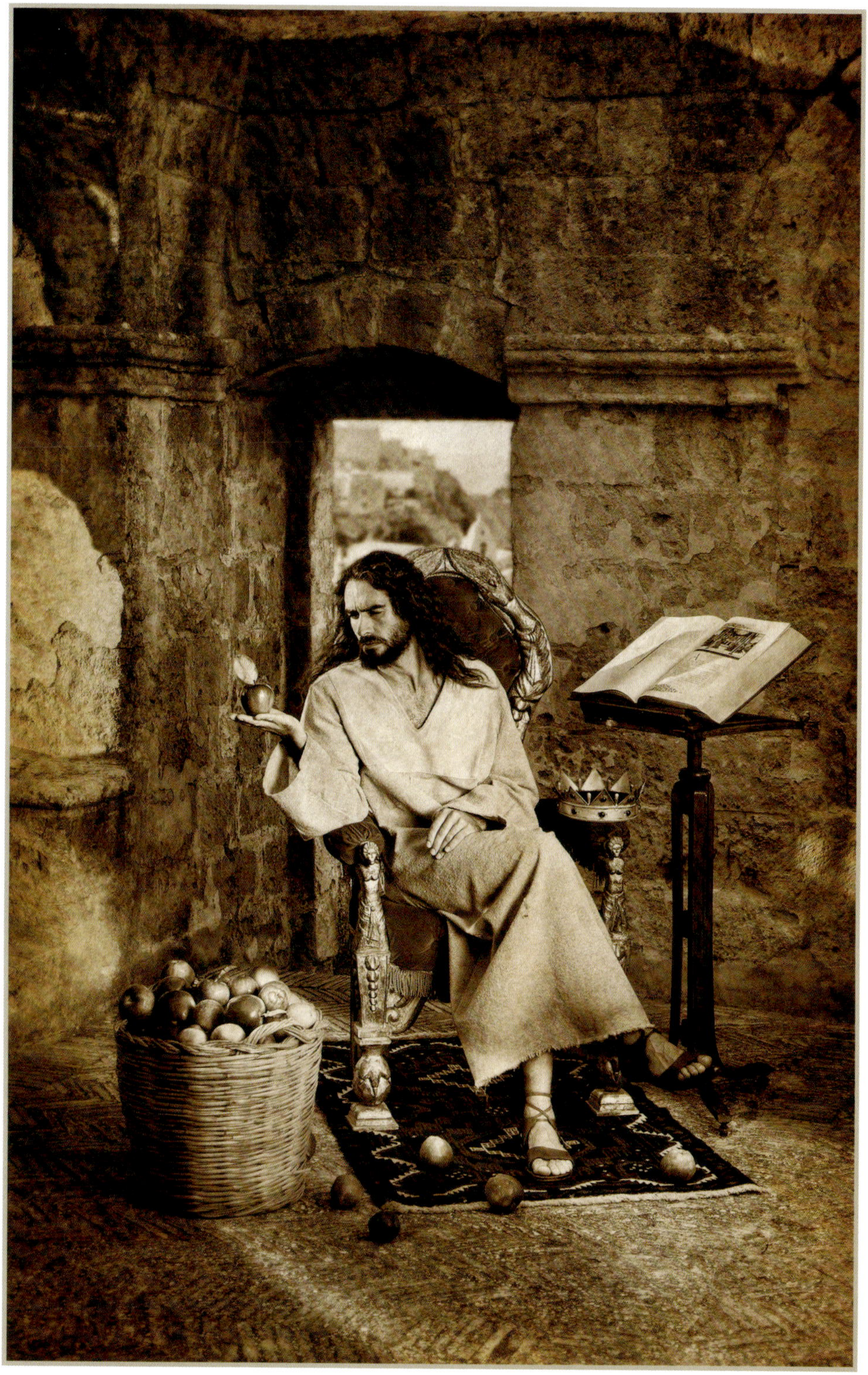

by some incredible writers who seemed to have looked for the same answers. These were classic writers like C. S. Lewis and Oswald Chambers and more contemporary writers like Josh McDowell and Lee Strobel.

I was especially attracted to something C. S. Lewis wrote:

> *A man who was merely a man and said the sort of things Jesus said would not be a great moral teacher. He would either be a lunatic — on a level with the man who says he is a poached egg — or else he would be the Devil of Hell. You must make your choice. Either this man was, and is, the Son of God or else a madman or something worse. You can shut Him up for a fool, you can spit at Him and kill Him as a demon, or you can fall at His feet and call Him Lord and God. But let us not come with any patronizing nonsense about His being a great human teacher. He has not left that open to us. He did not intend to.*
> — C.S. Lewis, Mere Christianity.

C.S. Lewis' explanation resonated with me! This was a brilliant scholar saying that Jesus was either who He said He was or He was not, and it appeared there was real evidence on which I could base my decision.

I will not pretend that I found answers quickly or that I know most of them…not even close...I'm still looking while the journey is unfolding! However, what I have discovered thus far has been fascinating and I'm confident that I have a grasp of the most significant truths of Jesus Christ. If you already know Him, perhaps this book will inspire you to know Him more. If not, maybe you will consider taking a closer look at Him.

To understand why I needed Jesus in my life, I started by building a foundation of some fundamental truths. The first truth I discovered was "God is holy." Holy is defined as perfect and flawless. The nature of God's holiness is that He creates perfection in everything and, in Eternity, He cannot be in the presence of anything or anyone less than perfect.

While I was traveling as a photographer, taking photographs of beautiful models and witnessing breath-taking places and scenery, I realized that everything I photographed had already been created by a Master Artist. I was just capturing His work! When I added these experiences to all of the National Geographic and science specials I had watched, it was easy for me to believe in God as the grand designer of the universe — one with infinite intelligence and imagination.

So, as I approached the *Story of Creation* in the Book of Genesis, I was confident that God existed. Genesis means origin and the book's first four words are, "In the beginning, God!" Genesis is God's story describing His creation of a perfect universe along with perfect directions by which everything He made would function perfectly. We refer to God's directions as "laws and commands."

God created natural and physical laws that included chemistry, physics and the natural elements where, for example, sodium and chloride combine to create life-sustaining salt. God also created laws of mathematics whereby "2 + 2" will always equal "4" and never any other total. Without this law, mankind could not have advanced past the stone age since so many advances depend on mathematics.

Everything God creates works perfectly. Yet when these laws are disobeyed, they can cause unfavorable and even deadly consequences. For example, a person can experience the consequence of violating the *law of gravity* by parachuting from an airplane.

While God was creating the world, He also created the first man and woman, Adam and Eve. At first, their creation story sounded fictional to me, but as Adam and Eve's history unfolded in the Bible, I discovered they had a family, a farm, and two sons — one who murdered the other (Genesis 2-4). These details made their story sound real and anything but fictional!

With the introduction of the human race, God created additional directions we call "moral laws." Moral laws show us how to live in right relationship with God and with our fellow man. These laws, known as *The Ten Commandments*, form the foundation of God's moral directions. They point us in the right directions and warn us which way not to go (Exodus 20, 24:12).

We can think of God's laws and commandments as we do the instructions that come with a new product. Instructions allow us to experience the purpose for which the product was made while warning us of the hazards of misuse. In the same way, God's laws and commandments are His "instructions." He provides them so that we may enjoy life to its fullest while being warned of potential dangers along our way. God's laws were created to add to our lives, not to take anything away from them.

As an example, one of God's commandments is, "Do not commit adultery" (Exodus 20:14). This command does not say, "Do not have sex!" In fact, it is just the opposite! God designed sex so that it would be enjoyed to its fullest with only one spouse through the commitment of marriage. Included in this command is a warning that sex outside of marriage can be highly destructive and result in emotional pain for us and others. Again, God's commands are only for our benefit!

The following statement is one of the defining truths about God's laws that helped me understand, "Why I needed Jesus in my life."

There cannot be a law
unless there is a price to be paid for breaking that law.

In other words, if there is a law, but there is no fine for breaking that law, then there really is no law! At most, there is only a suggestion. As an example, a stoplight represents a law. If you do not stop when it is red, you may be arrested and have to pay a fine. Or, you may crash into another car and suffer injuries and be fined or imprisoned for causing injuries to others. On the other hand, you could pass through the intersection without crashing or without a policeman stopping you for breaking the law.

So breaking God's physical or natural laws may or may not always result in a fine to be paid. However, the fine for violating any of God's moral laws is the death penalty. I will explain this later.

Adam and Eve were similar to animals in rudimentary ways. Still, they were created differently in that they were given a soul and a mind and the ability to think, understand, and form judgments and make decisions. God placed them in a perfect garden in Eden where they would live forever with everything they would ever need. God loved Adam and Eve but also gave them the freedom to choose whether they would love Him or not. The nature of love is that it requires choice. It cannot be forced.

In the Garden of Eden where Adam and Eve lived with God, two specific trees are noted: The *Tree of Life* and the *Tree of the Knowledge of Good and Evil.* God told Adam he could eat from the first tree (and from the abundance of other trees), but he would die if he ate from the second tree (Genesis 2:15).

There was a serpent in the Garden. In Revelations, Satan is called "the ancient serpent," which refers to the snake in the Garden in Genesis (Revelation 12:9, 20:2). The serpent (Satan) seduced Eve into believing that she and Adam could eat from the *Tree of the Knowledge of Good and Evil* and not die; that the forbidden fruit would make them "like gods, knowing good and evil" (Genesis 3:1-5).

Disobedience is defined as a failure or refusal to obey rules or someone in authority. In the Bible, disobedience to God's laws or commands and authority is called "sin." Adam and Eve were faced with a choice. They could believe and trust that God's directions were good and true and for their benefit, or they could choose to disobey Him and eat from the tree. They chose poorly! (Genesis 3:6).

As stated, disobedience to God's law is called sin. Like the fruit of the forbidden tree, sin looks good and initially tastes sweet until it creates flaws or imperfections in our character.

As established earlier, God is perfect and by His Holy nature, He cannot allow anyone who is not perfect to be in His presence. By their disobedience to God's command, Adam and Eve were flawed by sin and had to be banished from the garden.

The Tree of Life, which is also symbolic of God as the source of eternal life, was in the center of the garden. Unless Adam & Eve could get back into the garden with God and *The Tree of Life*, they would die and mortality would become a part of the human experience. When the Apostle Paul wrote, "The wages of sin is death" (Romans 6:23), it was in reference to this dilemma. Adam and Eve did not die directly from eating the forbidden fruit. They eventually died from their choice to disobey God — a sin that left them flawed and imperfect and separated from *The Tree of Life* and God, the only one who can provide eternal life.

:::::

Note: *When Adam & Eve disobeyed God by eating the forbidden fruit, their eyes were opened to the knowledge of evil and the darkness of sin and they hid in shame when they realized they were naked. Shame is the feeling we have when we know we have been disobedient to what is morally right. Genesis 3:21 says, "The Lord God made garments of skin for Adam and his wife and clothed them."* **To get the skins to cover their shame, God had to kill or sacrifice an innocent animal!**

:::::

Again, there cannot be a law unless there is a price to be paid for breaking that law. Adam and Eve have broken God's law — they have sinned through their disobedience to Him. So here is the question that leads to *"Why I need Jesus in my life."* **What happens if we break the law and cannot pay the fine?**

If we are caught disobeying the law by speeding, there is a price we will be required to pay to settle the fine. However, we can pay the fine only in the currency that is accepted by the court. If the court accepts only cash, we cannot pay with a credit card or check. Thus, **disobeying God's law comes with a price we cannot pay** because, metaphorically speaking, we have no valid currency for God's Kingdom. Stated another way, an imperfect man has no way of paying the price to remove the sins that keep him separated from Holy God. Although God will forgive us, the fine must still be paid; the sin must be removed or we remain separated from God and eternal life!

Fortunately, our dilemma can be reconciled, but not through anything we can do on our own. God knows we are helpless to save ourselves. Yet He loves us so much that, rather than see us die an eternal death, He offers the only perfect payment worthy of paying for our sins: **Himself!** That's right! God came to earth in human form as Jesus, to pay our fine — to pay for removing our sins — by giving His perfect life in exchange for ours. He was the only one who could because He is the only who is perfect. Jesus said, "Anyone who has seen Me has seen the Father." John 14:9)

Imagine it this way: You are sitting in jail and have been sentenced to death. There is nothing you can do to avoid it. Then one day the jail keeper comes to you and announces that you are free to go because another man has offered to be put to death in place of you. You ask the jailer, "What is this man guilty of?"

He replies, "Absolutely nothing! He is innocent!"

"So, why would he do this?" you ask.

The jailer replies, "I don't know. He just said that he loves you too much to let you die!"

Jesus said that there was no greater love than to lay down one's life for their friends. (John 15:13). He said it and then He did it! Jesus allowed Himself to be sacrificed like the innocent animal whose blood God shed to make skins to cover the shame of disobedience of Adam and Eve.

Yet, we have hope because there is a happy ending. God raised Jesus from death three days later just as Jesus predicted (John 2:19). He did this as proof that there will be eternal life after earthly death and to show us that Jesus was and is who He said He was.

We cannot make atonement for ourselves. Reconciliation with God has to be made for us. That is what Jesus did on the cross by being sacrificed to pay the price we could not pay for our sins of disobedience to God's authority and commands. If, by chance, you have not yet acknowledged this undeserved gift of God's amazing grace by accepting Jesus as Savior and Lord of your life, the opportunity is before you now.

When you confess that Jesus is Lord and believe in your heart that God raised Him from death, your sins and imperfections will be erased, and you will be reconciled

— restored from sin to perfect harmony to be with God. You will be made Holy and perfect as "the blood of Jesus washes all your sins away" (1 John 1:7). The gates to the *Garden of Heaven* will be opened, allowing you to step into God's presence when your time comes to an end on earth. A penalty you were incapable of paying is paid once and for all so that you will never perish, but spend life in eternity with Him. And, like me, you won't need to ask anymore, "Why do I need Jesus in my life?"

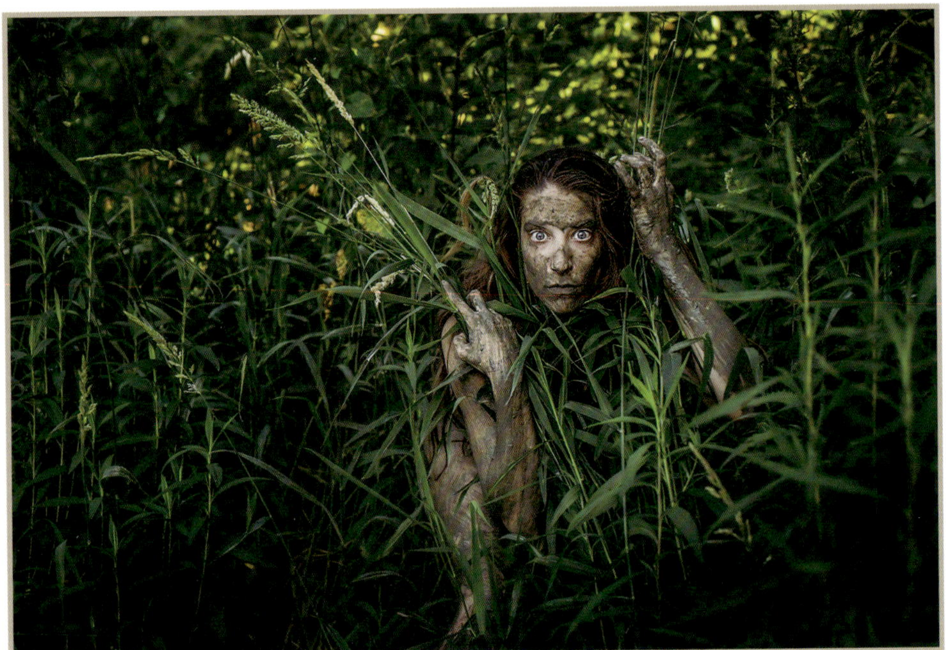

Shame is the feeling we have when we know we have been disobedient to what is morally right.

Thoughts to Ponder

View film at ▶ journeyswiththemessiah.org

An answer to "Why do I need Jesus in my life."

- God is Holy, which means perfect. Think of God's Holy domain as an airtight bubble. If anything penetrates it, His domain will be contaminated and no longer perfect.
- God can create only perfect things. He is the creator of life and the only one who can give eternal life which exists only in Eternity (Heaven or Paradise) with Him.
- God's plan = His directions = His laws and commands. They guide us how to live with Him and our fellowman and warn us how not to live. All of His laws are for our benefit and enjoyment.
- A law cannot exist unless there is a price that must be paid for breaking it.
- Breaking God's physical laws come with a price called consequences. Breaking God's moral laws come with the price called death, because it leads to eternal separation from Him.
- To live in Eternity with God, one must be Holy — free of sins (imperfections). This creates a dilemma since everyone has sinned and no one can cleanse themself of their sins.
- Solution to the dilemma: God came to earth in the form of a man — Jesus the Son of God — to give His sinless life as payment for our sins (of breaking His laws) which has left us flawed and imperfect. Atonement cleanses us of our sins, making us Holy (perfect) and reconciling us back to God.
- God raised Jesus from death for all to see that Jesus is who He said He was and to show that there is eternal life after death — either with God in Paradise or separated from Him in Hell.
- We receive eternal life with God by believing and confessing Jesus as both Savior and Lord of our lives; believing that God raised Him from death. Salvation through God's grace is truly "the deal of a lifetime."

22

Rest for the Weary

Time Out from the Burdens of Life

View film at ▶ journeyswiththemessiah.org

As Jesus' ministry grew, large crowds began to follow Him although few understood the life to which He was calling them. On one occasion, He warned them, saying they should consider the cost of following Him. "For which of you, desiring to build a tower, does not first sit down and count the cost." (Luke 14:28)

When I sensed God leading me to create Journeys' images, I made a business plan with a production budget and schedule. I thought I had counted all of the costs. Yet over the next years, I discovered my estimates were inaccurate. The actual costs grew to be staggering, while the physical price to me was exhausting.

At the outset, I was excited by the opportunity to create and produce a new project, especially one of its size and significance. Although my career as a fashion photographer was exciting and even glamorous at times, it was also hard work. Many locations were like being on vacation, while others were in the heat of the desert or the freezing cold. Some photoshoots lasted for days, while others went on for weeks. There were times when our plans came together seamlessly, while others were challenged by unexpected problems.

I recall a photoshoot in Jamaica when it rained like a monsoon for days while the expenses piled up as we waited. On another job in a foreign country, our equipment and the client's clothing samples were confiscated and held for ransom by dishonest customs agents.

I remember occasions when the pace of work, combined with life's trials, became physically and mentally overwhelming. I became weary and needed rest. So as I began this project, Jesus' message of "Come to me, all you who are weary and burdened, and I will give you rest" (Matthew 11:28) was on my mind. It became the inspiration for the photograph *Rest for the Weary.*

With the excitement of planning the images and production of Journeys, I sprung out of bed each morning energized to start the day in my new role. I no longer needed rest nor was I weary, although it would not be long before I was!

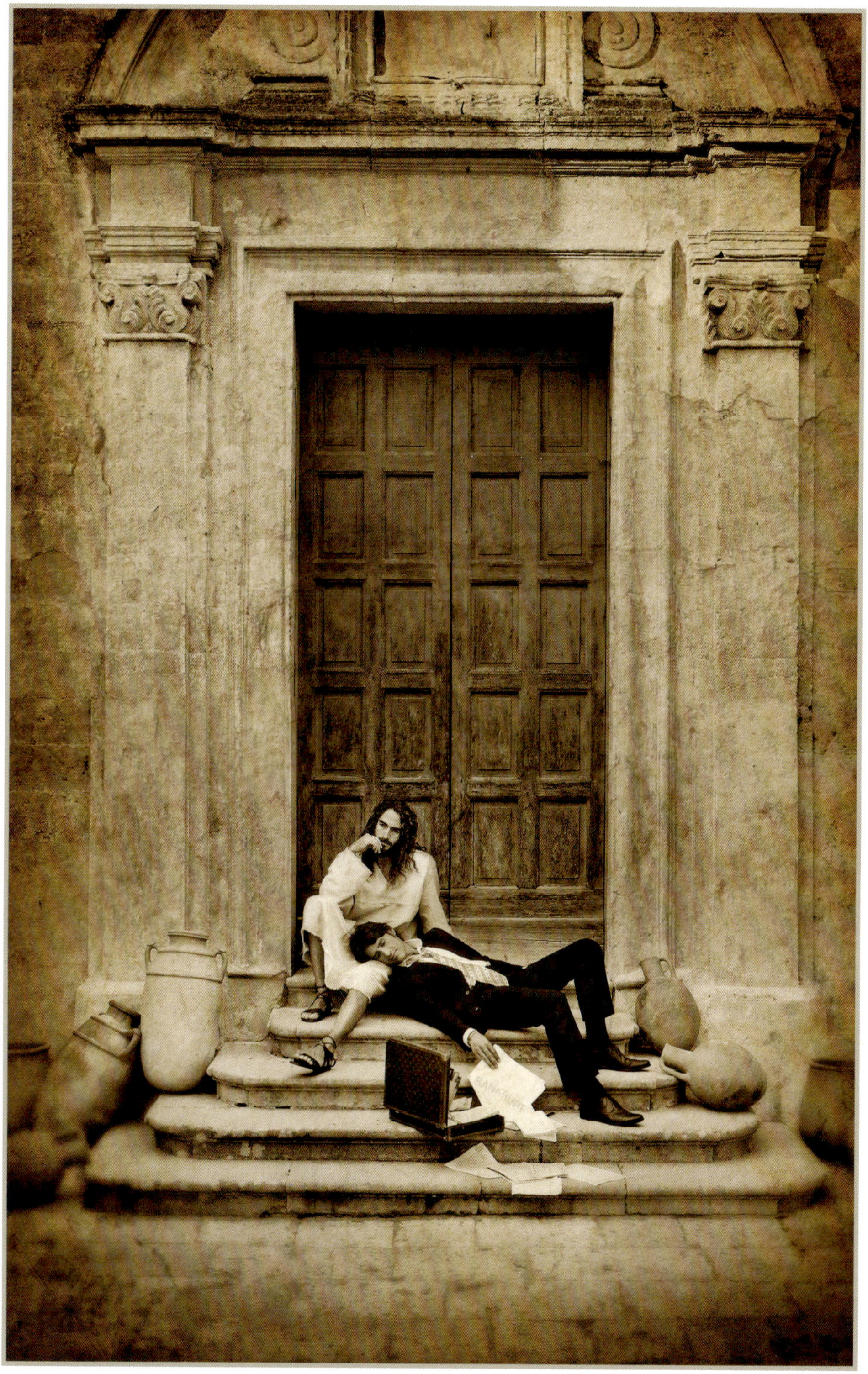

Most of 2008 was spent creating the concepts for the photographs and planning the production. In my fashion advertising company, the details of a project — locations, models, props, travel, lodging, catering, etcetera — were delegated to my staff. Now, without a budget for extra personnel, all of those details were falling on me. Producing the project in Italy, where initially I had no contacts and didn't speak the language, made it even more difficult.

Jesus said, "Count the cost!" In the beginning, I thought I had, yet my imagination for these images had grown considerably, tripling the budget! I had always kept my fashion client's expenditures in line, but this was my project and at my expense. Plus, I believed I was on a valuable mission and at the time, my wife and I could afford it. Then, the financial tsunami hit!

In the fall of 2008 as we arrived in Italy to begin production, the stock markets began to decline. As each day of production went by, market values around the world fell even further. This caused the U.S. dollar to drop in value against the European currency which caused a considerable increase in our production costs. The rising costs, on top of running the multiple aspects of the project, created so much anxiety that I just wanted to crawl up into Jesus' lap and have Him tell me, "It's all going to be okay!"

By the time we arrived home a month later, forty percent of our savings had evaporated and we owed our Italian production company the equivalent of a small fortune. It was evident that I had not accurately "counted the costs!"

Then, when we thought it could not get worse, the next wave of the financial tsunami hit as the housing markets collapsed. This was a huge blow to us because my wife and I counted on the value of our real estate to cover the massive losses we were taking in the stock market. Meanwhile, the costs of the project continued to climb. Unlike the man in our photograph, I was not yet financially bankrupt, but like him, I was quickly becoming physically and emotionally bankrupt from the stress of it all.

Many years went by before I truly understood the relevance of this financial calamity and what it would ultimately reveal to me about Jesus. In retrospect, it appears that God had combined my love of photography with the excitement of creating a collection of artwork in Italy to intentionally lure me into Him. Now I realize that God, the Master Artist, didn't need my photographs! He wanted to draw me closer to Him.

As I left for Italy to begin producing these images, I thought I knew Jesus. Yet, it has only been through these trials that I have really come to know Him. I've learned that life as a follower of Jesus does not mean life gets easier. It means God will challenge you to grow in your faith while He makes you stronger. That's why He told the crowds that, before following Him, they needed to count the cost" ((Luke 14:28). Then He said, "When you grow tired and weary and burdened by life, come to Me and I will give you rest" (Matthew 11:28).

As it turned out, I am the man in this picture and you may be too! Life can make us weary and the trials of life can add many burdens. Yet maybe we assign too much importance to many aspects of our lives that, in the end, will be of little consequence. Let's make sure that we do not end up bankrupt in the ways that really matter!

Jesus said, "Count the cost," but He also said count the rewards! I have experienced some of the costs and I know that there will be more to come. Yet I would do it all over again to discover that a relationship with Him is the reward! When I grow weary and seek Him for rest, He reminds me that I can tap into His energy to carry me through. I work for His Kingdom now.

Investing in business ventures comes with risks while investing in a relationship with Jesus comes with guarantees. If you want to draw closer to Him, tell Him you are available and ask Him to show you the way.

"Come to Me, and I will give you rest." It's a great offer! Let's take Him up on it!

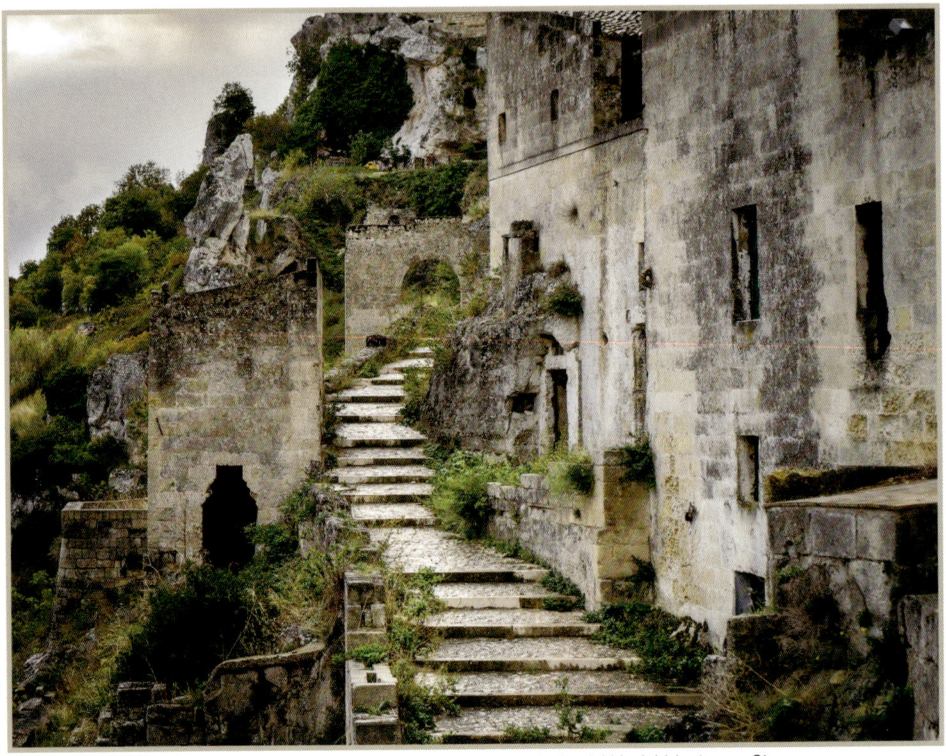

"The stones of Matera." Sassi di Matera, Italy. A World Heritage Site.

Thoughts to Ponder

View film at ▶ journeyswiththemessiah.org

- Large crowds began to follow Jesus as His ministry grew, yet few people understood the life to which He was calling them. He even told them they should "count the cost" before following Him. If you have followed Jesus, reflect on your life since accepting Him as your Lord and Savior. Do you feel it has come at a cost or not!
- Think of a time you invested in a business venture, purchased a new home or car or jumped into a relationship. Did you count the cost or did anyone advise you to "count the cost" first? Do you recall how it turned out?
- Have you been on a mission trip or volunteered for a Christian project thinking that "you were doing something good for God?" Did you discover that He was actually doing something good for you?
- Although the trials of life can naturally cause us to grow tired and weary, we can also grow anxious and depressed by assigning too much importance to things that, in the end, will be of no consequence. Take time to ponder this statement!
- When I grow tired and weary, I often picture myself as the man resting in Jesus' lap. Jesus' invitation is always open: "When you grow tired and weary and burdened by life, come to Me and I will give you rest." Try it!
- Although we should count the cost of following Jesus, we should also count the rewards! Make a list of "the costs" and "the rewards" you have experienced in following Him.

23

Safe Harbor

A Light to Guide Our Way

View film at ▶ journeyswiththemessiah.org

I recall a movie years ago in which there was a wedding scene in a garden and a bride and groom standing under a flower-covered arbor; seems it was near a cliff with the ocean in the distance…maybe California. The official performing the wedding ceremony made a comment I have remembered all these years. He said, "Marriage should be like a safe harbor." I recall thinking, "A safe harbor? That sounds so comforting. Boy, does my life need a safe harbor!"

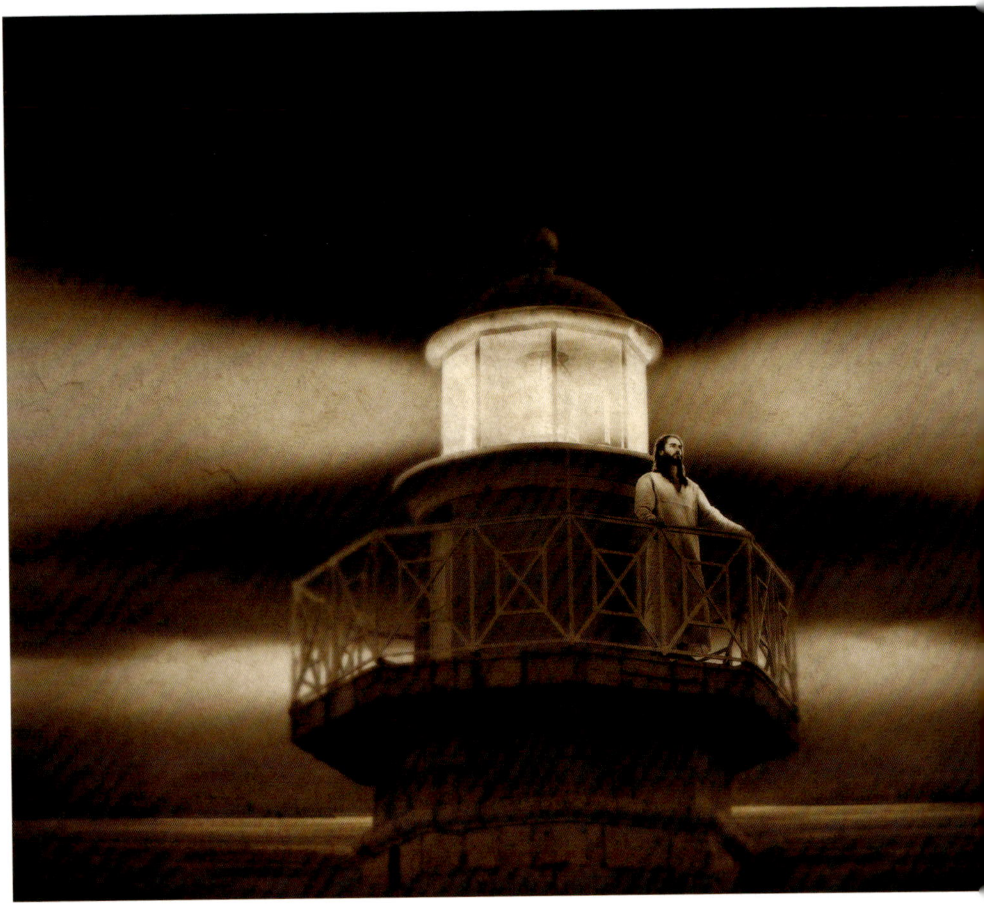

Harbors are often marked by lighthouses that project beacons of light to guide sailors in the night. The harbor can offer calm from a storm or just rest for the sea-weary. The lighthouse directs sailors to the harbor and warns them of the potential dangers of rocks, shallow waters and approaching coastlines.

While planning the images for Journeys with the Messiah, I recalled the statement made in the movie, "Marriage should be like a safe harbor." I envisioned a lighthouse guiding ships from the turbulent sea to the calm and protected waters of a safe harbor. The thought of a lighthouse also reminded me of Jesus' statement that *He was the light of the world bringing light to the darkness* (John 8:12). I thought, "Jesus is like a lighthouse!"

I immediately sent a message to our producer in Rome, asking if his team could locate a lighthouse on the Adriatic seacoast near Matera, Italy, where most of our photographs would be created. After several weeks of searching, one was eventually found in the ancient seaport of Molfetta.

Throughout the Bible, light is used metaphorically to represent righteousness and goodness. Since the opposite of light is dark, then darkness signifies evil and sin. The Gospels have a lot to say about God and Jesus and light, especially in John's Gospel.

- "God is light, and in Him is no darkness at all. If we claim to have fellowship with Him and yet walk in the darkness, we lie and do not live out the truth" (1 John 1:5-6).
- "The true light that gives light to everyone was coming into the world" (John 1:9).
- Jesus said, "I am the light of the world. Whoever follows Me will never walk in darkness, but will have the light of life" (John 8:12).
- Speaking to Pontious Pilate, Roman Governor of Judea, Jesus said, "In fact, the reason I was born and came into the world is to testify to the truth (by shining light into the darkness). Everyone on the side of truth listens to me" (John 18:37).

I have taken the liberty of combining these verses as a way of understanding the significance of light and darkness in scripture relative to Jesus: *While the Pharisees and other religious leaders stood by, Jesus told the Roman Governor of Judea, Pontious Pilate, that He was the True Light of righteousness and goodness; that He had come into the world for the purpose of shining God's light of righteousness and goodness through the darkness of evil an sin to reveal the truth of Himself—God in the flesh—for all the world to see.*

Just as the moon is revealed to us by reflecting the light of the sun, Jesus is revealed to us as He reflects the light of God. And, as the moon lights the night, God brings light to our darkness by revealing the truth of Himself through Jesus. Whether we are looking for the way home or we are caught up in the turbulent seas of life, the light of Jesus invites us into His harbor where we can find rest and safety from life's storms and trials. And, like the lighthouse, Jesus' teachings also warn us of hidden dangers as they light our way, keeping us from stumbling in the dark.

The first book of the Bible begins with, "In the beginning God said, let there be light, and there was light. God saw that the light was good, and He separated the light from the darkness" (Genesis 1:1, 3-4). Thousands of years later, God came into the world as a man, as Jesus, to light the darkness, revealing God's truth to our fallen world.

Despite how brightly Jesus' righteousness and goodness shines, many people have chosen the darkness of sin and evil. Jesus said, "People loved darkness instead of light (truth) because their deeds were evil. Everyone who does evil hates the light for fear that their deeds will be exposed" (John 3:19-20). It's no wonder that many crimes and evil deeds are done under the cover of darkness where people think they will not be exposed. If only they knew or recall that God sees all!

As the years goes by, it appears to many people that the world will be overcome with the darkness of sin and evil. Yet we are instructed not to lose hope for God's word assures us that, "In Him [Jesus] was life, and that life was the light of all mankind. The light shines in the darkness, **and the darkness has not overcome it**" (John 1:4-5). We can be confident that there is no darkness, evil or sin we will face that Jesus' light, righteousness and goodness cannot overpower with the light of God's truth.

God saw the light, that it was good;
and God divided the light from the darkness.
—Genesis 1:2-4

Jesus is the light. His light and life are reflected now through us to shine into the darkness of this world ! And, like a town built on a hill, that light cannot be hidden unless we put it under a bowl instead of placing it on a light stand for everyone to see (Matthew 5:14-15). The truth will not be overcome by the darkness, which means there will be a safe harbor for everyone as we go into the world and let our light shine before others.

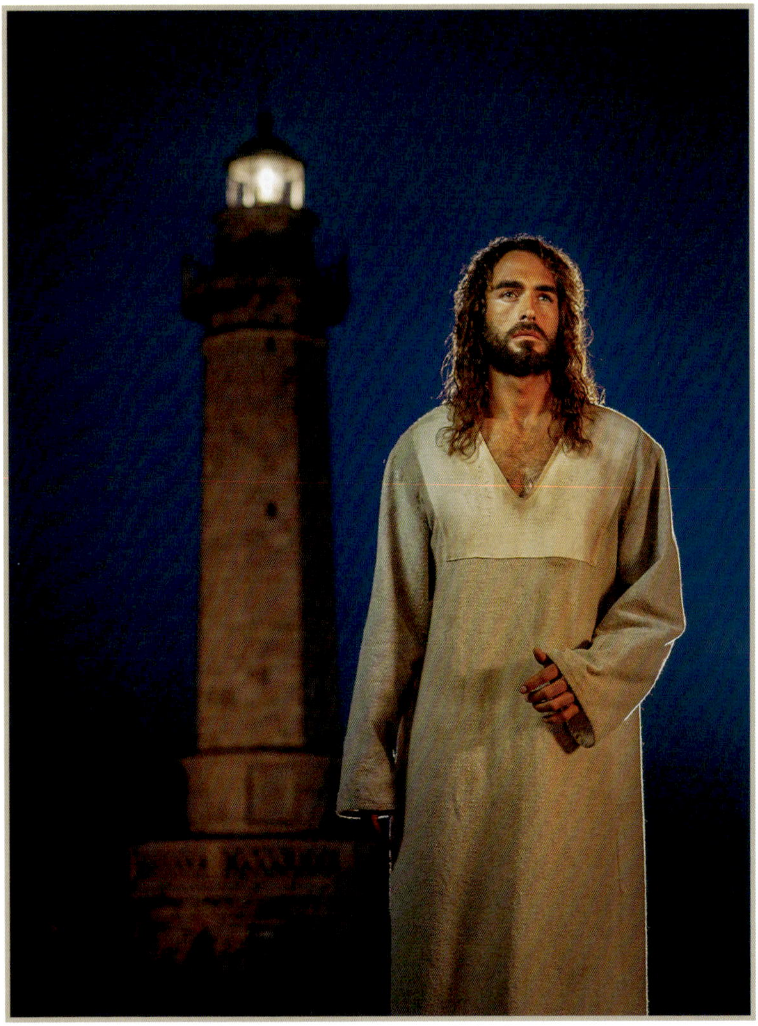

The Light guiding us to safe harbor.

Thoughts to Ponder

View film at ▶ journeyswiththemessiah.org

- The image *Safe Harbor* was inspired by a wedding scene in which the person officiating said that a marriage should be like "a safe harbor." Take inventory of your marriage, family, best friend, leaders, workplace, town, country, and environment. Which ones provide safe harbors?

- Before the modern-day technology of Global Positioning Satellites (GPS), lighthouses were long-trusted aids to navigation. Their messages were simple: ***Come this way. Stay away! Be aware of danger!*** Consider Jesus' role as the lighthouse in your life as He offers the same messages to you.

- The moon is revealed as it reflects the light of the sun, lighting the night. Jesus is revealed as He reflects the light of God. God's light shines truth into the darkness, overcoming all things that are not good. When you feel overcome by the darkness of worry or fear or anything that is not good, invite Jesus in and imagine Him as a lighthouse beacon shining light into your soul.

- John 1: 5 states, "The light shines in the darkness, and the darkness has not overcome it." I'm writing this in October 2020. The world is in a major pandemic (Covid-19) that threatens life and our way of life. There is rioting in our cities while our country faces one of the most divisive Presidential elections in our nation's history. I can find peace in knowing that there is no darkness or evil that Jesus' light cannot overcome. He is my "safe harbor!"

- Like a "safe harbor," Jesus offers us a place of safety from the storms of life. However, let's not forget that He is also a great place to spend the day even when our seas are calm!

- Jesus' light is available to shine into the world through us! We have been commanded to let our light shine before others so that they may see God's righteousness and goodness reflected in our good deeds, which glorifies our Father in heaven. (Matthew 5:16) So, let your light shine!

24

Salvation

Confession of the Heart

View film at ▶ journeyswiththemessiah.org

When I was a child, our family loved to play the board game, *Monopoly*. Like everyone, I hated it when I landed on the "Go to Jail" square and loved it when I drew the "Get Out of Jail Free" card, which I could use whenever I needed it. What if life had a "Get Out of Jail Free" card that we could use to cancel a debt, change a doctor's diagnosis or even have a do-over on something we wish we hadn't done?

"Salvation" is one of Christianity's central tenets. There have been times when I have questioned the simplicity with which the Christian invitation to salvation — "to be saved" — is offered and, perhaps, misunderstood... "Just accept Jesus as your Lord and Savior and you will have it all — redemption from sin and a seat in Heaven!"

Please don't misinterpret my purpose in making that statement. I make it to make a point, yet I don't wish to be insensitive. I actually do believe the acceptance of God's gift of salvation can be just that simple. However, I believe that there is more to being saved than just giving Jesus a thumbs up.

Webster's dictionary defines salvation as preservation or deliverance from harm, ruin, or loss. Christians believe this harm, ruin, or loss is the consequence of disobedience to God, while deliverance is brought about by faith in Jesus Christ.

As I have written in other chapters, the long term consequence of sin is eternal separation from God. Since God is the only one who can offer eternal life, it means there will be no life with Him in Eternity if we are separated from Him after our physical death on Earth.

While planning the production of our photographs and films, I researched what it means to be saved and what it takes to be saved. Using the words "preservation and deliverance" in Webster's definition, one could say that, *"Salvation is the process by which we are preserved or saved from death in this world and delivered into the arms of God in Eternity."* I like the way that sounds! Through salvation, we are preserved from death to be delivered into Eternity with God!

There are many books on this subject, and the Internet is filled with answers about

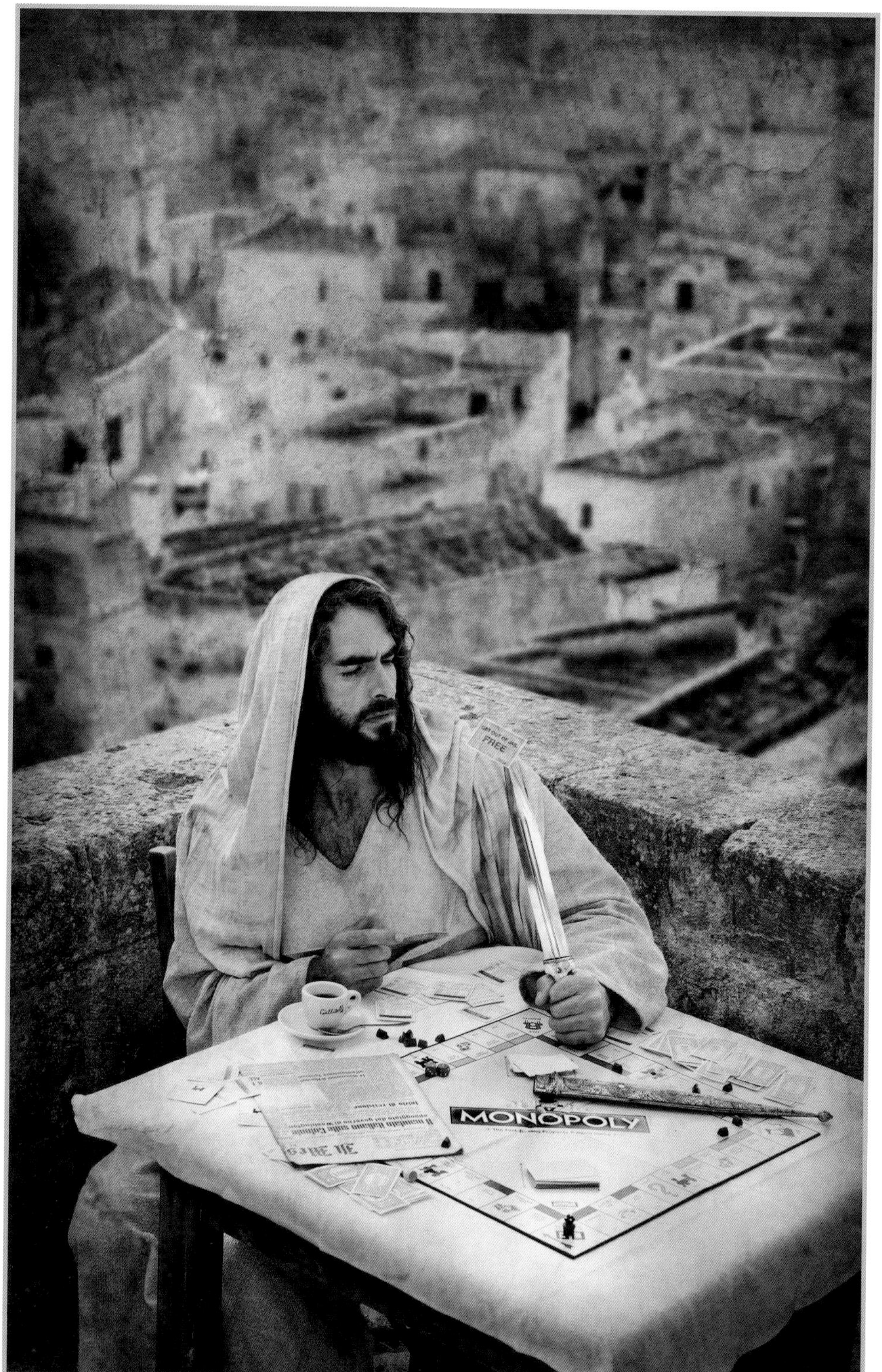
FREE
MONOPOLY

how to be saved. Many of them describe a similar process, while some are not aligned with what the Bible teaches. We know for sure that one cannot work their way into being saved and that salvation is not universal, which means not everyone will be saved. We also know that we cannot be saved through adhering to a list of "do's and don'ts," and salvation is not even slightly similar to the Eastern concept of enlightenment through self-awareness.

Since God is the source and the authority on the subject of eternal life, we should turn to Him to be sure that we know the truth regarding what is required to be saved. What did He say?

The divinely inspired words of John's Gospel about Jesus' life provide the answer. John 3:16 states: "For God so loved the world that He gave His one and only Son, that **whoever believes in Him [in Jesus] shall not perish but have eternal life.**"

This is saying that God loves you and me so much, that He allowed His Son, Jesus, to be sacrificed as atonement for our sins. And, whoever believes in Jesus, will not die upon death but will live in Eternity with Him. Sounds simple enough! Yet, where I think many people misunderstand this scripture is in the phrase *"believes in Him."*

Most of us know people know who say they are saved and say they believe in Jesus, yet their lives appear to be no different from people who say they do not believe in Him. Though they call themselves "Christians," they gossip and lie about others, commit adultery, cheat their business partners and worse.

Perhaps they accepted God's gift of salvation while thinking that it was the way to avoid a date with Hell. Maybe they view the gift of salvation as a "Get Out of Jail Free" card they can use upon death! Many who say they have accepted Jesus go on living as if nothing has changed. They go to church on Sunday, give a portion of their income and maybe sing in the choir or serve on a committee, yet they are void of any spiritual life!

Are they saved? Honestly, I don't know! It's not for me to say! What I am compelled to ask is, "Would God have taken the sacrificial death of His Son so lightly?"

The dictionary defines "believe" as accepting something as being true. However, the Greek translation implies that it is more than just "knowing and accepting;" it includes "taking action on what we know." For example, I can believe in helping the starving people around the world while doing absolutely nothing about it. Or, I can believe in helping the starving people around the world by donating food and supplies, giving money and volunteering my time to organizations that feed them.

So, believing in Jesus is more than just saying we believe in the existence of a man.

After all, that is what evil spirits did as described in Mark 3:11: "Whenever the evil spirits saw Him, they fell down before Him and cried out, 'You are the Son of God.'"

"Whoever believes in Him" means accepting that Jesus sacrificed His life for ours by dying a brutal death on a cross. It means that He overcame death when God raised Him to life again, showing us that there will be life after death for those who believe.

"Believing in Him" also means believing what He taught; that we are to "love God with all our heart, soul and mind" and "love our neighbors as ourselves" (Matthew 22:37,39). Believing in Him means caring for the sick, the widows and orphans, for those in prison, and for those who need food, shelter, and clothing, or just a friend or neighbor who needs someone to listen. As James said:

> *"What good is it, my brothers, if someone says he has faith [believes] but does not have works? Can that faith save him? If a brother or sister is poorly clothed and lacking in daily food, and one of you says to them, "Go in peace, be warmed and filled," without giving them the things needed for the body, what good is that?" —James 2:14-16*

Accepting God's gift of salvation through believing in Jesus should bring about a noticeable change in us; not because of anything we do but because of what He does through the Holy Spirit (1 John 3:17). Believing in Him should encourage us to let go of anger, greed, and jealousy, while desiring His joy, peace, love, and contentment.

When a person accepts Jesus as their Lord and Savior, I can't tell you how quickly these supernatural changes will appear, but I can tell you that God pursues each of us relentlessly! So, if our confession of belief in Jesus is from the heart — not just words from the mouth — change should begin immediately upon acceptance of Him and continue until we arrive in Eternity.

Jesus cautions us that this is a difficult road and few will choose to follow Him. But for those who do, He will stay by our side as He leads us on an exciting journey back to His Father in Heaven. On His *Monopoly* board, we won't need a "Get Out of Jail Free" card. Our salvation has already released us from prison to live in Eternity with Him forever!

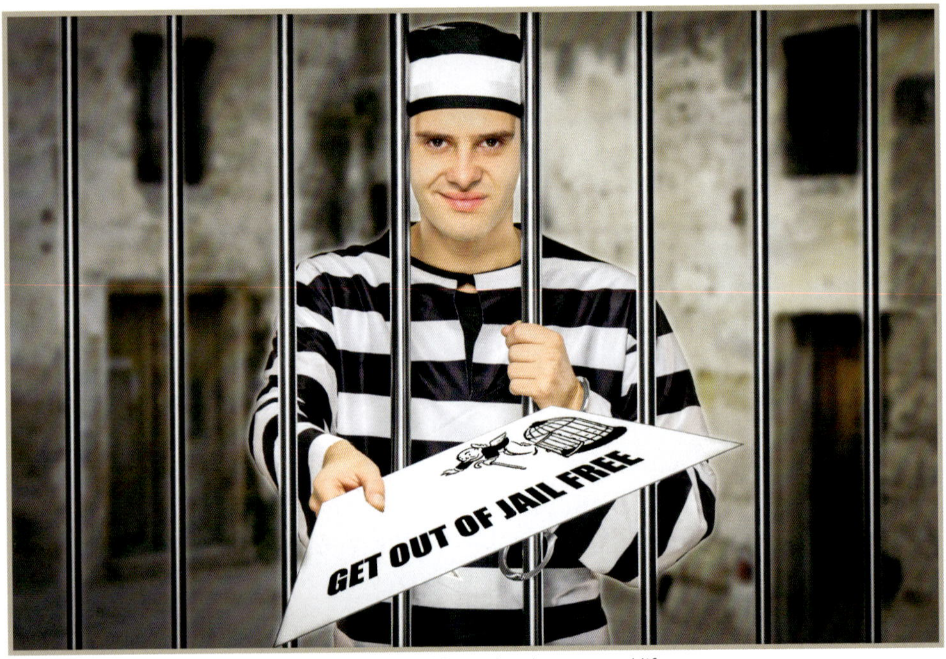

Salvation. Saved from death to eternal life.

Thoughts to Ponder

View film at ▶ journeyswiththemessiah.org

- Is there more to salvation than being saved? If you are "saved," what have you been saved from? What have you been saved to?
- "Whoever believes in Him" means accepting that Jesus sacrificed His life for ours by dying a brutal death on a cross. It means that He overcame death when God raised Him to life again, showing us that there will be life after death for those who believe.
- While the Bible says that everyone is offered salvation, it is also evident not everyone will be saved? Do you know of anyone who is not saved whom you would like to be saved? What can and will you do to assure that they know God's offer of saving grace?
- Salvation is a gift from God through Jesus. It is a supernatural process that brings about change in the person who has been saved. (See the chapter and film, "Metamorphosis.") What changes have you seen through salvation — your own or that of others?
- There are many scriptures like John 3:16 that offer conditions by which one can receive salvation. Many Christians and others do not clearly understand what one must believe to be saved. Perhaps the following scriptures will help provide clarity.

"For by grace you have been saved through faith, and that not of yourselves; it is the gift of God, not of works, lest anyone should boast." Ephesians 2:8-9

"For He made Him who knew no sin to be sin for us, that we might become the righteousness of God in Him." 2 Corinthians 5:21

"Truly, truly, I say to you, whoever hears my word and believes him who sent me has eternal life. He does not come into judgment, but has passed from death to life." John 5:24

"Behold, I stand at the door and knock. If anyone hears my voice and opens the door, I will come in to him and eat with him, and he with me." Revelation 3:20

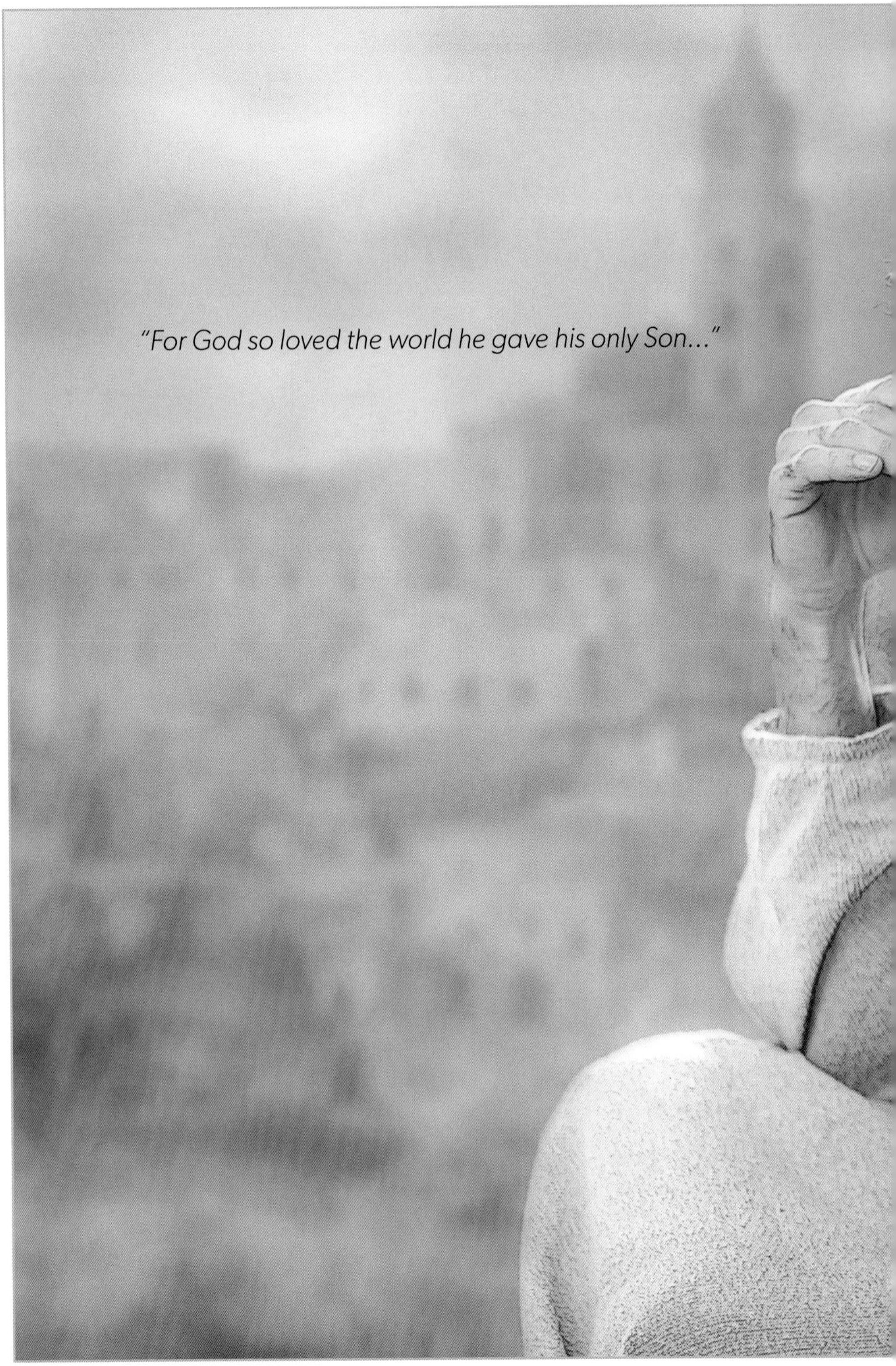
"For God so loved the world he gave his only Son..."

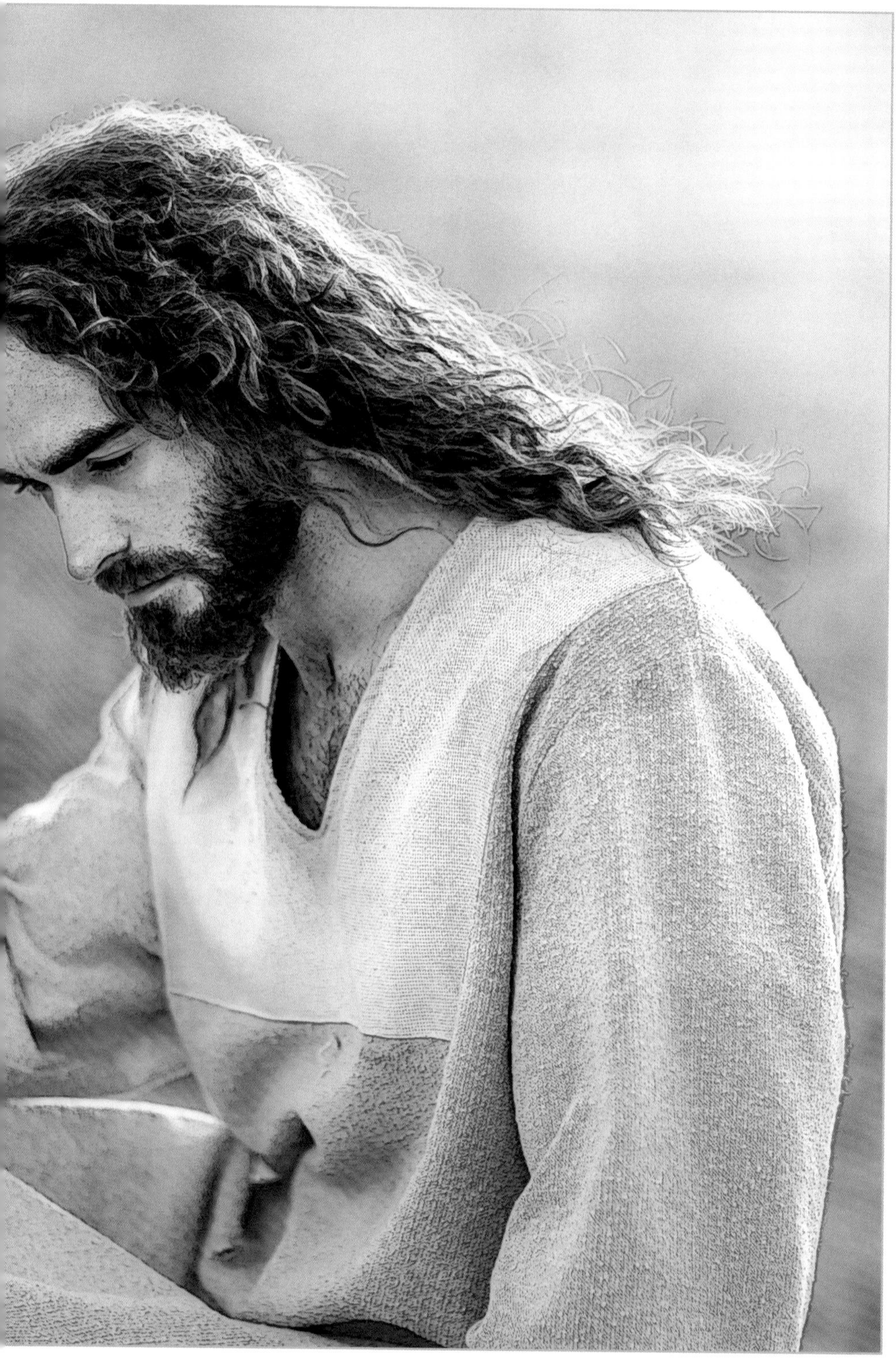

25

Staying Focused

God's Secret to Success

View film at journeyswiththemessiah.org

In 1961, President John F. Kennedy challenged the United States to put a man on the moon. At that time, no one knew how to achieve such a monumental task. Yet, just eight years later, mission commander Neil Armstrong and pilot Buzz Aldrin radioed back to planet earth, *"Houston. Tranquility Base here. The Eagle has landed."* Mission success! Man had landed on the moon!

When I searched the Internet for "ways to achieve success," I found topics that included *Guides to Success, Success Laws, Keys of Success, and Success Principles.* I read an article about billionaires that offered tips like, *"always be true to yourself, get ready for rejection, remember to maximize for happiness, not money."* At the last suggestion, I thought, "Give me a break! Maximize for happiness, not money? That can't be too difficult when you're a billionaire!"

Actually, I was not surprised that money success was the primary type of success mentioned in my initial search. However, let's be clear that money is not success, although it can be a by-product or the gauge by which many people measure success…their own and others.

If you asked highly successful people what brought about their success, most of them could provide insight, yet only in hindsight. No one knows in advance if the path they are taking will lead to success. Nevertheless, I am convinced that successful people would agree that they were focused on **"what"** they wanted to achieve rather than **"how"** they would achieve it.

Putting a man on the moon was President Kennedy's challenge of **"what"** to achieve, but did anyone know **"how?"** After all, the moon was nearly a quarter of a million miles from the Earth, it was circling the Earth while the Earth was rotating on its axis and orbiting the sun. Just the mathematical calculations required to pursue such an endeavor was beyond anyone's comprehension.

Yet, focused on **"what"** was to be accomplished, **"how"** it would be achieved continued to reveal the answers until 10:56 p.m. EDT on July 20, 1969, when astronaut Neil Armstrong stepped onto the moon's surface 240 thousand miles

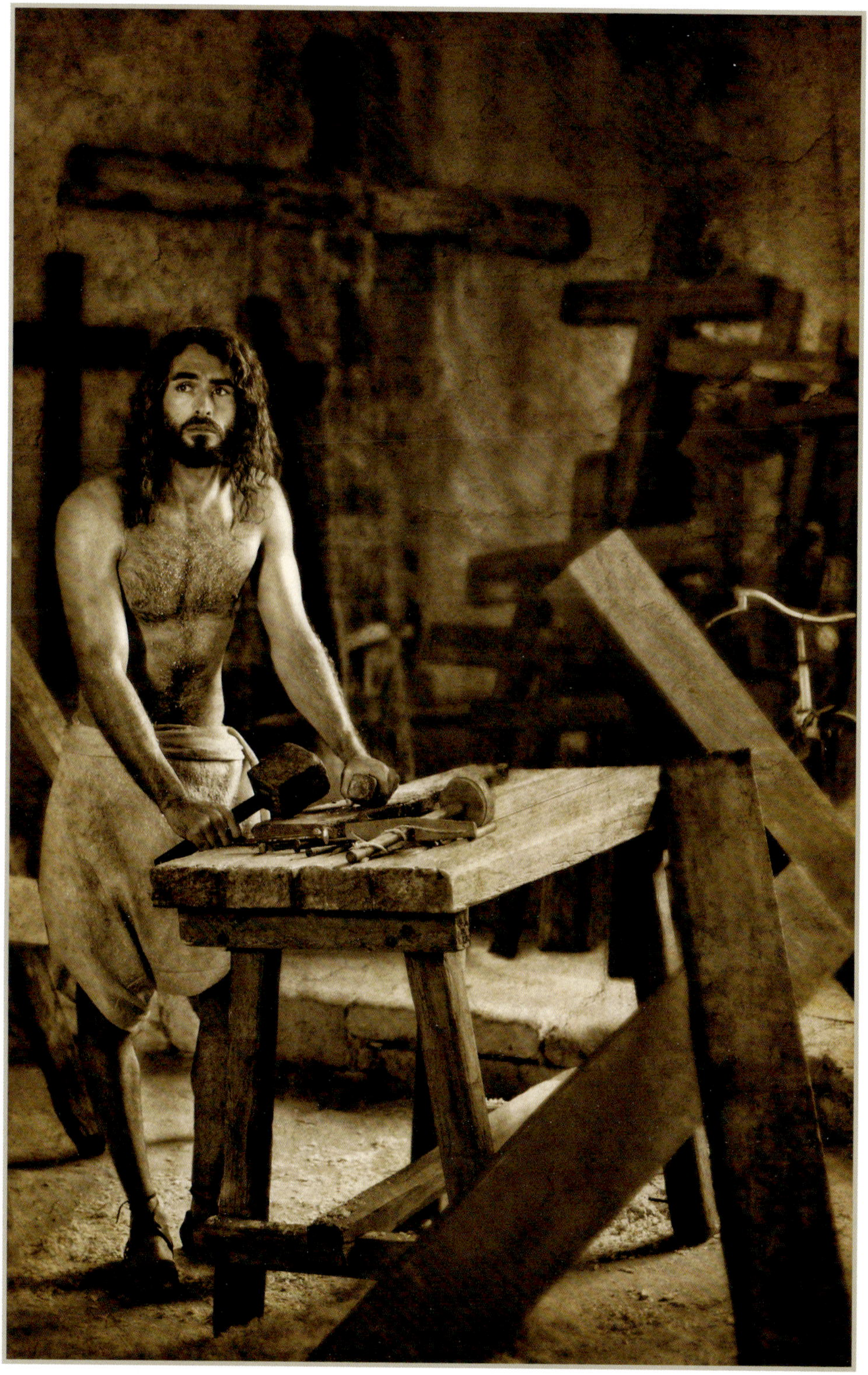

from Earth. He radioed Mission Control in Houston, "That's one small step for a man, one giant leap for mankind!"

When I began my career as a fashion photographer, I had no reason to believe I could be successful. At the time, I was a salesman for a leading clothing company and was knowledgeable of the men's fashion industry. Yet, the odds were highly against an inexperienced amateur photographer going to New York City and becoming a successful fashion photographer. In fact, the idea borderlined rediculous! The only sure thing in my defense was I knew **"what"** I wanted to do.

After a year of struggling and only enough money to make one last trip to New York, the **"how"**of how I would achieve my dream began to fall into place when I was hired for a substantial project by a leading company. My "lucky break" led to validation and credibility and over time, it led to a contract to produce the first J. Crew Catalogs and the original ad campaigns for Nautica. It also paved the way for travel to Paris for Christian Dior and into the Outback of Australia on assignment. It led to having my images in the pages of *Vanity Fair, Elle, GQ* and many other upscale publications.

Today, when young people ask me **"how"** I became successful? I tell them I had no specific formula other than staying focused on **"what"**I wanted to do.

Success is relative. I was paid extremely well for my work (more than most) while others made much more. Success in one part of life does not always mean success in another. Michael Jackson was a musical success, earning more than a billion dollars in his career. When he died of a drug overdose, it was reported that he was $500 million in debt. He was a success in music, but I'm not sure he would say that his overall life was a success.

In the eyes of some people, I was considered to be a success. Yet the year I made the most was also the year I was the most miserable. I experienced success as a fashion photographer, yet on a spiritual level I was a failure. My life was empty of substance and meaning. I wanted significance beyond taking a good photograph. At the time, I did not know how to find it. I just knew what I wanted!

The theory of focusing on **"what"** rather than **"how"** was indirectly supported in Richard Bach's book, *Illusions: The Adventures of a Reluctant Messiah*. In his book, Bach wrote, "You're never given a dream without also being given the power to make it true."

I'm not sure where Bach thought the power came from, but I knew God was the "giver of dreams!" When God gives us a dream of **"what"**is possible, He also provides us with the power of **"how"** to do it. Unfortunately, many of us get consumed in achieving _our_ dreams rather than the dream God has for us. Yet, we often find that our dreams are challenging to sustain because we try to fuel them with self-sufficiency, whereas God dreams run on God-sufficiency.

Jeremiah 29:11 says, "For I know the plans I have for you, declares the Lord, plans to prosper you and not to harm you, plans to give you hope and a future," and Psalm 37 tells us that, "If we delight in Him, He will give us the desires of our hearts." Although God was speaking through Jeremiah to the Israelites about His future plan of Jesus, I believe He is also speaking to us; saying that we can have the hope of dreams that He will place in our hearts when we delight in Him.

During the last years of His life, Jesus was focused on His mission of **"what"** His Father sent Him to do, which was to lay down His life for all us. As Luke writes, "As the time approached for Him to be taken up to Heaven, Jesus resolutely set out for Jerusalem" (Luke 9:51). I suggest that "resolutely" mans He knew **"what"** He was going to do!

Can you imagine setting out for the town where you will be crucified? Jesus had to be tired and, near the end, He was frightened as any man would be. He even asked His Father to consider calling it all off (Luke 22:38-39). Yet He knew that the cost of failure was unacceptable as it would mean the loss of all mankind.

God's plans and dreams for us come in many shapes and sizes. Whether you are planning to sail around the world, find a cure for cancer or be the greatest stay-at-home mom you can be, Jesus said that we are to "Seek first His Kingdom and His righteousness, and all these things will be given to you as well" (Matthew 6:33). I believe Jesus is saying that we are to stay focused on **"what"** God wants for our life and then leave it to Him to work out and reveal to us **"how"** it gets done.

Having God as the focus of our lives guarantees a path to success. Now that's a path worth taking!

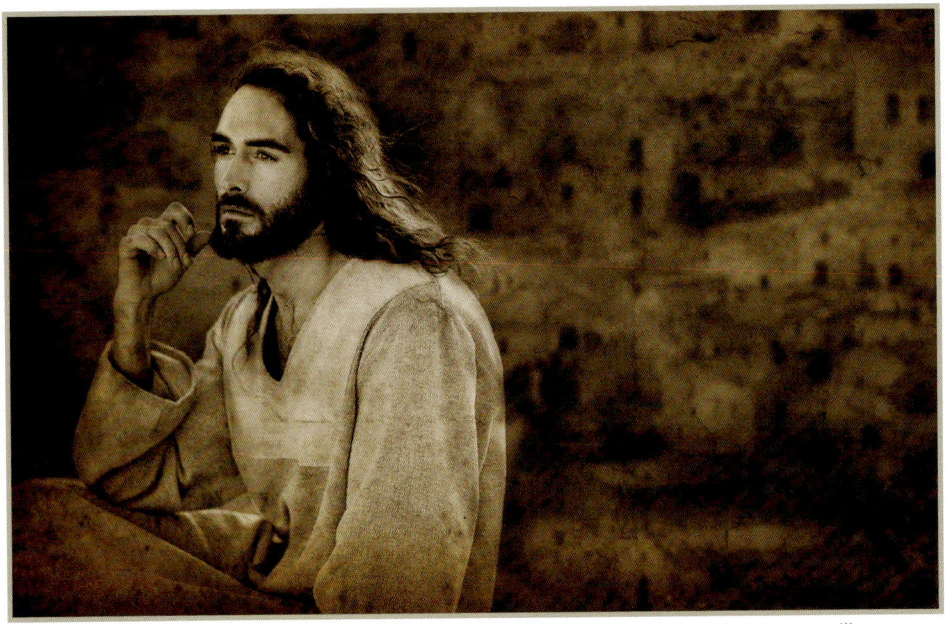

"If it be possible, let this cup pass from me; nevertheless, not as I will, but as you will.

Thoughts to Ponder

View film at ▶ journeyswiththemessiah.org

- Is money success?
- Have you been successful or considered to have been successful in business or any other endeavors? Do you recall how you became successful? Did you know you would be successful when you began?
- Do you see how focusing on **"what"** is to be achieved can lead to **"how"** to achieve it?
- Can you also see why starting with **"how"** to achieve something might provide so few answers that you could become disheartened and quit before you have a chance at success? (See the link to inspiring stores below.)
- Which is more important to you: Achieving success or achieving significance? Being happy or feeling fulfilled? (Your answer may vary based on age and which if either, you may have already achieved.)
- I asked my friend and founder of Cloudwalk Ministries, Larry Green, what part we play in achieving our ministries' funding. His response: "If it's ministry, we play no part! That's God's job!" By the same token, if you believe that God has given you a dream to do something for His Kingdom, do you believe that He will also supply your needs to make it happen?
- Jesus is an excellent example of being focused on **"what"** to achieve since He knew **"how"** it would be achieved was up to His Father. He even said so: "Seek first His Kingdom and His righteousness — **the what** — and all these things will be given to you as well" — **the how**. (Matthew 6:33)

Inspiring stories: https://students-residents.aamc.org/choosing-medical-career/medical-careers/inspiring-stories/

26

Supernatural Peace

Peace through Contentment through Him

View film at ▶ journeyswiththemessiah.org

Have you noticed that the days of our lives don't always work out the way they were planned? Troubles that can come in "threes" also come in "fours, fives and sixes." We learn to cope with most of the day-to-day problems, but what happens when we find ourselves in one of life's raging storms and feel we are sinking. What happens when a child dies, a spouse leaves, or a job gets terminated and there are no savings to fall back on? How do we self-service our needs at times like these?

As a fashion photographer, my work allowed me to travel to beautiful locations around America and, at times, around the world. Friends and others would say, "How exciting your life is…jet-setting to exotic locations to photograph beautiful models!"

I'll admit it was often exciting and mostly enjoyable. However, there were also flight delays, lost baggage, unexpected bad weather, cost overruns and snippy clients with demanding deadlines that sometimes made my job less glamorous than one might think. Then, if my personal life wasn't running on all cylinders, my dream job could be more like a nightmare. Those were the times I would have traded everything just to have peace.

If you have owned or managed any business, you understand the cycles and fluctuations in revenue and cash flow. As the old saying goes, "You must make hay while the sun is shining." Translated: You need to take advantage of opportunities while they are available.

In the world of fashion advertising, the periods of work fluctuated as fashion clients ramped up for each coming season. The windows of opportunity were often very short, requiring that I take on all of the assignments my staff and I could manage before the window shut. During those times, we worked on multiple jobs simultaneously. I would finish one photoshoot only to hop on a flight to the next. Some projects lasted a day or two, while others could go on for weeks.

Photography was only one component of my responsibility. As the owner of my own agency, I also had to manage the design, copywriting, and production

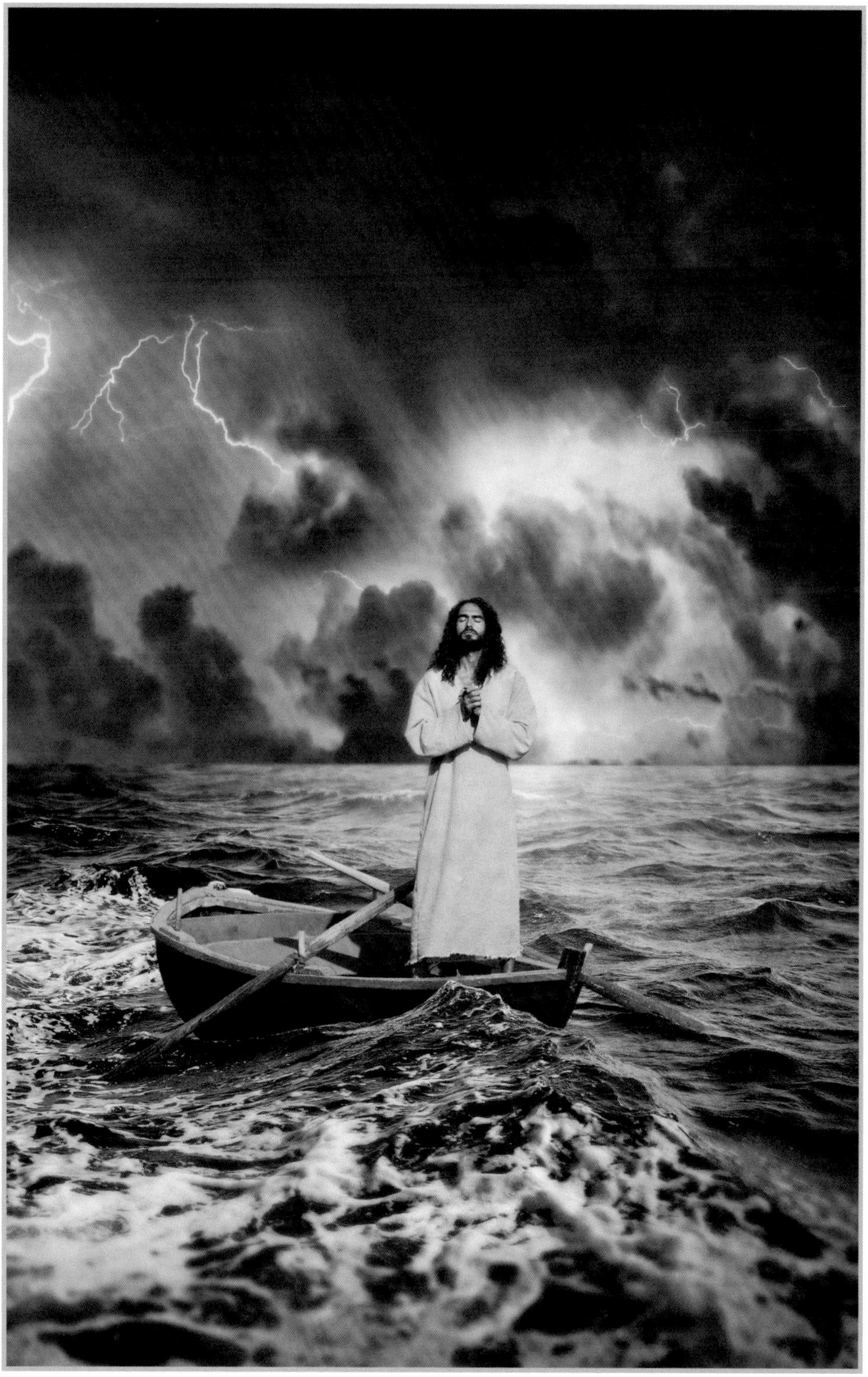

of brochures and ad campaigns, plus manage the planning and production of photoshoots. Because of the "make hay while the sun shines" mentality, taking on more work was the norm rather than the exception. Life was always in the fast lane. Anxiety, tension and frustration were the emotions of the day.

In 1955, Anne Lindbergh, wife of the famed pilot Charles Lindbergh, wrote a book after a vacation on the beaches of Florida's Captiva Island. In her book, *A Gift from the Sea,* she reflected on her life and experiences. Her inspiration came from the shells on the beach.

The book was a gift to me by a friend when we were in high school. I don't know why I was so moved by this book at such a young age, yet I even memorized a paragraph I thought to be profound and meaningful. Within that paragraph, Anne Lindbergh wrote, "We have so little faith in the ebb and flow of life…We leap at the flow of the tide and resist in terror its ebb. We're afraid it will never return."

Lindbergh was writing about love and relationships. Yet her words are relevant for all aspects of life. Leaping at the flow of life's tides while resisting its ebb is what many of us do. Even though we have seen the tide come in and go out over and over, we still have no faith that it will ever return.

Having no faith in the tides of life usually means having no faith in God; it means having no faith in His promises or knowing that He is in control (so we don't have to be)! The only way we cannot have faith in God is if we simply don't know Him.

Webster defines peace as "tranquility and calm and freedom from disturbance." I can make peace with a friend, our country can be at peace with other nations and I can be at peace — free from anxiety and stress. Personal peace is a supernatural condition that comes only from God, whereas anxiety and stress are conditions that come only from man.

While sharing His last supper with the disciples on the night of His arrest, Jesus told them He would be put to death, but they should not be troubled or afraid. Then He said, "Peace I leave with you; My peace I give you. I do not give to you as the world gives. Do not let your hearts be troubled and do not be afraid" (John 14:27).

Do you see that? Jesus said it was *"His peace"* He would leave them, not the world's. He was saying that He would leave them with *"His supernatural peace!"*

I believe that peace is the result of being content even as the tides of life flow in and out. In his letter to the Philippians, the Apostle Paul wrote,

> *"I've learned by now to be quite content whatever my circumstances. I'm just as happy with little as with much, with much as with little. I've found the recipe for being happy, whether full or hungry, hands full or hands empty. Whatever I have, wherever I am, I can make it through anything in the One who makes me who I am."* —Philippians 4:11-13

Our lack of trust in the ebb and flow of life stems from our lack of knowing the Author of Life. So our nature is to want the tides "coming in" all of the time. When the tide flows out, people will scurry about trying to manipulate the tides to keep the feeling of the high tide going. When we lack patience to wait on God's timing for the tide to return, we often make bad choices.

God makes it clear that the tides of our lives are continually changing. Sometimes the "tides of plenty" come in, while it goes out at others. Sometimes the "tides of happiness" come in, and at other times they ebb. God tells us that we can have contentment through faith in Him regardless of our circumstances; that we do not need to be anxious when the tide flows out. They'll come again!

I believe that peace through contentment is the single most blessing everyone is seeking…whether they know it or not. An entrepreneur seeks contentment through financial success. A musician seeks it by performing well and an athlete through victory. If you are a mom, you seek the contentment that comes when you know your children are safe and happy.

I am blessed to have learned that I can be content and free from anxiety when I trust God's timing for the tides' ebb and flow. I am free to be content wherever I am with whatever I have; to know that I can make it through anything by trusting in *The One* who makes me who I am; and to know, when all else fails, He will not!

Bask in the glow of His Supernatural Peace!

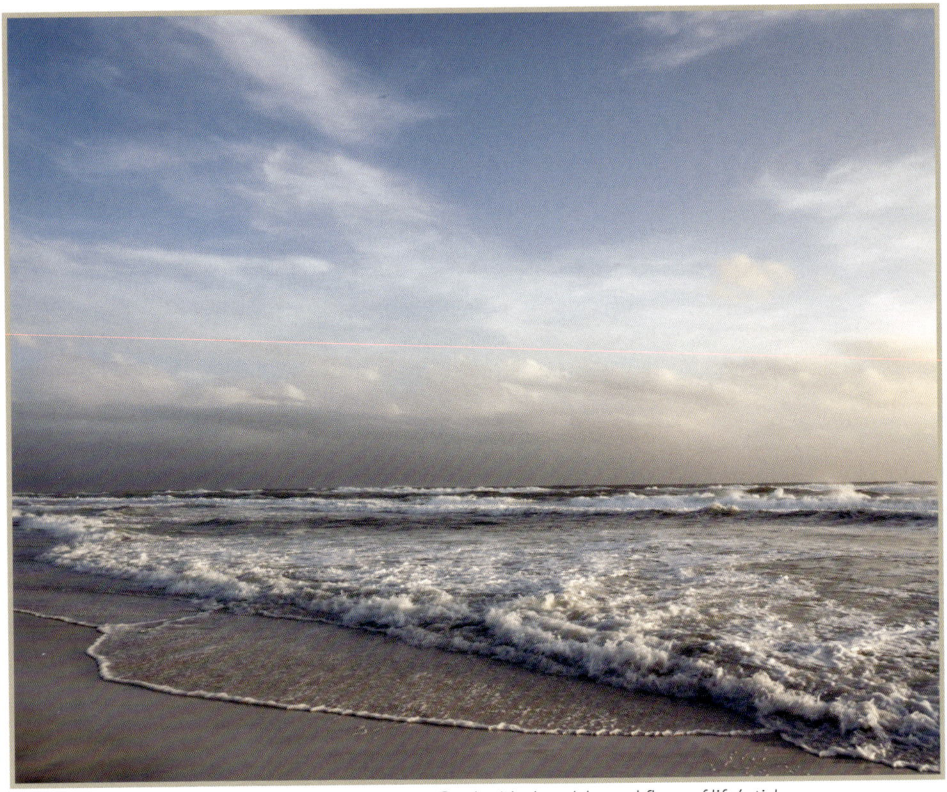

Whether in or out, we can trust God with the ebb and flow of life's tides.

Thoughts to Ponder

View film at ▶ journeyswiththemessiah.org

- We manage day-to-day problems as a part of life, but where do we turn when tsunami-size waves of troubles follow one another in succession? Many times during this project I cried out to God, "I just can't take anymore." Yet, He has shown me that I can! All things are possible with Him.

- Anne Lindbergh's book, *A Gift from the Sea,* uses the ebb and flow of tide's to describe relationships. The flow of the tides are also a great example of the events of our lives, especially in relationship to our Lord. Consider the ebb and flow in the history of "tides" in your life?

- When we "leap at the flow of the tides of life" and then "resist in terror its ebb," it is an indication that our faith is fragile — strong in the good times, weak when not. Go to the beach or watch a YouTube video showing tides coming in and going out. They never stop! They never will! We can count on them as surely as we depend on God. Does your faith stay constant or flow with the tides of your life?

- Personal peace is a supernatural condition that comes only from God, whereas anxiety and fear come from man. God's character is peace, joy, and contentment in all circumstances, whether the tide is in or out.

- I believe that peace is the blessing everyone desires, whether they know it or not. Peace is the feeling that results from contentment, and contentment comes from faith in God. The Apostle Paul said that he had learned to be content in all circumstances — tide in or tide out. Note that Paul said he had "learned" to be content. We can learn it too!

27

The Promise

Making Everything New

View film at ▶ journeyswiththemessiah.org

When I was a child, it was easy to be frightened by some of the hellfire and brimstone preaching that was prevalent in those times. I heard that the earth would be destroyed by fire and I got the impression that I would be sent to Hell if I was a bad boy. It was pretty scary stuff! Maybe the strategy was literally to scare the Hell out of me!

On a flight to New York in my early thirties, I recall reading an article about an minister being asked to leave a country after several days of a crusade. The article said, *"The story of Jesus Christ is a story of love, but this minister makes it sound like a threat!"* I'll have to admit that it was more of the threat I knew as a child before I was introduced to the story of Jesus' love.

Although the Bible is filled with volumes of encouraging messages, it would be foolish for us to ignore its warnings about the end times (the end of the earth) and life after death. Perhaps we are at a time in history when the world could profit from a description of Hell and the world's catastrophic end. Maybe a little wake-up call about these negative consequences can be a positive thing!

As to the biblical descriptions of the end of the world, I'm confident that we can have faith in the Bible without immediate understanding of everything in it. For example, although some of the writings in the Gospels of Matthew, Mark, Luke, and John may at first appear to have inconsistencies, when the Gospels are viewed for their overall content, they firmly agree and testify to the same truth.

The Second Book of Peter tells us that, "No prophecy was ever made by an act of human will, but only by men who were moved by the Holy Spirit spoken from God" (2 Peter 1:21). Through Peter, God is telling us that we can trust everything written in the Bible as having been written by His inspiration and direction, although written by the hands of men.

In the Gospels, Jesus talked more about Hell than Heaven. He compared Hell to Gehenna, an area in the valley of Hinnom very close to Jerusalem. Gehenna

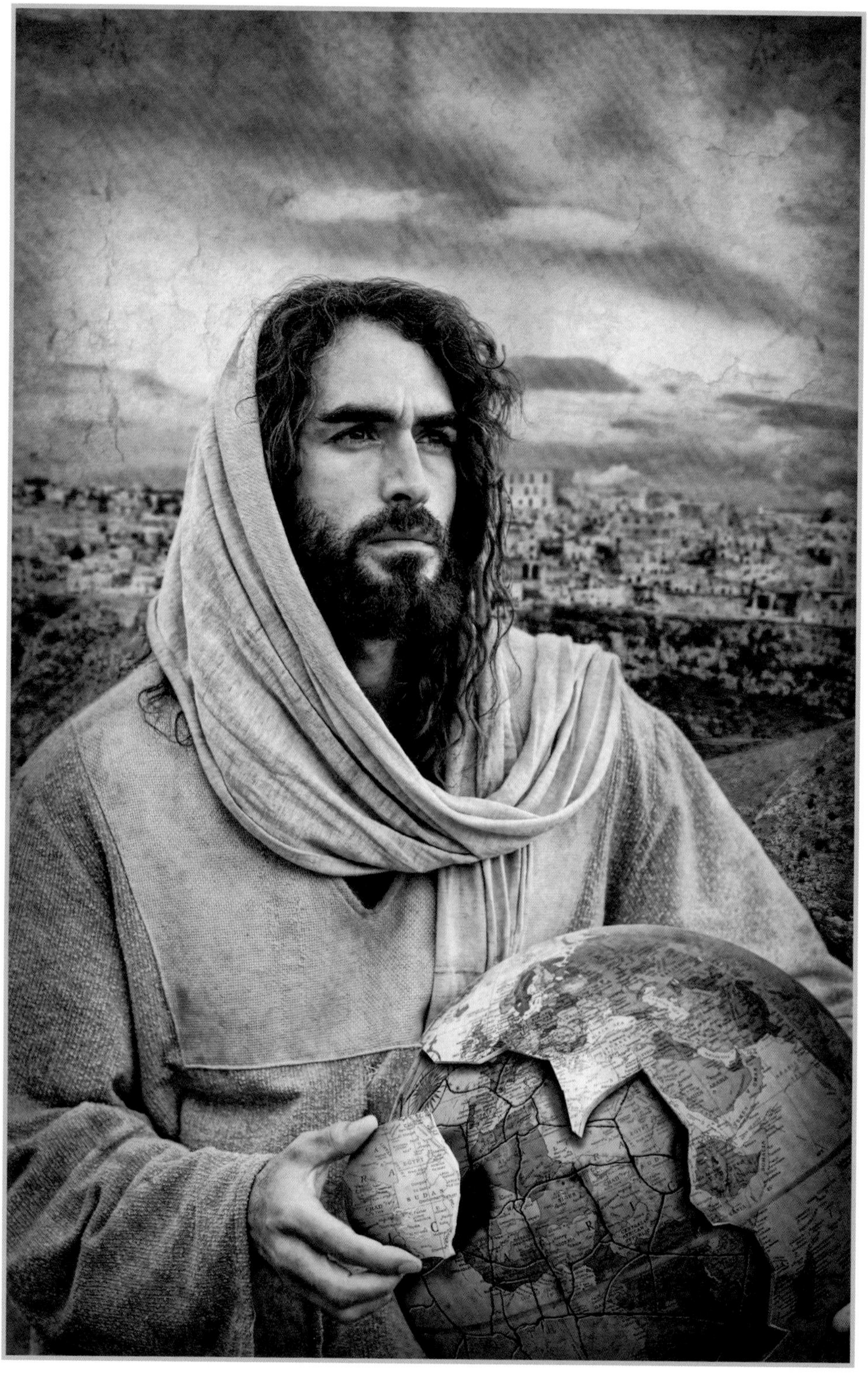

had become a vast public rubbish dump where dead bodies and trash burned in continually smoldering fires. People listening to Jesus would be familiar with Gehenna and have a clear picture of what He was saying.

In the story that Jesus told about "*Lazarus and the rich man,*" Jesus said that there was a great divide between Heaven and Hell. On one side, there was life in Eternity with God the Father. On the other side, life was separated from God forever. The divide was permanent. Once crossed, a person could not cross back over. In His story, Jesus was saying that if a person dies and has not accepted Him as Savior and Lord, it will be too late to turn back even if they discover later that His story and promises are true (Luke 16:19-31).

As I searched for answers about God's nature and His plan for mankind, a consistent theme was revealed to me about how much God loved the world and the people He created for it. In the Book of Genesis, there are five times God pauses to observe His creation and declares His work as "good" (Genesis 1:10, 12, 18, 21, 25).

Later in the Bible, through the inspired writing of the profit Jeremiah, God tells the Israelites about the good plans He has for them (Jeremiah 29:11). These good plans ultimately lead to good plans for you and me through Jesus Christ. So we can believe with confidence that God loves us and has good plans for us.

Studying these scriptures made me wonder, "If God has looked upon His creation and declared it to be good and also has plans for mankind that are good, why would He destroy the Earth and His creation?" Yet Jesus warns that "Heaven and earth will pass away" (Matthew 24:35).

Depending on the Bible version one refers to, Isaiah 24:1 has many varying descriptions about the Earth's end. They include, "destroyed, emptied and made desolate, lay waste and devastate, and distort its face and turn upside down." I found it difficult to understand exactly what will happen, yet my sense is that "how or what" may not be important.

Regardless of how this cataclysmic event occurs, it appears to me that God is going to wipe the earth clean of all evil and everything that is not a part of His original design. Perhaps it will be like a remodeling job whereby the Planet Earth will be gutted, leaving only the original shell. In any case, after the earth is wiped clean, it may be like God having a new canvas on which He can re-create the world.

The author of the Book of Revelations was given a vision by God, "Then I saw a new heaven and a new earth" (Revelations 21:1) and a vision of Jesus sitting on the throne saying, "I am making everything new!" (Revelations 21:5). That's huge! Jesus is not making just some things new; He is making everything new!

The author of Revelations continues to describe it this way, "I saw the Holy City, the New Jerusalem, coming down out of Heaven from God, prepared as a bride beautifully dressed for her husband. And I heard a loud voice from the throne saying, 'Look! God's dwelling place is now among the people, and He will dwell with them. They will be His people, and God Himself will be with them and be their God'" (Revelations 21:2-3).

Does that sound familiar? At first, maybe not, but I think it is this scripture from Revelations that we acknowledge each time we recite the Lord's prayer: "Thy Kingdom come, thy will be done on earth as it is in Heaven" (Matthew 6:10). God's Kingdom will come to Earth, and His will...will be done on Earth! "He will wipe every tear from our eyes. There will be no more death or mourning or crying or pain, for the old order of things will pass away" (Revelations 21:4).

Jesus says, "To the thirsty, I will give water without cost from the spring of the water of life" (Revelations 21:6). "Without cost?" This must mean that we can cut up our credit cards! Everything will be free…forever! The earth will be restored to its Garden of Eden condition before the first sin occured. Sin will be no more!

"All things new!" Hallelujah! What a promise!

The Book of Revelations continues with Jesus saying, "Those who are victorious (meaning everyone who has confessed Jesus as Savior and Lord) will inherit all this new and eternal world." He says, "I will be their God, and they will be My children" (Revelations 21:7).

What I hear in all of this in all of this is that God comes seeking us. He reaches down to us because He wants no one to be separated from Him by the great divide that Jesus tells us about in the story of Lazarus (Luke 16:19-31).

I will admit that many biblical passages can be challenging to understand at first. Revelations is no exception. I'm always searching for understanding through the opinions of scholars and others. Yet I'm reminded of what God says in Isaiah: "For my thoughts are not your thoughts, neither are your ways my ways. As the heavens are higher than the earth, so are my ways higher than your ways and my thoughts than your thoughts" (Isaiah 55:8-9). It is not always possible to understand the spiritual thoughts of God's infinite mind with our limited carnal minds.

There is a great story about Mother Theresa and John Kavanaugh when John went to Calcutta, India to work with her. The trip came as John was seeking God's direction for the future. So the story goes, when he met with Mother Teresa, John asked her to pray for him. Mother Teresa asked him what he wanted her to pray for and John replied, "Clarity! Pray that I might have clarity!" To his surprise, Mother

Teresa refused and said that she would not pray for clarity for him.

She said, "Clarity is the last thing you are clinging to, and the last thing you must let go of."

John responded by asking, "Surely, Mother Teresa, you have found clarity in all your years serving the poor and dying?"

She laughed at that suggestion. "I have never had clarity; what I have always had is trust. So I will pray that you will trust God."

Perhaps we do not need to spend our time seeking clarity about how the world will end. After all, Jesus has told us that we will not know when it will occur (Matthew 24:36).

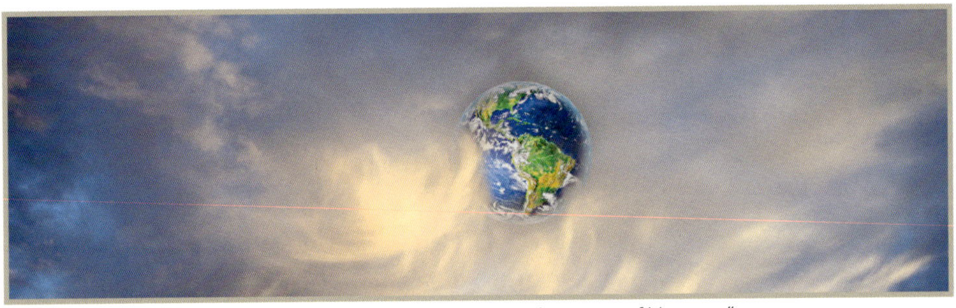

"And I saw a New World coming down out of Heaven."

As Mother Theresa prayed that John Kavanaugh would trust God, we must also trust that God has everything planned and under control. Our focus should not be on what happens to the world, but what happens to us when it ends or, more importantly, when we die. If you have confessed Jesus is your Lord and Savior, then the only question to consider is, "Who else can I tell about Him before I go?'

On the other hand, if He is not the Lord and Savior of your life, I encourage you to at least consider examining the evidence about Him before you make a decision. Jesus promised that "He will make all things new," including you. So, on behalf of everyone who has accepted Jesus Christ as Lord and Savior of their lives, you are invited to join us for this glorious ending, which never ends!

Thoughts to Ponder

View film at ▶ journeyswiththemessiah.org

- Regarding the "end times," are you clear on it, confused by it or haven't given it much thought?
- There are differing opinions and interpretations of scriptures regarding the "end times." How do we know which is correct? Perhaps God wants us to pursue the essential — life in Eternity with Him — rather than the non-essential details of how the end times might occur.
- If we are not convinced that the Bible is God's inspired word, we may choose only the scriptures we understand and believe to be true. That's a slippery slope that can lead to confusion and away from God.
- God is love! The Bible is the history of a Good Father who loves His children even when He admonishes them!
- When I read the Bible, I make sure I have immediate access to resources that can provide explanations for scriptures I do not understand. It makes reading scripture fun and fascinating!
- Two criminals were crucified with Jesus. One acknowledged his guilt and said to Jesus, "Remember me when you come into your kingdom." Jesus answered, "Today, you will be with me in paradise." I don't know about you, but *"today in Paradise"* is all the explanation I need about what happens when I die! Paradise is the heavenly abode of God, where the people who have a relationship with Him will go as soon as they die! (See Revelation 2:7) Now that's something to ponder!
- As amazing as Heaven (Paradise) will be, it is still not the final stop on our eternal journey. According to Revelation, someday, we will return with Jesus to "The New Heaven and New Earth."

Check out Randy Frazee's book, "What Happens After You Die."
Two favorite resources: GotQuestions.org and the Ask Pastor John App.
www.desiringgod.org/messages/today-you-will-be-with-me-in-paradise

28

The Road Less Traveled

The Cost of Following Christ

View film at ▶ journeyswiththemessiah.org

It was around 1980 when I first picked up M. Scott Peck's best-selling book, *The Road Less Traveled.* I clearly remember the first sentence which read, "Life is difficult!" I quickly closed the book while thinking, "That's the last thing I need to hear right now!" I didn't pick it up again for many years. As it turned out, it was an excellent book with many good thoughts about life, including the fact that "Life is difficult!"

In 1916, the New England poet, Robert Frost, wrote one of the most memorable poems in history, *The Road Not Taken*. In his short poem, he describes two roads that diverge in the woods. Frost was sorry that he could not travel both, and at the end of his poem he wrote, "I took the one less traveled by, and that has made all the difference."

During the hundred years since the poem was written, many people have thought that Frost meant the road he chose, "the one less traveled," was the better road because he said that choosing this road "made all the difference."

Over the years, people have interpreted the phrase "the road less traveled" as meaning unique or unconventional; to think or do things differently. Today we say, "Learn to think out of the box!" We even admire famous people and celebrities we think fit these descriptions, saying they have taken "the road less traveled." Perhaps we give them this distinction without a proper understanding of which road they have taken!

I prided myself as being one who chose the road less traveled. For me, that road was synonymous with "standing out from the crowd" and "marching to the beat of a different drummer." My mantra was, "If I am just like everyone else, how will I know who I am?" My need was the need to be different at all costs. When all of my friends decided to belong to the most popular high school fraternity, I chose the least popular. When many of my friends went to one of the two largest universities in our state, I selected a small university that was far away.

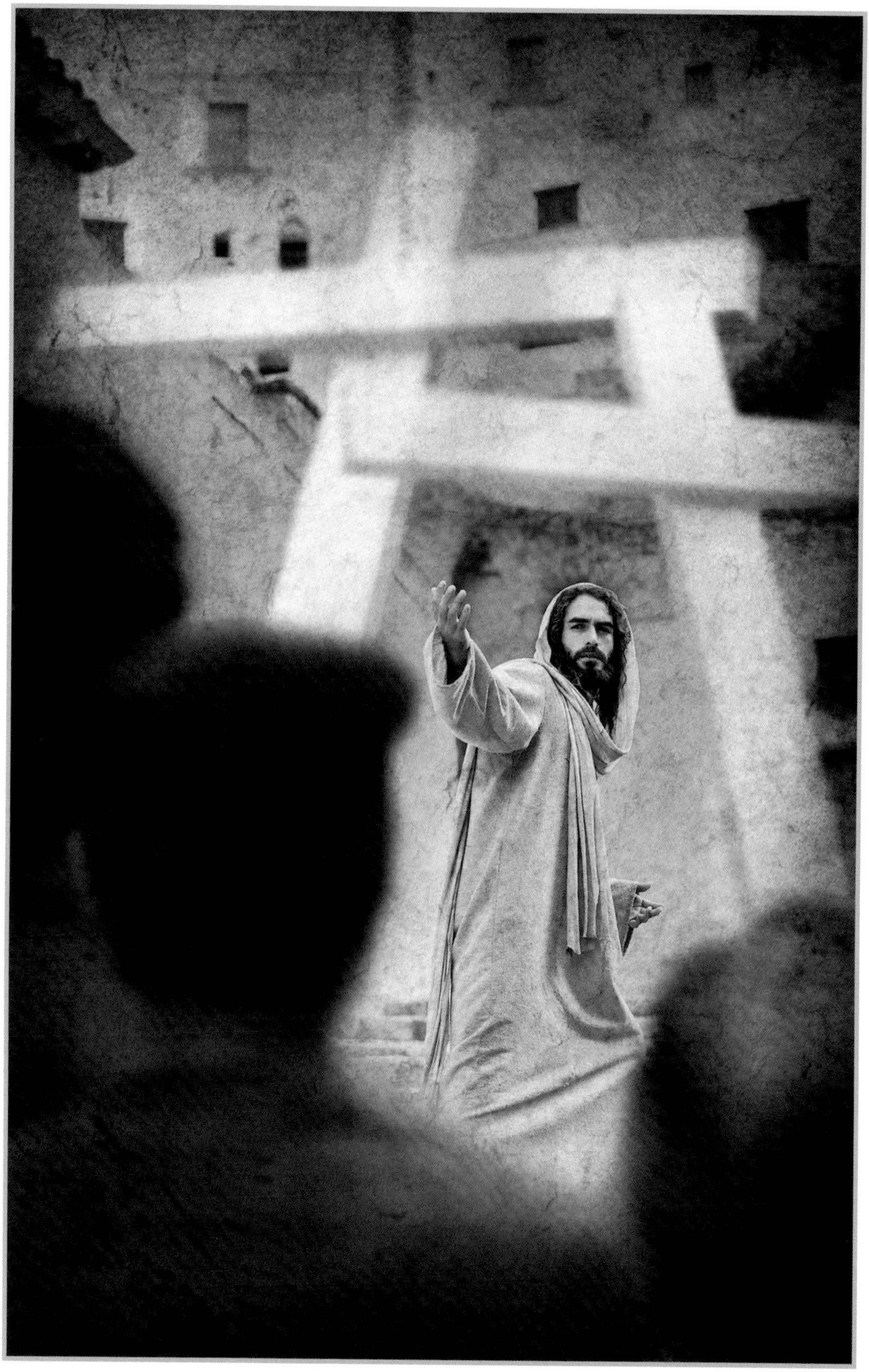

I cannot testify now that choosing "the road less traveled" was always the best choice. In retrospect, many of my choices became testaments to the first sentence of Scott Peck's book, "Life is difficult!"

However, I may have steered you off track a bit as critics believe we have misread Frost's intention. Frost did not name his poem *The Road Less Traveled*. He called it *The Road Not Taken*. There is a huge difference! His poem is really about choice!

Life is very much like the diverging roads in the woods. Since we cannot go down both roads, at least not at the same time, we are faced with which one to choose. If we take the road on the left, we miss taking the road on the right or *the road not taken.*

Frost considers both roads before making his choice. Whichever he chooses, he thinks he can return someday to take *the road not taken.* Looking back years later, he believes that he chose the less traveled road and says that it "made all the difference." Yet there is no indication of what the phrase "all the difference" means. Some people think the poem suggests that he may regret the one he chose.

As I read Frost's poem, I could immediately recognize the two roads. Actually, Jesus identified them long before Frost, and they are described in Matthew 7:13-14 as "the broad road" and "the narrow road."

The road Jesus called "the broad road" is the one that is defined by the world. It is characterized by success, wealth and self-sufficiency. It is lived by clamoring to get to the front of the line, and it thrives on convenience. Its favorite words are "me" and "my," and it comes with membership in *The Club of Instant Gratification.*

The other road is characterized by a "narrow road with a narrow gate." Jesus' description of it doesn't sound too inviting. Travelers on this road are asked to forgive others time and time again (Matthew 18:31-22). They are told to pray for their enemies and anyone who persecutes them or says ugly things behind their backs (Matthew 5:44). On this road, one is asked to feed the hungry, care for orphans and the elderly and to visit people in prison (Matthew 25: 35-36).

Jesus also talked about being charitable on this road. He said that if the amount you are giving does not cause you discomfort in at least some small way, it's because you're not giving enough! (Luke 21:4). Jesus told a *Rich Young Ruler* to sell everything he had and give the money to the poor before starting down this road with Him (Luke 18:18–30).

When we consider everything Jesus said about taking this road less traveled (the one with the narrow gate), we will agree with Him that, anyone who thinks they might want to take this road, better count the costs first! (Luke 14:28). Faced with "the broad road" and "the narrow road," most of us will choose the broad road. Let's face it, human nature desires comfort and pleasure! Jesus knows that most people will turn and run at the thought of denying their own desires.

As far as "the narrow road with the narrow gate," Jesus said that ultimately it will be an exclusive club, but its membership is currently opened to everyone. He noted that few will take it! On the other hand, "the broad road" was non-exclusive. It will be packed with people like the highways leaving cities at rush hour. (Matthew 7:13-14).

But just suppose we did not want to follow the crowd and decide to follow this "narrow road with the narrow gate," *the road less traveled?* Is there an upside?

Jesus says this road leads to His Father's Kingdom where there are many mansions (John 14:2). Although it can be a challenging journey, He will make the trip with us (John 16:33). He will protect us in the dark valleys, lighten our load when it gets too heavy and give us supernatural peace when encountering storms. However, once we reach His kingdom, the storms will end. There will be no tears, no sorrow, no sickness, hatred, jealousy or fear...and no death! Life will be eternal; we will live forever (Revelations 21:4).

In Robert Frost's poem, two roads diverge in the woods and ultimately it did not seem to make much difference which one was taken. Yet, in God's world, your choice does matter! Jesus says that "the broad road" leads to destruction — the traveler's destruction — in the sense that the road eventually comes to an end. The other road, "the one with the narrow gate," continues on into eternity with God (Matthew 7: 13-14).

I spent many years on "the broad road." Since I began following Jesus on "the narrow road," I am in awe of what I have seen, heard and experienced. On this *road less traveled*, I have never thought that maybe I should have taken the other road, *the road not taken.*

Jesus is inviting everyone to join Him on "the narrow road,"(aka Highway to Heaven). It leads to a journey of a lifetime that ends in life! He promises, you'll never look back!

The Road Not Taken

by Robert Frost

Two roads diverged in a yellow wood,
And sorry I could not travel both
And be one traveler, long I stood
And looked down one as far as I could
To where it bent in the undergrowth;

Then took the other, as just as fair,
And having perhaps the better claim,
Because it was grassy and wanted wear;
Though as for that the passing there
Had worn them really about the same,

And both that morning equally lay
In leaves no step had trodden black.
Oh, I kept the first for another day!
Yet knowing how way leads on to way,
I doubted if I should ever come back.

I shall be telling this with a sigh
Somewhere ages and ages hence:
Two roads diverged in a wood, and I—
I took the one less traveled by,
And that has made all the difference.

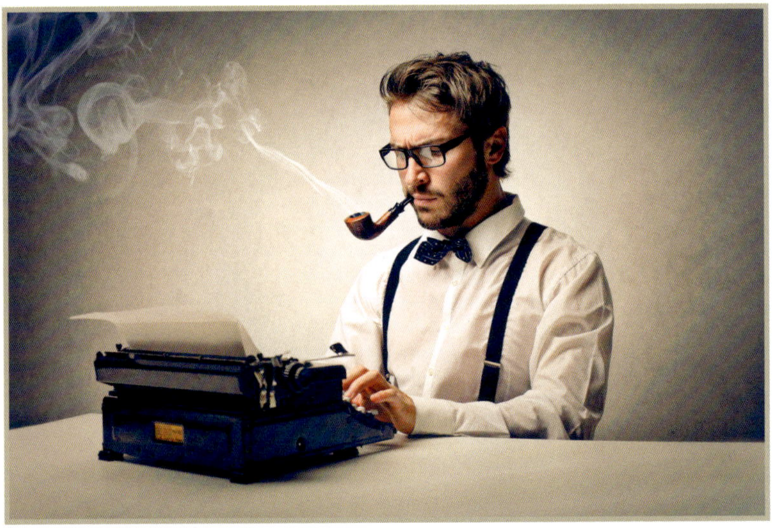

Thoughts to Ponder

View film at ▶ journeyswiththemessiah.org

- In his book, The Road Less Traveled, Scott Peck wrote, "Life is difficult!" Do you agree? If yes, why do you think it's difficult? How can it be, or have been easier? If you answered, "No," please write a book to share with the rest of us!

- Were you familiar with the phrase,"the road less traveled?" Which road defines your life: "The road less traveled" or "the road not taken?"

- This chapter points out that there is a vast difference between "the road less traveled" and "the road not taken." I loved talking to my mother and father about "the roads not taken" in their lives. Consider "the roads not taken" in your life — both secular roads and spiritual roads — and whether you feel they made a difference.

- In Frost's poem, he describes "two roads that diverge in the woods." They coincide with the two choices Jesus identified: "The broad road" and "the narrow road with a narrow gate." Re-read the description of each on page 180. Have you taken one or the other or find yourself spending time on each?

- In Frost's poem, it didn't seem to make much difference which road was taken. Yet, in God's world, the choice of the two roads matters! Why?

29

The Second Mile

The Joy of Forgiving

View film at ▶ journeyswiththemessiah.org

Where does a mother find the courage to stand in a courtroom and forgive the man who murdered her daughter? How does a wife or husband forgive their spouse for breaking their marriage vows? How do Jews forgive the German Nazis for the horrendous crimes they committed in the Holocaust of World War II?

Jesus understood that forgiving someone for the wrong they have done can be the

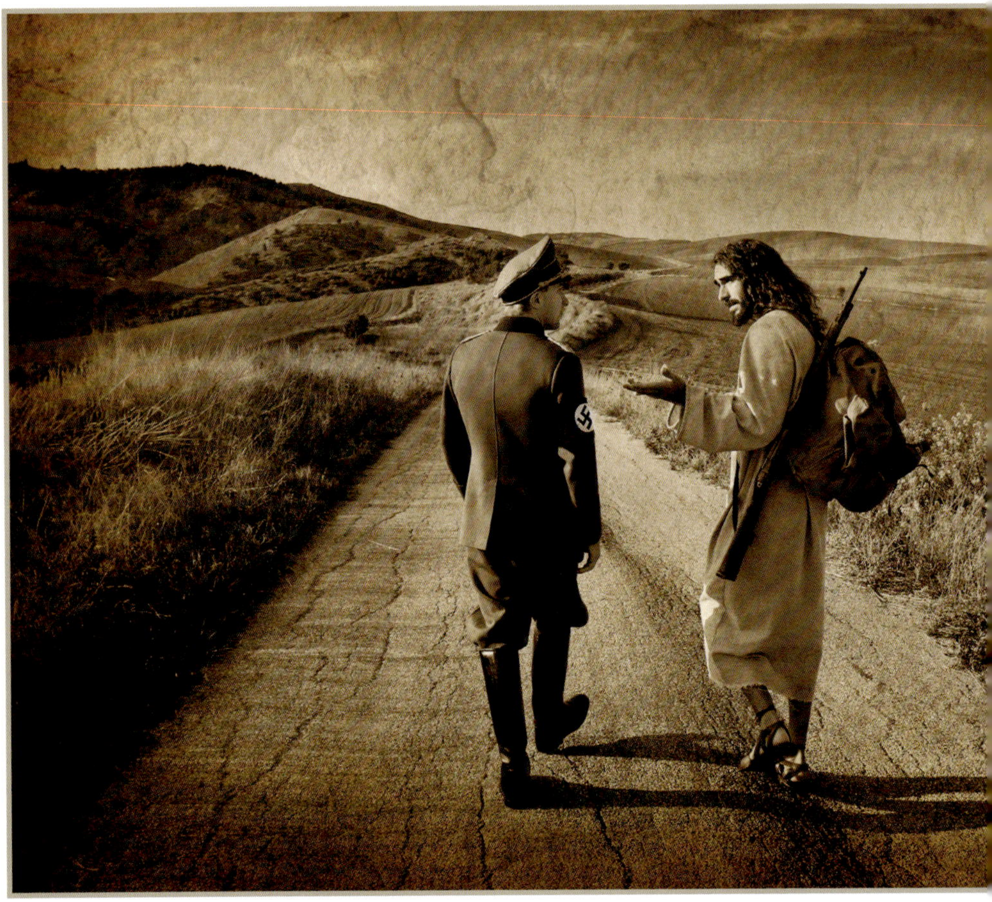

most challenging experience we will ever encounter? Yet he still campaigned for it. Why?

There was a period in my life when I read several pop-psychology self-help books. Most of them attempted to be motivating. Many of them included comments and instructions on forgiveness — forgiving others and forgiving oneself. Years later, as I was growing in my knowledge and understanding of Jesus — who He is and how He was changing my life — I found that He had a lot to say about forgiveness.

There was an occasion when Jesus told a Roman governor, "The reason I was born and came into the world is to testify to the truth. Everyone on the side of truth listens to me" (John 18:37). A part of that truth would be His instructions about forgiveness. His teachings on forgiveness were revolutionary: "Love your enemies as yourself. Pray for those who persecute you (Matthew 5:44). Forgive people seventy times seven (Matthew 18:22). If you go to the altar and remember you have an issue with someone, go settle it and then come back." (Matthew 5:23-24).

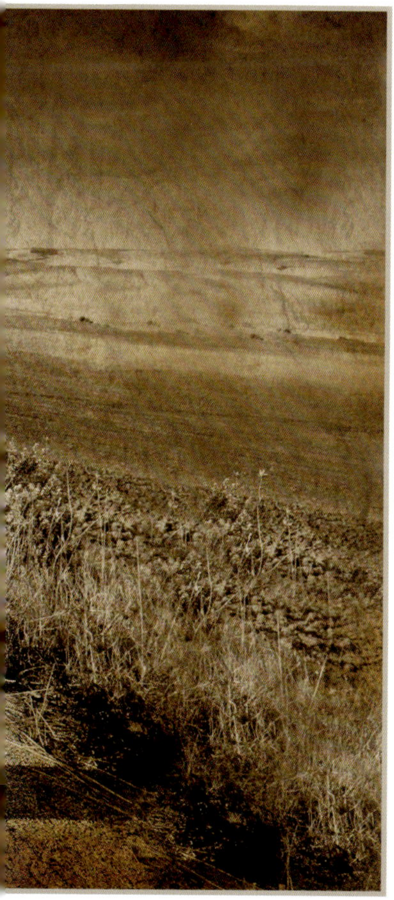

C.S. Lewis wrote in his book *Mere Christianity*, "Everyone thinks forgiveness is a lovely idea until they have something to forgive." Yet Jesus knew that our feelings of anger, resentment and bitterness would always hurt us far more than the person we need to forgive.

When planning the images of Journeys with the Messiah, I wanted to create a photograph that would speak to Jesus' teachings on forgiveness. I had also planned an image that would explore His statement, "If someone slaps you on the right cheek, offer the other cheek or, if a soldier demands that you carry his gear for a mile, carry it two miles" (Matthew 5:39,41).

As I thought about how to depict forgiveness in a photograph, I wondered, "How difficult would it be for a Jew to forgive the Nazis for the horrendous crimes they committed during the Holocaust?" I quickly recalled, "Jesus was a Jew!" And concerning Jesus' instructions, "If a soldier demands that you carry his gear for a mile, carry it two miles," (Matthew 5:41) I thought, "What if the soldier Jesus was referring to was not a first century Roman soldier, but a German Nazi from World War II?" So, I decided to combine these two scenarios into one image depicting forgiveness.

Jesus' instructions for us to let go of our bitterness and resentment through the act of forgiving actually become personal blessings to us. Just saying, "I forgive you," releases us from the intense feelings of bondage and removes the emotional roadblocks that keep us from moving forward in life.

We have no control over the reaction of the person who is forgiven. So, forgiving someone with expectations that they will respond positively may not provide the response we seek. However, we can be assured that in forgiving them, we will be set free. The person who wronged us will no longer have any power over us. This allows us to move on with life and experience God's glorious plans. Theologian Lewis B. Smedes wrote, "To forgive is to set a prisoner free and discover that the prisoner was you."

In the early days of our project, my wife and I were attacked by people who made false accusations. The influence they had on others would cause the cancellation of plans for a major event. Their attack escalated to legal levels requiring the advice of an attorney who believed that we needed to respond in the name of justice. I needed time to ponder what was happening.

It is no coincidence that I was reading the second chapter of First Peter during that time. When I arrived at the twenty-third verse, I was amazed at what was written concerning Jesus' false arrest before His crucifixion: "When they hurled their insults at him, he did not retaliate; when he suffered, he made no threats. Instead, he entrusted himself to Him, who judges justly" (1 Peter 2:23). Sensing that God was speaking directly to me, I phoned our attorney to tell him to disregard their attorney's letter. We would not respond; it was no longer necessary to defend ourselves. We would walk away from their attack and place our case in God's hands. He would judge fairly in His own time.

It was the most challenging thing I have ever done. Emotionally and physically, the injustice of it all seemed unbearable at the time. Yet I can look back with thankfulness that God inspired Peter to write those words that would be a perfectly-timed message to me. Turning to God as "the judge" has been a beacon to guide me in many circumstances since then.

Please do not misread what Jesus is saying. Forgiveness does not necessarily mean there will be no consequences for the guilty party. The man who was forgiven for murdering the woman's daughter was still required to face the consequences of his action. It should also be noted that forgiving someone does not required that we become bosom buddies going forward, though it can repair friendships and start new ones.

Yet, by not forgiving others, we are attempting to usurp God's power as the judge, and He has said, "Vengeance is mine; I will repay" (Deuteronomy 32:35). Plus, Jesus warned in Matthew 6:15, "If you do not forgive others their sins, your Father will not forgive your sins." He also reminds us, "He who is without sin should be the one to cast the first stone" (John 8:7). I can assure you that will not be me!

So, let's put down our rocks and stones of anger and resentment and offer the same grace of forgiveness to others that God offers to us. For as Jesus has spoken, "For if you forgive other people when they sin against you, your heavenly Father will also forgive you" (Matthew 6:14).

We all sin, so we all need forgiveness. As C.S. Lewis pointed out, "To be a Christian means to forgive the inexcusable because God has forgiven the inexcusable in you."

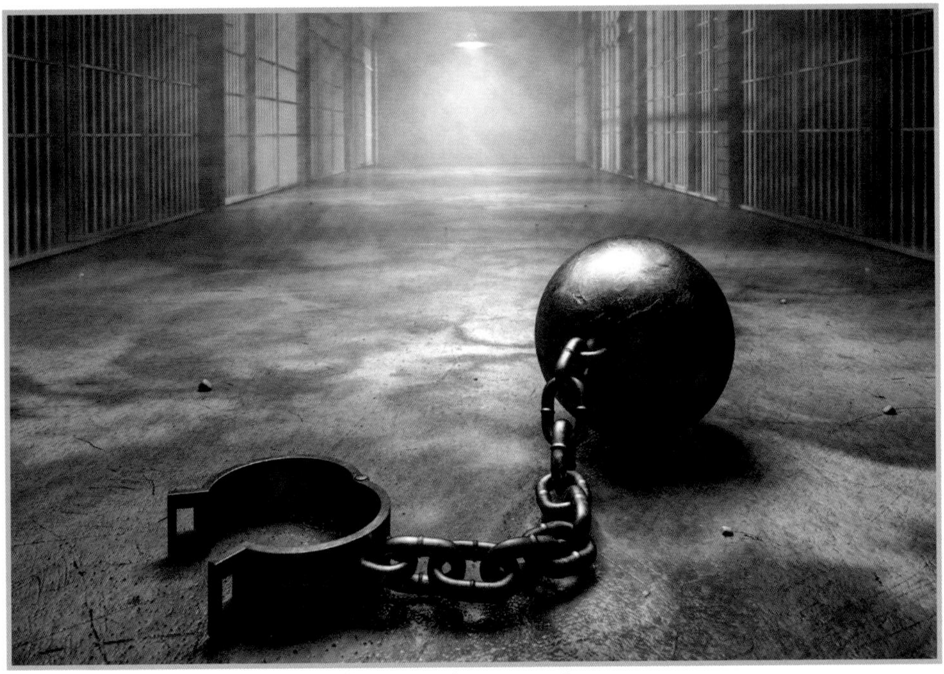

Forgiving others sets us free.

Thoughts to Ponder

View film at ▶ journeyswiththemessiah.org

- C.S. Lewis wrote: "Everyone thinks forgiveness is a lovely idea until they have something to forgive." Jesus understood that forgiving someone for the wrong they have done can be the most challenging experience we will ever encounter? Recall your experience of forgiving someone or the feelings you have when you think about someone you need to forgive.

- Who is the primary benefactor of forgiveness? What do they get in exchange for what they give?

- Lewis B. Smedes wrote: "To forgive is to set a prisoner free and discover that the prisoner was you." Have you made that discovery?

- 1 Peter 2:23 describes the example Jesus set of how to respond when we are offended in any way. Turn back to page186 to read His response. Consider how His response can be your response in the future.

- True or false? A forgiven person is not required to face the consequences of their actions? Does forgiving someone include making them your friend going forward?

- Are there instances when you are allowed to seek vengeance against someone who has done wrong to you? Why or why not? See Deuteronomy 32:35.

- Biblically speaking, are we allowed to choose who to forgive and who not to? Are there consequences for us if we do not forgive? (Re-read Matthew 6: 14-15)

- C.S. Lewis wrote, "To be a Christian means to forgive the inexcusable because God has forgiven the inexcusable in you." Consider that you were once (or still may be) sentenced to death. Ponder C.S. Lewis' statement until you explode into a happy dance of thanksgiving for what God has done.

30

The Winning Hand

Trusting God with the Good Hands and the Bad

View film at ▶ journeyswiththemessiah.org

In 1976, Don Schlitz wrote a song he titled *The Gambler*. Although it was recorded by several artists, Kenny Rogers made the song a mainstream success, winning him a Grammy Award in 1980.

The song is a story of two men — a gambler and a man down on his luck — who meet on a "late-night train to nowhere." The gambler gives advice to his traveling

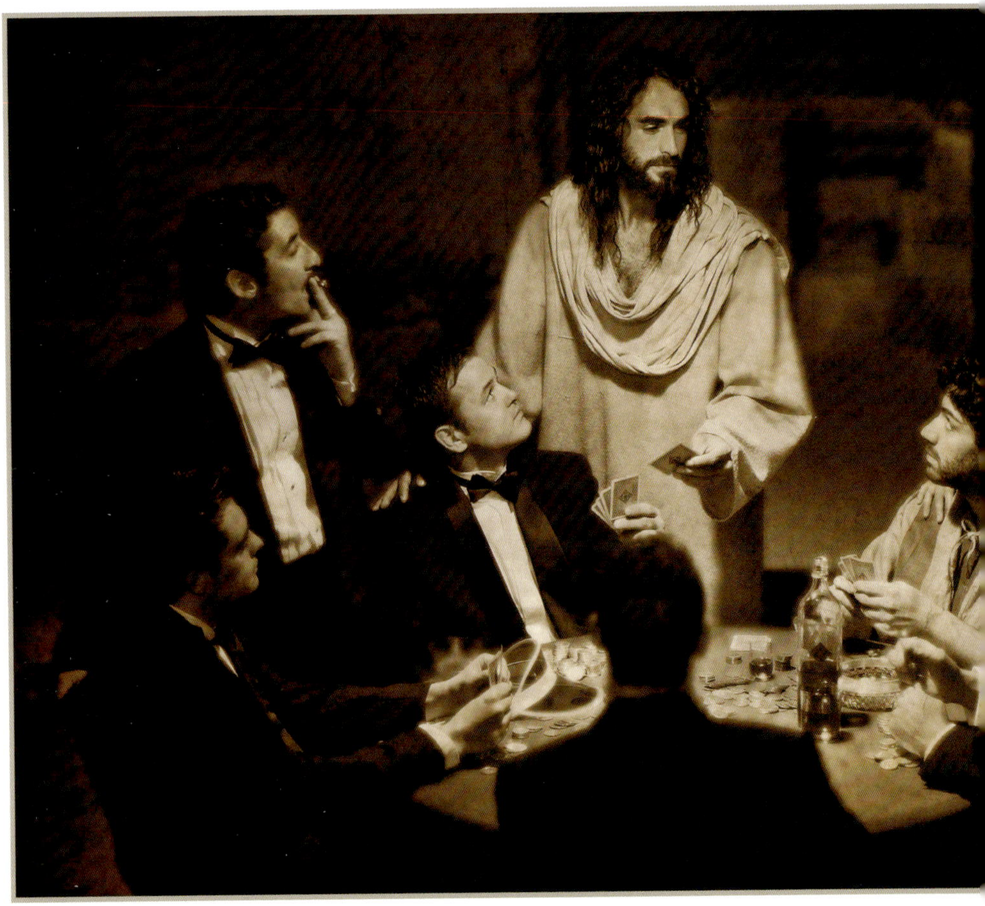

companion, but does so in the form of strategies used in the game of poker — *"You've got to know when to hold them, know when to fold them, know when to walk away, know when to run."*

Poker is one of the oldest and most popular card games in history. It's played with real money in casinos, but it's also a game for family fun using play money and chips. One of the game's strategies is called "bluffing," which is a form of deception. A player will use bluffing to induce others into believing that he has better cards than he actually does, although he may not have the winning hand.

Like the powerful imaging found in good advertising, Journeys with the Messiah's photographs were designed to capture the viewer's interest, hopefully to the point that the viewer will want to read, watch or listen to the message. The message in the image *The Winning Hand* is about choice.

We all have choices, even when it appears we have no choice. My desire was to photograph a poker scene as a way to depict that we do not choose which cards or circumstances are dealt to us in life, but we can choose how to play them or how we will respond. Spiritual gambling begins when we play our cards without seeking God's guidance. The consequences can go as far as to put our lives at stake!

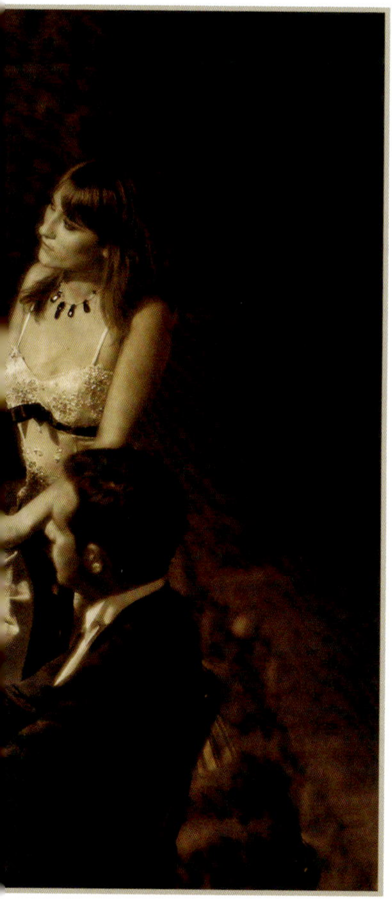

When I began this project, I actually believed that creating this collection of images was something I was doing for God. Over time, He showed me that the project was not about my photographs, it was about my relationship with Him. He was using the talents and resources He had given me, plus my love of photography and travel, to draw me into Him. God is always the one who is pursuing us — pulling us into problems, projects and life circumstances so that He can reveal more of Himself to us.

When the stock and housing markets crashed in 2008, eventually taking our life savings with it, I suddenly needed this project to be a financial success, although that was not our initial goal. I soon found myself struggling as I desperately tried to move this project forward on my own.

Frustration set in as I continued to be dealt cards I didn't like. Without seeking God's wisdom and guidance, I was gambling and couldn't understand why it seemed I was losing at every turn.

Now I look back to see that God allowed these trying times to occur out of His love for me. My self-sufficiency had gotten in the way of our relationship. He needed to remove it so I could surrender to Him as the sovereign Lord of my life. When we seek God, He reveals what we need to know, how much we need to know and when we need to know it.

One evening, I watched a movie where there was a poker scene similar to the one in our image. The betting had narrowed to two men when one of the players pushed his entire stack of poker chips to the center of the table. Then he said, "I'm all in," which meant that He was betting everything on the belief that he was holding the winning hand.

I stared at the television screen and asked God, "Am I all in?"

A similar question was asked by Jesus to a Rich Young Ruler. The wealthy young man had asked Jesus what good thing he must do to get eternal life — to go to Heaven. Jesus challenged the wealthy young man to follow Him, but only after the young man had sold all of his possessions and given the money to the poor (Matthew 19:16-22).

In essence, I think Jesus was asking him, *"Do you want to go all-in with Me? Do you want to bet everything you have, including your life, that I am the one; that I am the way, the only way to the Father in Heaven?"*

This presented a quandary for the young man because he was very wealthy. The scriptures say that he went away sad as he chose his wealth and worldly life over the eternal life Jesus offered.

When we come to the place in our life when we know Jesus is the one; that He is *our winning hand* and with Him we cannot lose, but we do not choose to go all-in, we will go away sad. A life divided in this way can never be whole. The Rich Young Ruler may have kept his wealth and lifestyle, but knowing Jesus and not choosing Him would leave the young ruler forever unfulfilled without eternal life with God.

If you feel the discomfort of living a divided life, one in which you know Jesus is the winning hand but you have not gone all-in, I encourage you to ask God to reveal what is holding you back? Going all-in means a daily commitment to trust God with the good hands and the bad by surrendering them to The One who never loses.

"Know when to hold them and know when to fold them, know when to walk away and know when to run."

That's the advice *The Gambler* offered. Yet, when we allow Jesus to play the hands of our lives — the good and the bad — it doesn't really matter which cards we are dealt. We learn to be content with all of the cards as long as we have gone *all-in* with Him!

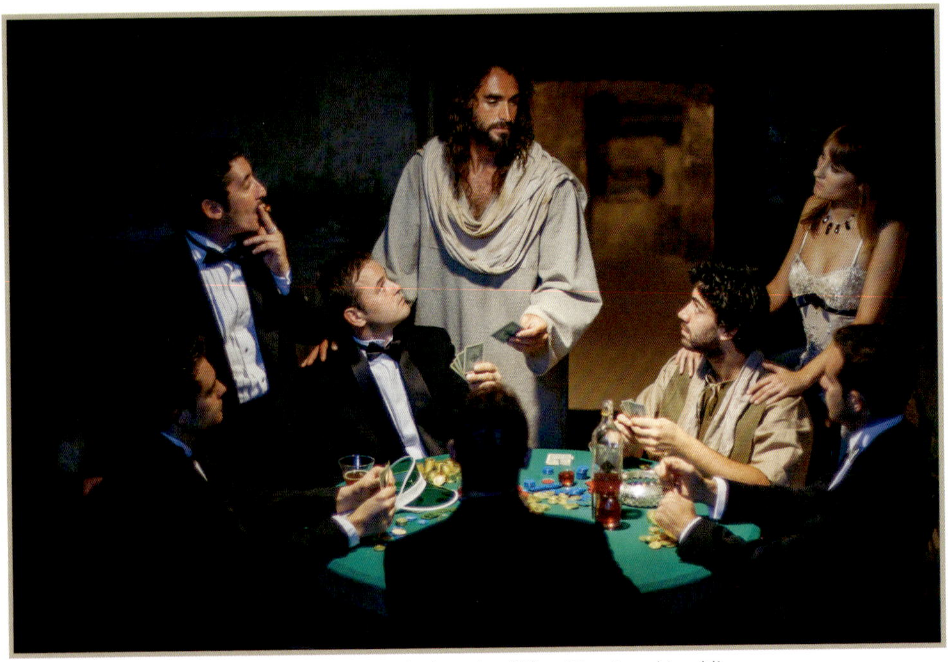

Gambling is playing the hands of life without seeking Him.

Thoughts to Ponder

View film at ▶ journeyswiththemessiah.org

- Consider how the words from *The Gambler* could be substituted for biblical discernment. *"You've got to know when to hold them, know when to fold them, know when to walk away, know when to run."* From God's perspective, could you profit from such advice?

- The difference between bluffing and lying is the intended outcome. Lying states a falsehood, whereas bluffing allows both parties to decide whether they think the other is telling the truth. There are times in life when it's good to know the difference!

- Circumstances are often dealt to us like poker cards — we don't choose which ones we get. Some are good while others are not. Approaching circumstances as they are instead of how we want them to be, allows us to be at peace while we seek God's guidance in how to respond to them.

- "I'm all in!" is a phrase used in poker for betting everything one has in the belief they have the winning hand. Similarly, followers of Christ will say, "I'm sold out for Jesus" if they believe they have surrendered everything — money, possessions, time, dreams — and made them available for His purposes. Consider if you would want to go "all-in," remembering what Jesus said, "With man this is impossible, but with God all things are possible."

- Jesus is our winning hand. We cannot lose when He guides us on how to play each "hand of circumstances" dealt to us. Yet, we all have the tendency to try to play some of hands ourselves. Consider making a conscious decision that, everytime the cards are dealt, whether good hands or bad, you will turn to Him for guidance.

31

Vacancy

A Cross for Everyone

View film at ▶ journeyswiththemessiah.org

The Romans were not the first civilization to devise barbaric ways to execute their fellow man. Developing unique ways to inflict pain on each other goes back to just after God banished Adam and Eve from the Garden of Eden. Still, the Romans were unusually skilled at devising methods for executing people. Their techniques included beheading, burning alive and crucifixion — whereby they tied or nailed

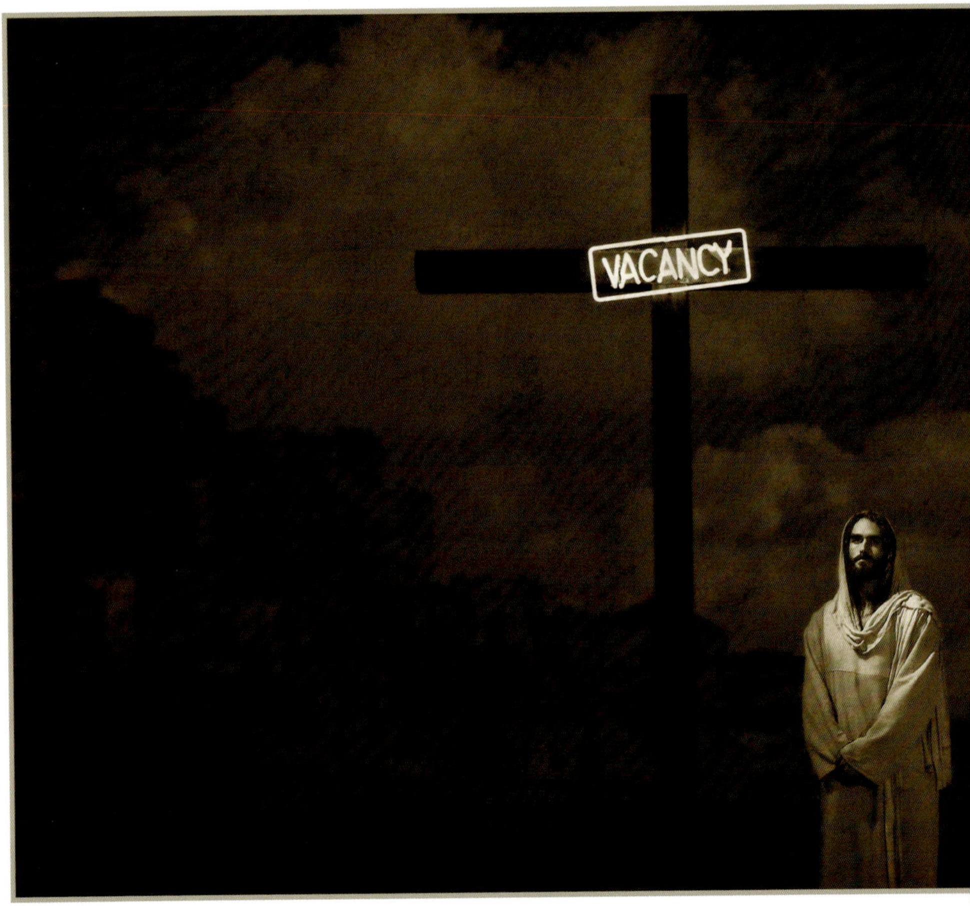

a person to a cross. There was one method so horrific that I will probably have nightmares for just having read about it!

There are many resources where you can read all the gory details of crucifixion. However, I created the image *Vacancy* not to tell how Jesus died but to show how we can live!

When I was in my early forties, my dad, brother and I took a whitewater rafting trip on the Rogue River in Oregon. It was an exciting but exhausting three-day trip following several days of travel on the Oregon coast. When our trip came to its end, I dropped my dad and brother at the local airport and began driving toward Montana, where I would begin a fashion photo shoot four days later.

On the evening of my second day of driving, I arrived in Coeur d'Alene, Idaho to find no hotel rooms available within a hundred miles. Every direction I turned, the signs read, "No Vacancy!" It was already late and I was tired, so trying to make it to Montana that night would have been foolish.

As I sat outside a lakeside restaurant pondering my predicament, a young couple walked by. I asked, "By any chance have you heard of any place with a vacancy?" To my surprise, they answered, "Yes," and pointed to an inn across the lake. I awoke the next morning to a heavenly view of the lake and mountains. It was such a pleasant place, I wanted to stay forever.

When I began planning these images, I wanted to create a photograph of the crucifixion of Jesus, yet not the conventional one of Jesus on a cross. I'm not sure when or where the idea of a cross with a neon vacancy sign came to me. However, there were many times that I had thought back to that miraculous night in Idaho, the night I found a vacancy when "No Vacancy" was the only message in sight.

Although the cross is the instrument on which Jesus died, for Christians it has become the symbol by which we live. After all, who but God could take the cross, a barbaric tool of execution, and turn it into a symbol of hope and faith, a signature representing all that is good and righteous in the world?

There is a wealth of understanding to be discovered through Jesus' death on the cross. In the historical accounts of Jesus' birth, Mary and Joseph arrived in Bethlehem to find no place to stay...no room in the inn...No Vacancy! Yet, thirty-three brief years later, there was plenty of room for Jesus on the cross as He was nailed to it.

His death announces there is room at the cross, and in His Kingdom, for you and me. When we arrive at the foot of His cross, we learn to die to our own needs while learning to live for the needs of others. We learn to die to wanting everything our way and learn to follow a better way...His way. And, we learn to die to the darkness of this world while He opens our eyes to the light of God's world.

Jesus fulfills more than three hundred Old Testament prophecies that detail His coming as The Messiah. In the 2,000 years since then, we have accumulated an abundance of documented evidence testifying to His death and resurrection from death. As Josh McDowell points out in his book by the same name, "It is evidence that demands a verdict."

Consequently, for anyone who has examined the evidence and then states they are still waiting on The Messiah, I would have to respectfully respond, "If you cannot see that He has already come, it is unlikely that you would recognize Him when He does!" Yet, even with this rich profusion of evidence, there will always be the need for faith.

The Book of Luke records a story about an encounter that occurred on the Sunday after Jesus' crucifixion as two men were traveling on the road to the village of Emmaus about seven miles from Jerusalem. While they talked with each other about all that happened regarding Jesus' death and rumors of His resurrection, Jesus himself came up and walked along with them. The scriptures state they were kept from recognizing Him. He asked them what they were discussing? They replied, "About Jesus of Nazareth" (Luke 24:13-19).

The two men told their new traveling companion how the chief priest and rulers had crucified Jesus. They were disheartened as they believed that Jesus was the Messiah who would redeem Israel. Then they told Him the exciting news about the report of the empty tomb (Luke 24:19-24).

Jesus said to them, "How foolish you are, and how slow to believe all that the prophets have spoken! Did not the Messiah have to suffer these things and then enter his glory? And beginning with Moses and the Prophets, he explained to them what was said in the Scriptures concerning Himself." (Luke 24:25-27).

When they arrived in Emmaus (still not recognizing that it was Jesus), they urged Him to stay for the evening and dinner. At the table, as the stranger broke the bread, the two men recognized that it was Jesus who was with them. Then, at once, He disappeared. The two men asked one another other, "Were not our hearts burning within us while He talked with us on the road and opened the Scriptures to us?" (Luke 24:28-32). For me, this scripture is convincing and convicting!

You see, I can tell you what I know about Jesus and show you the evidence about Him that has been revealed to me. I can give you great books by brilliant men who know far more about Him than I do, and I can read biblical accounts of Him to you forever. However, in the end, I know what I know because, like the two men on the road to Emmaus, "my heart burns within me" with what I know is true.

As the renowned newscaster David Brinkley said about his stellar career in broadcasting, "Our only real purpose in life, and in work, was to tell people what we knew to be true." It's the same for me and millions of others living now and in the past. We have examined the facts with our minds and pondered them in our hearts and have come to only one possible conclusion: Jesus is the Messiah! He is the Son of God who was crucified to death, buried and was raised from death by God. It all happened just as He said it would, showing that only through Him can we escape eternal death to have eternal life with God in Heaven.

Although millions of people worldwide believe this to be true, we have great respect for all those who do not. Therefore, we will make no attempts to sell them our belief or beat them into submission. We will not ask them to fall on their knees before Jesus and declare Him as Lord and Savior. We will tell them what we know, show them the evidence and provide a good answer for the hope we have. Then, they and God can decide what to do with it!

Jesus, the man, died on the cross. Jesus, the Savior of the world, is alive and well. And, just like my night in Idaho when a vacancy opened up with a heavenly view, there's a vacancy available for you in God's Kingdom, where you can in fact, stay forever!

Please make sure you have your reservations booked now!

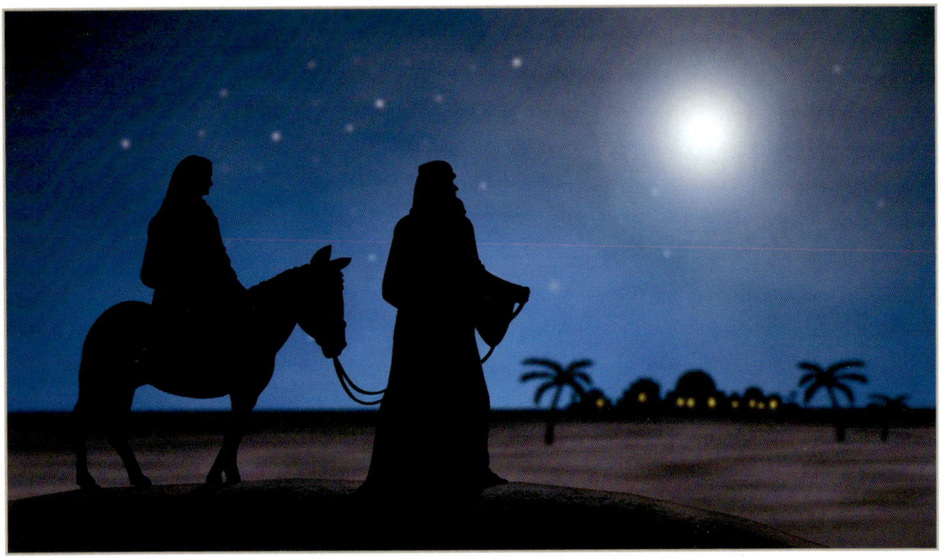

There is a room waiting for us at The Father's Inn.

Thoughts to Ponder

View film at ▶ journeyswiththemessiah.org

- Violence is part of our world's history, with the twentieth century being the most violent of all time. Everyone is affected by it. However, violence is less an issue of the times and more an issue of the heart. It is an issue that will be changed by blood, but only by the shed blood of Jesus Christ!
- The cross was a Roman instrument of torture, suffering, and defeat. In the fourth century, shortly after Emperor Constantine converted to Christianity and abolished crucifixion as a punishment, the cross became a symbol of God's Son and continues to be a symbol of triumph and salvation. Next time you see a cross, take time to consider it for what it is!
- I am thankful that God would allow me to tell this story through a neon vacancy sign attached to an old cross. Jesus died on a cross so that we may have eternal life. Review three ways we can die at the cross and three for which we live (p198).
- There has been more written about Jesus than any other subject in all of history. Yet, even with this abundance of evidence, people reject Him without knowing anything about Him. Consider reading *More Than a Carpenter* by Josh McDowell (over 15 million in print). It is one of the simplest, non-confrontational, and inexpensive ways you can strengthen and share your faith.*
- Please read the story of the men on the road to Emmaus and picture yourself with them (Luke 24:25-32). Allow your heart to "burn within you" as one who is privileged to know the truth of Jesus.

* *Best deal as of 11/11/20 at ChristianBook.com $4.99 or 30-pack for $2.17 each.*

32

Watch Your Step

Avoiding Religious Ditches

View film at ▶ journeyswiththemessiah.org

My desire to be artistically creative appears to have been a part of my life all along. Yet I was not consciously aware of it until I discovered photography in my early twenties. I recall the day I watched a friend develop prints from photographs. It was fascinating to watch the images appear like magic as they were immersed in the trays of chemicals. With Christmas just around the corner, I splurged on a personal gift — a 35mm camera and two lenses. I was mesmerized as I looked through the viewfinder to see the world from a different perspective. It was not long before I knew that I had an eye for photography!

After college, I accepted a sales job in New York with a leading brand of men's clothing. As a traveling salesman, my camera was my constant companion as I traveled the highways and byways of Georgia and South Carolina. The highlight of each trip was getting home to my darkroom to develop the photos I had captured along the way.

Several years into my job, our company created a small seasonal collection that deviated from the traditional styles for which our company was known. Although I had seen the new styles at a fashion show…and liked them, I felt my conservative retailers would not feel the same. So I had an idea!

I invited a friend to model the samples while I photographed him on a beach near my home. After developing prints of the best images, I put them in a binder and went on the road to show the new line of clothing to my clients. After seeing my samples and then objecting to the non-traditional styles, I opened my binder of photos to show them how great the new collection looked when worn correctly as part of an outfit.

After several weeks, the president of our company called to ask if there was anything special I was doing to sell these new styles. He explained that sales from the rest of our sales force were not good!

Immediately I thought, "I could make these photo binders to help other salesmen."

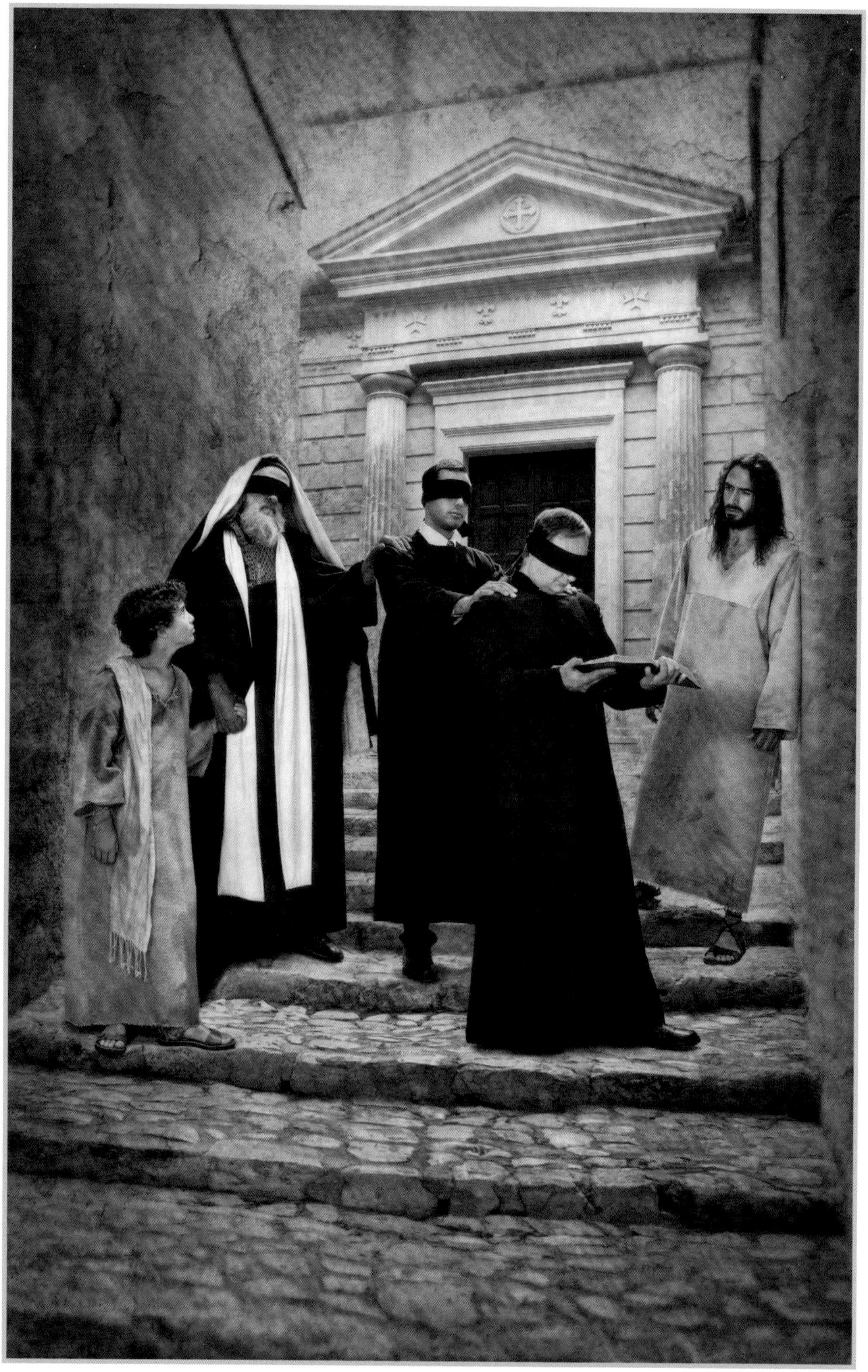

Then I thought, "I could make binders of photos for the salesmen of other companies." Finally, I landed on the idea that I could make them for other companies for all of their salesmen! After doing the math and coming up with a simple business plan, I resigned from my secure and prestigious job and headed off to New York to sell my new "Visual Marketing Program" to fashion companies.

As if almost by accident, I had combined my knowledge and love of the fashion industry with my limited knowledge of photography to become a fashion photographer and producer of fashion marketing, albeit in the simplest of ways. Although I struggled the first year, I still sprang out of bed each day to pursue my passion until my idea finally caught on.

Over time, my initial concept for binders with photos expanded to include brochures, then catalogs for J. Crew and advertising campaigns for Izod, Nautica and others. I traveled to beautiful and exciting locations all over the United States and around of the world.

As the years went by, the responsibilities that came with running an ad agency began to overshadow my initial desire to excel as a photographic artist.

Tabloids and celebrity magazines are filled with stories of actors and actresses, musicians and others who began their careers doing what they loved to do, only to get lost in the process that goes with it. Human nature is seldom content or satisfied —we want more! We want to climb to the top, be celebrated stars, or become the head of our own company. The climb often comes at a price!

Whether you are a mom, business executive, rock star or school teacher, burnout looms large. At a workshop I attended at his church in Albequerque, Father Richard Rohr say, *"Your gift can become your sin,"* or as I like to say, "We get tied up in the process and lose sight of our purpose." I started out with the purpose of being a creative photographer. Over time, the process turned me into a corporate manager.

At the time of Jesus' ministry in the first century, the Pharisees were the religious party who spoke for most Jewish people. Unfortunately, they made up hundreds of rules and regulations that went beyond the Commandments and laws of Moses. These "Pharisaic" laws became a crushing religious burden on the Jewish people and this was of deep concern to Jesus. He rebuked the Pharisees, saying their laws were a burden and they were not doing anything to help their people (Matthew 23).

The New Testament has many accounts of Jesus confronting and being confronted by the Pharisees. He told the crowds to be careful to do everything the Pharisees told them to do, *"but do not do what they [the Pharisees] do, for they do not practice what they preach"* (Matthew 23:3). Jesus called them hypocrites for telling the people to follow the laws which they did not practice.

On several occasions, the Pharisees tried to trick Jesus with questions about divorce, adultery, taxes and the legality of helping someone on the Sabbath. With each answer Jesus gave, it became more apparent to them that He spoke with authority that could only have come from God. When they asked Jesus why His disciples broke with tradition by not washing their hands before eating, Jesus responded, "A man is not defiled by what enters his mouth, but by what comes out of it." (Matthew 15:1-2,10).

When Jesus' disciples told Him that the Pharisees were offended by His teachings, Jesus said to disregard them, "They were like the blind leading the blind and they would fall into a pit" (Matthew 15:12,14). The Pharisees had become absorbed in the process of religion and had lost sight of their purpose, which was to lead people into a closer relationship with God.

During this time, people were watching for signs of the promised Messiah. If Jesus was the Messiah, the large crowds that would follow Him could overpower the authority of the Pharisees. If the Pharisees let things get out of hand and could no longer control the Jewish people, the Roman authorities would respond by significantly limiting their power.

> *"Then the chief priests and the Pharisees gathered a council and said, 'What shall we do? For this Man works many signs. If we let Him alone like this, everyone will believe in Him, and the Romans will come and take away both our place and nation.'"* —John 11:47-48

Jesus' threat to their power and their way of life was of great concern, so they plotted to kill Him!

Watch Your Step was inspired by Jesus' statement that the Pharisees were like "the blind leading the blind." It depicts how power and authority — and the wealth that usually comes with it — can cause people to lose sight of their purpose as they get tangled up in life's processes.

The Pharisees probably started out with a sincere and humble purpose of helping people in their relationship with God. However, many of them allowed religion, power and privilege to cause them to lose sight of God's purpose.

In similar ways, there are those in our religious communities that have allowed the process of acting religious to overcome Christ's purpose. As Father Richard Rohr said in one of his daily meditations, *Jesus as Paradox*, "We've made Jesus a religion instead of following Him on the path that takes us to Eternity. The shift has made us a religion of belonging and believing instead of one of transformation."

Jesus came to invite us to know Him through a personal relationship and then make Him known to others. He offers us a revolutionary journey, one in which our personal walk through life will become a personal walk with Him as He leads us home to Eternity with God.

With our focus on Jesus and our compass pointed to Heaven, we are on the right path and in step with God's purpose. Just "*watch your step*" while you're on your way!

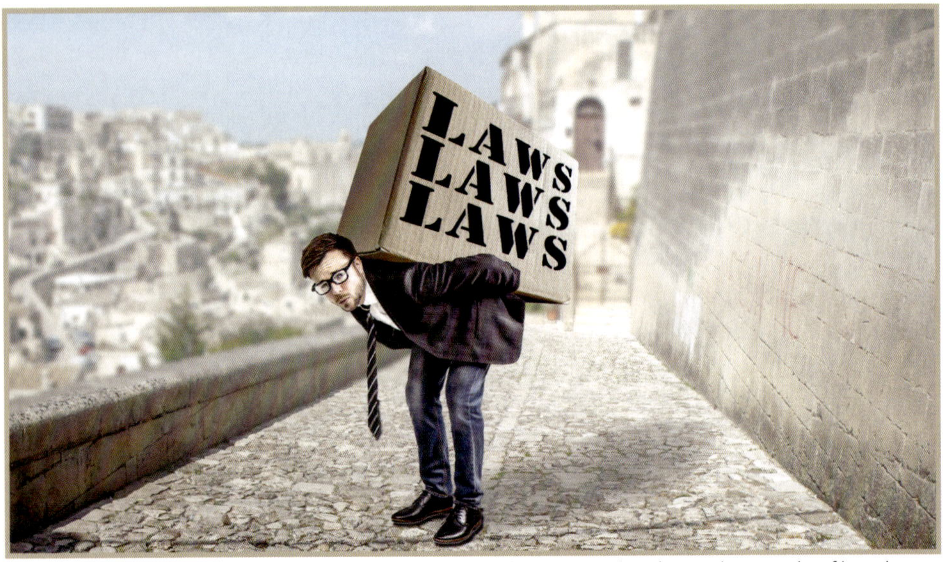

The Pharisees had created so many laws they had become a burden to the people of Israel

Thoughts to Ponder

View film at ▶ journeyswiththemessiah.org

- Looking back through and enjoying the thousands of photos in my files reminds me of my purpose in becoming a photographer. Can you identify with "getting tied up in the process" of your work while "losing sight of the purpose" for which you started it?"

- Father Richard Rohr said, "Your gift can become your sin." Consider God's gifts to you, such as your creative talent, being a good leader, a manager of people, effective educator, entrepreneurship and so on. Ponder how you have used these gifts.

- Jesus called them hypocrites for telling the people to follow the laws which they did not practice. We see similar things in our government, but also in our homes where "Do as I say, not as I do!" may be a popular directive!

- Jesus said, "A man is not defiled by what enters his mouth, but by what comes out of it." Proverbs 21:23 says, "He who guards his mouth and his tongue keeps himself from calamity." Thus, what comes out of our mouths can build up or tear down, educate or criticize, delight or destroy. It seems God has a purpose for our mouths beyond eating!

- The Pharisee's obsession with the process of creating religious laws caused them to lose sight of their purpose of guiding people to a closer relationship with God. Jesus told the Pharisees (and surely us as well) that when the process of what we do leads us away from the purpose of why we do it, we can become like "the blind leading the blind." We will fall into a ditch [of undesired circumstances].

- Many people are turned away by religion rather than by Jesus' teachings. Jesus is not a religion but our "guide for transformation" on our path to Eternity. Consider this when sharing your faith with others.

33

Without a Doubt

Evidence of the Resurrection

View film at ▶ journeyswiththemessiah.org

A marketing tactic of new car dealers is to entice potential customers to lease cars by offering low monthly payments. In the fine print of their advertisements, they also note a large sum of money that will be "due at signing." Referred to as "capital reduction," this large amount reduces the monthly payments, making the payment appear more enticing. However, when the total cost of the lease — total lease payments plus amount due at signing — is divided by the number of months in the lease, it reveals that the actual cost is much higher than the lease payment suggests.

Every direction we turn today, someone is offering a deal — 30% off, 50% off, 70% off. But off of what? We live in a deceptive world where this has become the norm, not the exception. Moreover, the people who deceive us often do so by encouraging us to deceive ourselves.

Too often, people do not examine the evidence before making a decision. By the same standard, many people do not know the facts before stating an opinion about things. I am amazed at the number of internet articles forwarded to me without the sender considering whether the article is accurate or even truthful.

In the Apostle Paul's First Letter to the Corinthians, he wrote, "When I was a child, I talked like a child, I thought like a child, I reasoned like a child. When I became a man, I put the ways of childhood behind me." (1 Corinthians 13:11). Paul was saying that, once we have grown up, we must first examine the evidence of any situation and then respond based on the evidence. We must stop acting like children by reacting without considering the facts.

Unfortunately, even when there have been eyewitnesses to an event, people will still view the event through the filters of their own beliefs, regardless of whether their beliefs are supported by evidence. For example, some people believe that President John F. Kennedy's 1963 assassination was a conspiracy. There are people who believe that the jets that flew into the World Trade Centers on September 11, 2001 were part of our own government's plot, and others do not believe that America's astronauts walked on the surface of the moon.

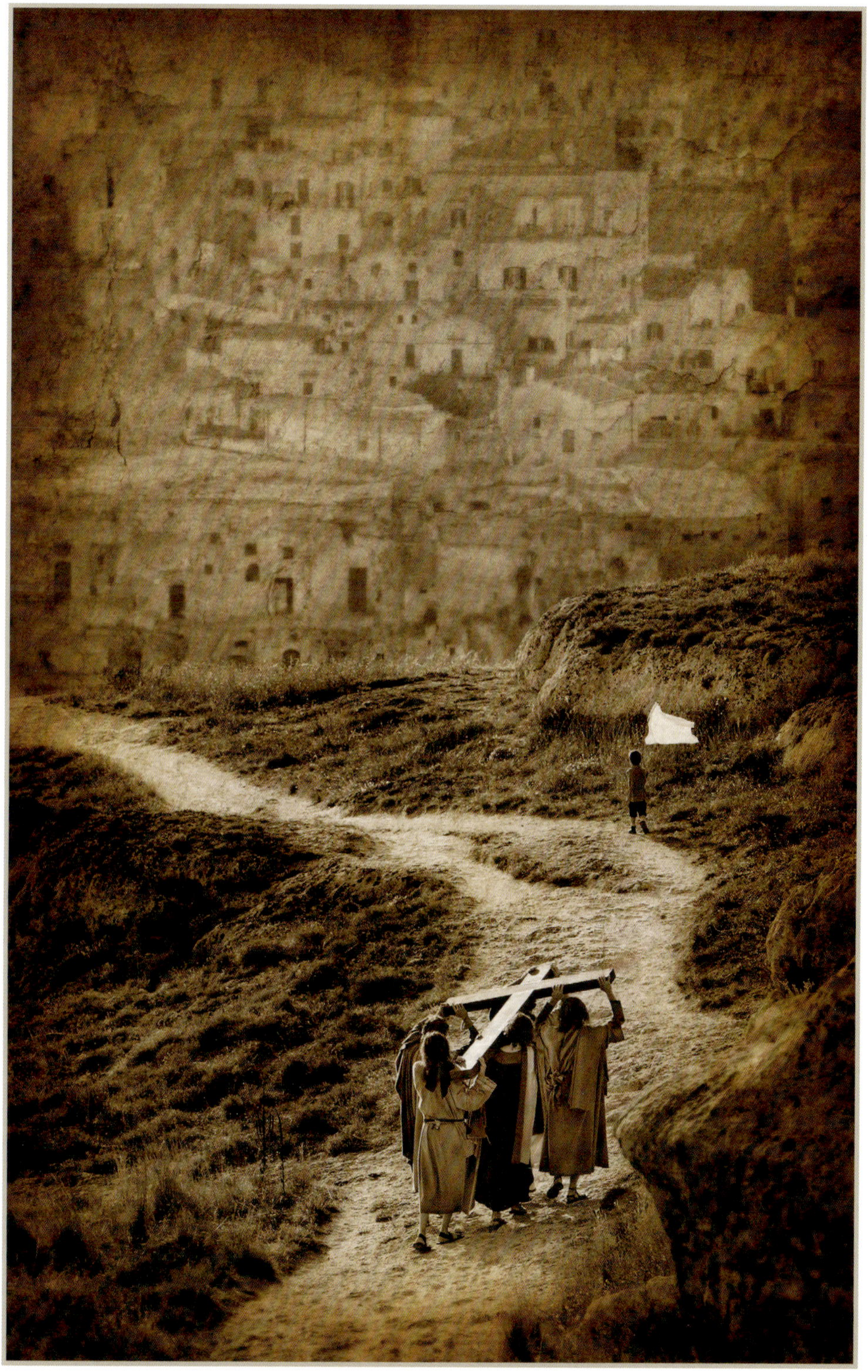

Furthermore, it is difficult to convince these people to change their minds despite the mountains of evidence that contradict their views.

Our perceptions can influence what we believe! This is often the case surrounding the life of Jesus. Many scholars believe the Old Testament books of the Bible point to a Messiah that God would send to save us from our own destruction and restore our relationship with God. These scholars interpret the meanings of passages from Psalms, Zechariah, Micah and Isaiah to point to Jesus of Nazareth as the Messiah.

In the New Testament, the books of Matthew, Mark, Luke and John are accounts of Jesus' life from birth to execution to His resurrection from death. Additional books record the testimonies of eyewitnesses who saw Jesus alive after seeing Him crucified to death on a cross. Yet, the Jewish leaders of Jesus' time, regardless of their motives, said that Jesus' resurrection did not occur; that the disciples stole His body! Yet no evidence exists — now or then — to support their theory.

The Roman government ruled Jerusalem during the time that Jesus lived. Jews were given a lot of freedom as long as the Jewish leaders kept order. Jesus dying on a cross and then rising from the dead three days later — if true — would create disorder as people would turn to this Messiah for authority rather than the Jewish leaders. Civil unrest could arise because of the hope it would provide to the people. In turn, it would result in serious consequences for the religious elite whose power would be removed by the Romans.

Some Jews were eyewitnesses to Jesus' resurrection and many became followers of Jesus in the days ahead. However, most Jews were told that He had not risen from the dead. That explanation became a tradition among Jews that has been carried forward for over 2,000 years. Jews and other religions will admit to Jesus being a great teacher, just not to being The Messiah.

Scholars have put together the writings of first-century historians to both support and deny the case for Jesus' resurrection. Historians and other scholars use detailed criteria for determining a document's legitimacy, including the number of existing manuscripts. The documents that carry more weight than any others in history are the Books of the New Testament. They have more complete or partial manuscripts still in existence today than any other ancient writing.

There are approximately 5,800 Greek manuscripts and a total of 24,000 when various other ancient language manuscripts are added in. The next closest document considered accurate is *Homer's Iliad*, estimated between 650 and 1,500 manuscripts. The New Testament documents were probably written during the 70-90 years after Jesus' crucifixion. This means there would have been many people still living at that time who could dispute the writings if they were not true. Yet, no credible historical evidence exists that contest them.

The bottom line is that there is more documented evidence attesting to the truth of Jesus' resurrection than to any event in ancient history!

After Jesus was nailed to a cross, His disciples, who believed that He was the Messiah, must have looked at each other and said, "Hey, we called this one wrong, let's get out of here!" They believed that Jesus was the Messiah and now they had doubts. They knew the authorities would come after them and they hid in fear for their lives.

Yet no documents have ever been presented that show evidence that any of the disciples ever recanted their faith. Several historical records suggest that all of the disciples, except John, were eventually martyred for believing in Jesus. So, **if they had doubts after His crucifixion, something must have happened to change them!**

In planning this project, I wondered, "How could I depict the evidence of Jesus' resurrection in a photograph?" The answer came to me in Matthew 16:24: "Jesus told his disciples, 'If anyone would come after me, let him deny himself and take up his cross and follow me.'" So, in my image, I would show the disciples literally carrying their cross as they followed Him — returning to Jerusalem to almost certain death. They had seen Jesus alive after His death and they could now be bold in their faith and go forward *"without a doubt!"*

Some people are willing to die for what they believe, but few are ready to die for what they know is a lie!

The Book of Acts supports this premise in an account of the Apostles Peter and John. After being arrested by the Jewish authorities and placed in jail for healing a man in Jesus' name, Peter and John were questioned by the Council while the man they healed stood by.

"By what power or what name did you do this?" the Council asked (Acts 4:5).

Peter and John responded, "By the name of Jesus Christ of Nazareth, whom you crucified but whom God raised from the dead and by whom this man stands before you healed" (Acts 4:10)."

When they saw Peter and John's courage and realized that they were unschooled, ordinary men, they were astonished and took note that these men had been with Jesus. But since they could see the man who had been healed standing there with them, there was nothing they could say" (Acts 4:13-14). So, they decided to let them go but commanded Peter and John not to speak or teach in Jesus' name (Acts 4:18).

Yet Peter and John were not willing to drop it. So, in response to being told they could not teach or heal in the name of Jesus, they replied, "Judge for yourselves whether it is right in God's sight to listen to you rather than God. [As for us], we cannot stop speaking about what we have seen and heard" (Acts 4:19-20).

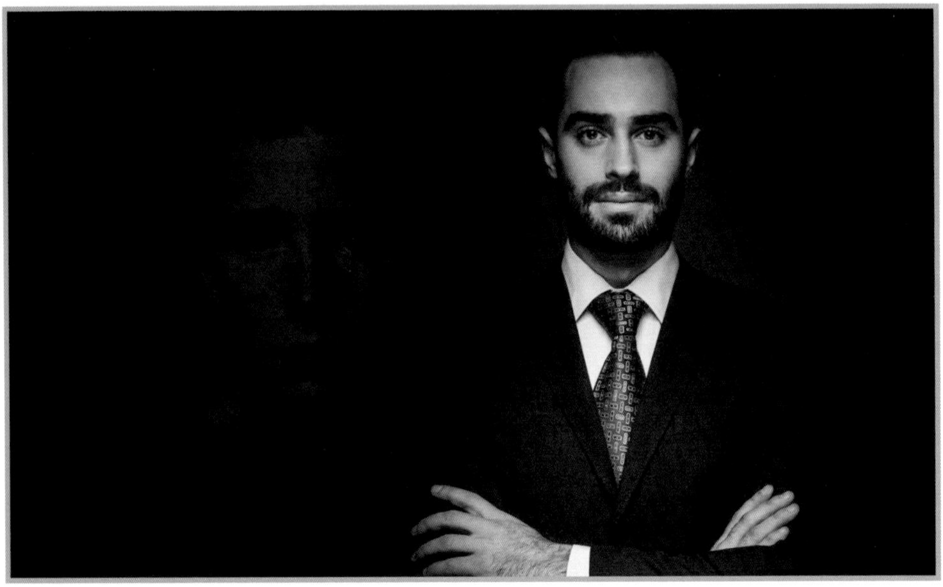

1 Corinthians 13:11 "When I became a man I put away childish things."

What do we do with all of this information attesting to the historical account of Jesus' death and resurrection? Do we react to opinions as a child or respond as adults after examining the evidence? If the story of Jesus Christ is in fact correct and He died so that you and I can have eternal life with God in Heaven (after our time has ended here), this is a serious matter! It's a matter of life and death!

I have examined the evidence and have come to a conclusion. But of more significance, I have looked into the mirror to see I have changed. I'm a new person since I encountered Him. The old life is gone and a new life began, of which there is no logical explanation other than the supernatural change Jesus has caused in me!

Ultimately, everyone must make their choice! As for me, like Peter and John, I just cannot stop talking about what I've seen and heard!

Thoughts to Ponder

View film at ▶ journeyswiththemessiah.org

- With instant access to virtually unlimited information, we should be a society who always examines the evidence before making a decision or stating an opinion.
- The Apostle Paul wrote in 1 Corinthians 13: "When I was a child, I talked like a child, I thought like a child, I reasoned like a child. When I became a man, I put the ways of childhood behind me." A child's nature is to "react" to situations without thinking them through to logical conclusions. An adult's responsibility is to observe situations, gather information and then "respond" appropriately after thinking them through to logical conclusions. Consider how peaceful the world could be if politicians, heads of nations, street gangs and you and me took time to think things through to logical conclusions and responded appropriately instead of reacting.
- There is more documented evidence attesting to the truth of Jesus' resurrection from death than to any event in ancient history! Muslims, Jews, atheists and many others do not accept this truth. However, they hold as tightly to their beliefs as I do to mine. Regardless, Jesus said that we are to tell the world the Good News, and 1 Peter 3:15 tells us to be prepared to answer everyone about the reason for the hope we have [in Jesus] and do this with gentleness and respect. We can do this in the comfort of knowing that everything else is between them and God.
- Imagine yourself as a disciple of Jesus who has been with Him for several years. You are sure that He is the Messiah. Yet, your hopes are crushed with His crucifixion. Now what? Stop to ponder what that might feel like.
- Then, as a sad and frightened disciple of Jesus after his crucifixion, you hear that He has risen from death; that He is alive and well after His brutal death. Now what? Ponder what that feels like.

The movie, "Risen," with Joseph Fiennes can help us imagine life with Jesus and the disciples in the days after His resurrection. I highly recommend it for a wonderful spiritual experience! It can be streamed from On Demand as of 2020.

34

You Feed Them

God's Unique Plan to Feed the World

View film at ▶ journeyswiththemessiah.org

If I offered ten loaves of bread to you on the condition that you give one to someone who is hungry, would you do it? Of course you would! What if I give you ten one-hundred-dollar bills with the agreement that you give one of them to someone who needs financial help? Would you agree? Would you still give one if there were no conditions? Or, let's say that I could get your employer to increase your salary by ten times, but on the condition that you agreed to give one-tenth of your raise to

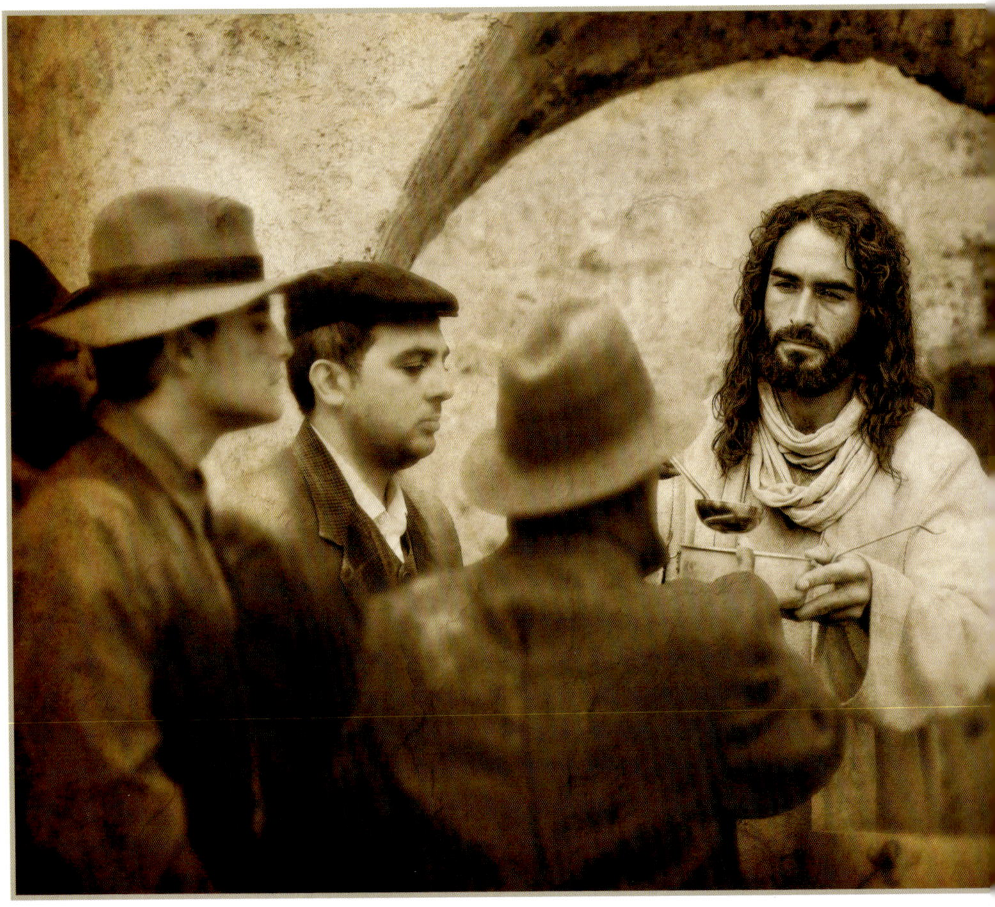

charities and people in need. Would you do it...even if there were no conditions?

One of the most successful television news programs in history was *The Huntley-Brinkley Report*. In an interview with David Brinkley years after the show ended. He said, "When television news began, they trusted us completely, and should have because none of us had any ax to grind; none of us had any political ambitions. Our only real purpose in life and work was to tell people what we knew to be true." He went on to say, "When we did the news, it lasted only fifteen minutes because there are only fifteen minutes of actual news in the world each day." If Brinkley was right—that there is only fifteen minutes of "actualy news" each day, then our 24-hour news channels would have a lot of space to fill.

Imagine a scenario in which the 24-hour news channels could cover only the good news taking place around the world each day? Twenty-four hours might not be enough time to get it all in! Organizations like Samaritan's Purse, Convoy of Hope, the American Red Cross and thousands of other organizations and individuals feed the hungry, care for the sick, educate the uneducated, build homes, schools and infrastructure across a broad spectrum of people throughout the world. Firefighters, police officers, soldiers, National Guard and others help protect and save people through acts of kindness and heroism. All of the people of these organizations are helping to make our world a better place.

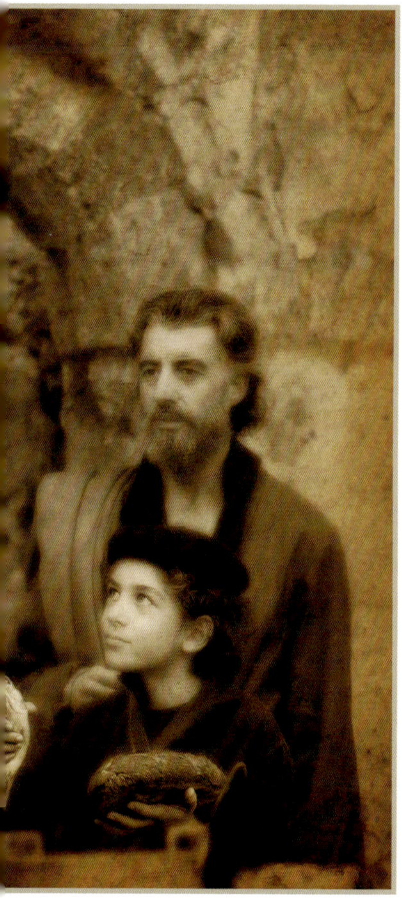

What if we had a steady stream of stories of people helping others? Might it rub off on us?

The Bible notes two occasions when Jesus performed miracles in which He fed thousands of people with an amount of food that, in reality, could feed only a few. Jesus' *Feeding of the 5000* is the only miracle, aside from the resurrection, recorded in all four Gospels. We must assume there is something special we need to learn from it.

The *Feeding of the 5000* took place in a remote area where Jesus went to be alone after the death of his friend, John the Baptist. However, the crowds followed Him, so Jesus began teaching.

When it was getting late in the day, Jesus' disciples came to Him, suggesting that Jesus send the crowds away to buy food and find lodging in nearby towns (Matthew 14:15). Jesus responded to them with a better idea. He replied, "They do not need to go away. You give them something to eat" (Matthew 14:16).

I would expect that their response was something like, "Do what? We have only five loaves of bread and two fish! You expect us to feed 5,000 people!" Those familiar with this story know that Jesus miraculously fed the crowd with what they had — five loaves of bread and two fish (Matthew 14:17).

Through this story, Jesus is clearly telling you and me that we are to feed the crowds with what we have. This begs the question, "What portion of our 'loaves and fishes' are we giving to charities, especially the ones that feed the crowds?"

The answer was not easy to define. However, it appears that the average giving for all Americans is around 3% of their incomes. However, the number is misleading because more than 40% do not give anything! It's interesting that the rich give more than the average and even more interesting, that low-income families give even more as a percentage of income! That's amazing! Those with the least give the most!

In the Old Testament books of the Bible, the giving standard commanded by God is called "the tithe" and represents 10% (Genesis 14:20, 28:22). Four hundred years before Jesus, God spoke through the prophet, Malachi, scolding Israel's people for failing to keep His commandment of giving the tithe. God said, "Will a mere mortal rob God? Yet, you rob me." The people of Israel respond, "How are we robbing you?" God replied, "By not keeping my directions for the giving of "tithes and offerings" (Malachi 3:8).

God provides for all of the world's needs. At different times He gives more to some than He gives to others. Still, at all times, He commands each of us to bring back a percentage to Him, as Malachi explains, "So that He may put it into His storehouse, so that there may be food in His house" (Malachi 3:10).

God's command was directed at the Israelites who had failed to bring the tithe into the storehouse. The tithe in question was 10% of food, including grain, livestock, crops, etcetera. The purpose of the food was to feed the Levites who were on temple duty. The storehouse was not the temple, but a barn-like structure where food could be stored.

This scripture is not a direct command that we give 10% of our income to the church. However, I believe there is much more we can gain in learning about it?

Fast forward 400 years.

In the New Testament, the principle for giving is to "give voluntarily." There is no percentage or amount directly commanded of us. Considering that at least 800 million people worldwide suffer from food shortage, inaccessible medical care, clean water, education and a host of other issues, I question if we are adequately disciplined to "give voluntarily," and more, will we give generously? Since Americans give only 3% of their incomes and over 40% do not give anything, the facts suggest the answer is "No!" Giving is not taken seriously by the majority of people, Christians included!

So, what does this mean for the people Jesus referred to as,"the poor who will always be among us?" (John 12:8). The answer: They go hungry! They go without, because as God said, we "rob Him" of what He intended for them when we give back less than the amount needed to care for them.

God is the source of our provision and we are His source for filling the storehouse from the amount He has provided to us. Again, people go hungry and have unmet needs when we fail to return the portion God intended for those in need. If you are blessed to have enough or more than enough, it's not a big deal. If you have less than you need, it's a real big deal!

So, can we benefit from the guidance God gave the Israelites through His command to tithe?

As stated earlier, the New Testament giving standard is to "give voluntarily" with no percentage commanded. The tithe was one of the Mosaic commands not carried forward. However, since the tithe was established thousands of years ago does that mean we are not to consider the tithe of 10% as the starting point when we "give vountarily?"

Let's play "What if?"

By averaging multiple resources, it appears that only 5% of churchgoers tithe or give 10% of their finances. In fact, Christians give on average only 2.5%. This average includes at least 40% who do not give. According to an article in Relevant Magazine by Mike Holmes, if Christian believers were to increase their giving to a minimum of 10% (the tithe), there would be an additional $165 billion for churches to distribute. Holmes suggests a few things the Church could do with that amount:

- $25 billion could relieve global hunger, starvation and deaths from preventable diseases in five years.

- $12 billion could eliminate illiteracy in five years.
- $15 billion could solve the world's water and sanitation issues, specifically at places in the world where 1 billion people live on less than $1 per day.
- $1 billion could fully fund all overseas mission work.
- $100 – $110 billion would still be left over for additional ministry expansion.

These are impressive numbers! Yet, regardless of whether we are commanded to tithe as in Malachi or we "give voluntarily," our personal standards for giving will not change until our hearts change to Jesus' standard: "Love the Lord your God with all your heart and with all your soul and with all your mind" and "Love your neighbor as yourself." Matthew 22:37,39

Giving is a heart issue, not a money issue!

The act of giving includes more than just a percentage of our money. It includes a portion of our time, talents and other resources. In addition to other types of Christian work that is needed, there must be people available to manage and distribute the bread and fish once it is brought into the storehouse.

In the *Feeding of the 5000*, Jesus performed a miracle by feeding over five thousand people from five loaves and two fish. Yet it is no less of a miracle that God provides the world with enough for everyone's needs if we do our part — if we give back one loaf of bread out of the ten He gives to us? We keep 90% and give back only 10%. What a deal!

Fortunately, many people recognize the grace under which we live and give more than 10%, which I believe should be the starting point of our giving, not the end goal to achieve. Regardless of what others give, God does not excuse anyone from giving, or as Malachi said, "an excuse for robbing God."

The Bible tells us not to test God. Yet, in Malachi 3:10, God offers an exception to show the Israelites the seriousness of keeping His command regarding the tithe. "Test me in this, says the Lord Almighty, and see if I will not throw open the floodgates of Heaven and pour out so much blessing that there will not be room enough to store it."

Although it was a great offer to the Israelites, it doesn't mean (as many have preached) that God will shower us with wealth if we are obedient to the Old Testament command to tithe. Go has already opened His gates and showered us with His love through the supreme gift of salvation through Jesus and promises to reward us in Heaven when we give generously while on Earth.

Again, regardless of whether we are commanded to give or we give voluntarily, giving is not a money issue, it's a heart issue. Jesus had a lot to say about both. His command is clear: "Anyone who has two shirts should share with the one who has none, and anyone who has food should do the same" (Luke 3:11). And, regarding the condition of our hearts, He said, "For where your treasure is, there your heart will be also" (Matthew 6:21).

Let's make "our treasure" a world in physical need and one in spiritual need. Then let's open our hearts and our finances until there is "so much blessing that there will not be room enough to store it."

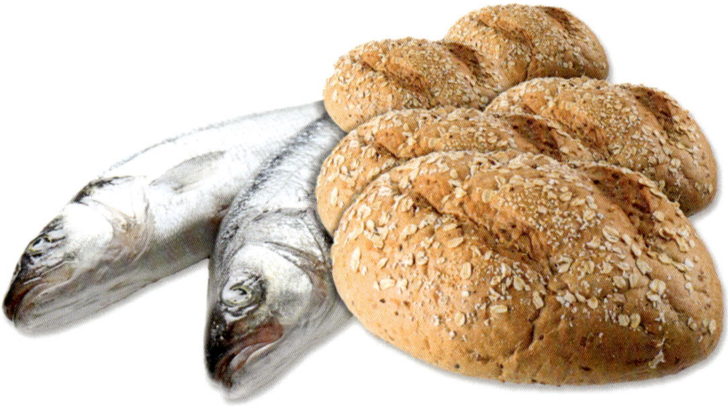

In God's economy, two fish and five loaves can feed thousands!

Thoughts to Ponder

View film at ▶ journeyswiththemessiah.org

- The *"Feeding of the 5000"* with two fish and five loaves of bread provides a view of God's economy whereby He can supernaturally multiply things beyond our wildest imagination. Think about this story relative to any insurmountable odds you may have faced or will face in the future.

- God does not feed the hungry directly! He feeds them by first giving to you and me and then allowing us the privilege and honor of being involved in His distribution plans.

- The tithe of 10% was not one of the Mosaic laws brought forward into the New Testament, but does that necessarily mean it was eliminated? Perhaps it was so ingrained in Israel's culture that no one considered it had not been carried forward! Perhaps 10% was the assumed starting point of giving since we now live under God's grace through Jesus!

- I began this chapter by providing hypothetically examples of giving back 10% of bread, hundred dollar bills, and salary raises offered to you. Almost everyone will quickly agree to give back 10% in these examples. So, why is it most people say "No" to giving back 10% of all the finances God has given to them?

- Jesus said, "For where your treasure is, there your heart will be also." Giving is an issue of the heart! Your "treasure" is anything that takes your heart to a place other than where God wants it to be.

(Although Cheryl and I have tithed for 25 years, it humbles me to know that I will never make up for all the years when I gave next to nothing!)

What now?

"Humanly speaking, it's impossible.
But with God, everything's possible."

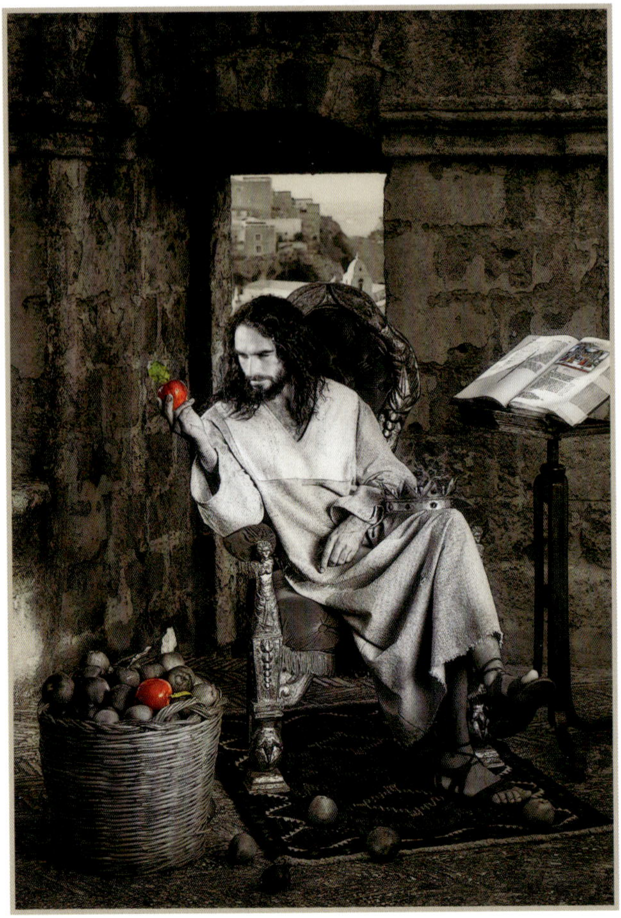

Hopefully you have arrived here after experiencing each chapter and companion film and contemplating the *Thoughts to Ponder.* The messages explore challenges we encounter like forgiveness (Jesus with the Nazi soldier), financial quandaries (Jesus with the Rich Young Ruler), faith and trust (Jesus with the wheelbarrow), and compassion (Jesus with the Woman at the Well).

Journeys with the Messiah's central theme is the gift of salvation and eternal life through Jesus. If you have accepted God's gift, congratulations, you have received the finest gift of all. If not yet, I hope you are inspired to consider Jesus and all He can be in your life.

So what now? If we embrace Jesus, which includes his teachings, commands and directions for life, how can we actually live by them day to day?

After we receive salvation, what do we do with it? Intellectually, we have accepted Jesus' sacrifice — His crucifixion and resurrection — and His promise of eternal life. Emotionally, we can appreciate and be thankful for God's love, mercy and grace. Yet how do we surrender our lives to the challenging life Jesus has called us? Then, how can we see the evidence of our journey with the Messiah?

Surrendering is not only difficult to do, *complete* surrender is pretty much impossible this side of Eternity. The Apostle Paul must have been pondering a similar dilemma when he wrote in Romans 7, "For I have the desire to do what is good, but I cannot carry it out. For I do not do the good I want to do, but the evil I do not want to do — this I keep on doing." In other words, Paul is saying that we know what we should do, and we want to do it, but we continually fall short of achieving it.

Moreover, we may think that we can live a good and fruitful life on our own, but Jesus explains we can't: "I am the vine and you are the branches. If you remain in me and I in you, you will bear much fruit; apart from me you can do nothing" (John 15:5).

In other words, Jesus said that He is the trunk of the tree that provides support for the weight of the branches, and is also the conduit for supplying the needed nutrients to blossom and bear fruit. If we stay attached to Him, together we will produce fruit. If we are detached, we will not produce any fruit on our own. "Fruit," in this instance, means efforts, acts or works that are worthy of God's Kingdom.

This is the key: We stay attached to Him.
"You remain in me and I in you; you will bear much fruit;
apart from me you can do nothing."

We stay attached in prayer. "Then you will call on me and come and pray to me, and I will listen to you" (Jeremiah 29:12). We stay attached by seeking Him through the scriptures and the abundance of resources that help us see Him more clearly. "You will seek me and find me when you seek me with all your heart" (Jeremiah 29:13).

God was speaking through Jeremiah to the Israelites in exile 600 years before Jesus. Yet, the words of these scriptures are the same today for us: Pray and He will listen. Seek Him and you will find Him. It can be that straightforward and uncomplicated: Seek Him with all our heart, day by day, moment by moment. When we pursue Him as relentlessly as He pursues us, the "fruits" of obedience, patience, contentment, joy, peace and others will begin to grow as His desires blossom to be our own.

It's my prayer that you have made profitable discoveries on your journey through the messages in this book and the accompanying films. And, I hope you will revisit them often in your daily devotions and in a small group as well. They are meant to be traveling companions for you and for others as you share your faith along your journey.

A few words of thanks!

In Chapter 3, *Lighten the Load*, I wrote, *"Jesus said count the cost, but He also said count the rewards."* The costs of producing this project — financial, physical and emotional — have been high, if not excessive! Yet the rewards have been priceless, like the actor, Sergio, who engaged the part of Jesus with such strength and kindness as if he was The Messiah. Maurizio, Gianni, Sandra and all the crews in Italy will be cherished memories forever.

We have met so many good people — some briefly, while others have been alongside from the start, like the leadership team at Ronald Blue Trust. Cheryl and I have been clients of Ronald Blue Trust for more than 25 years, and the company's advice has helped us with our financial journey, employing biblical principles into our finances. Journeys' parable-like way of telling Jesus' story has resonated with the leadership team and they have been a valuable source of guidance, wisdom and encouragement.

In 2014, we met Bob & Linda Taylor when they dropped by our home to purchase books after hearing me speak at their church. We invited them in for coffee and when they left, we had become best friends. Together, we've all been on a journey with Jesus. Since we met, Bob has been a continuous sounding board and encourager, a promoter of multiple connections and relationships, sometimes editor, occasional golf partner and dearest friend.

To the people who have made this project possible through the purchase and sharing of sixty thousand books, thousands of posters and DVDs, hundreds of pieces of original artwork, and while inviting me into your churches and organizations to present Jesus through these unique images, we couldn't keep going without you. Thanks to David Green, Founder of Hobby Lobby, for your friendship and sharing our books and artwork through your stores.

Walt Wilson and Global Media Outreach invited us to partner in a campaign called, "Something Better," designed to digitally present the Gospel through the Internet using Journeys' images and messages. Through 2020, over two million people have been reached in the United States with over 360,000 indicating their desire to be followers of Christ. Just Amazing! Thank you. Onward! (somethingbetter.us)

Last here, but first in my heart, my precious Cheryl, a true gift from God. Cheryl agreed for me to take one year away from my career to pursue this project. Twelve years later, we are still on this journey to share Jesus. Thank you for enduring the trials while making my life possible. Surely God is stacking up rewards for you in your mansion in Heaven.